THE HONEST RAINMAKER

The Life and Times of Colonel John R. Stingo

A. J. LIEBLING

WITH A FOREWORD BY
GARRISON KEILLOR AND MARK SINGER

NORTH POINT PRESS
San Francisco 1989

LIBRARY OF CONGRESS CATALOGING-IN-PUBLICATION DATA
Liebling, A. J. (Abbott Joseph), 1904–1963.
  The honest rainmaker.
  1. Stingo, John R., b. 1874. 2. Journalists—United States—
Biography. 3. Horse racing—New York (State) 4. New York
(N. Y.)—Social life and customs. I. Title.
PN4874.S6884L54   1989   070.92 [B]   89-8812
ISBN 0-86547-396-x

North Point Press
850 Talbot Avenue
Berkeley, California
94706

To the Châtelaine

Contents

Foreword

BY GARRISON KEILLOR AND MARK SINGER

*"All my life I have been faithful to one woman," the Count once said to
me,—"a fragile blonde with a morbid expression."*

*He found this woman in every country, and she never aged, although
the Count did. The fragile blonde with a morbid expression, wherever she
turned up, was in her twenties.* A. J. LIEBLING

A. J. LIEBLING was the wittiest American writer who ever lived, and though
he died in 1963 without ever enjoying a perceptible big success, a flash of
fame, or a bundle of money, it's enormously cheering for his supporters to
see the old master's reputation expand. Most of his fifteen books have been
reprinted, and in the second-hand book market, that true democracy where
literary reputations are tested by the pure interest of readers, Liebling's
work is in hot demand. A mint copy of *Back Where I Came From* will get you
$500, *The Telephone Booth Indian* about $200, with *The Road Back to Paris*,
The Sweet Science, *The Wayward Pressman*, and *Mink and Red Herring* all
running right around $100. We like to think how tickled Liebling would be to
hear what a good value he is, that old copies of his great books have been ap-
preciating at ten to twenty percent per annum, a better deal than U. S. Steel.

We loved him the moment we took up his books as college boys, and read
him fast, over and over, finding him funny—laugh-out-loud-pee-in-your-
pants funny—and yet passionate in his loyalties and full of feeling; a comic
outsider and a rebel against convention and at the same time a man of the
world who enjoyed himself hugely and whose best stuff was all about himself
having a hell of a good time. Liebling was no puritan or academic. He
sneered at "the boys from the quarterlies." He never quoted Thoreau. He
enjoyed crowds, noise, drunkenness, hype and hurly-burly, overstatement
brought on by the "divine inflatus," big dinners, and close pals, one of whom
is the subject of *The Honest Rainmaker*, a New York racing writer (for the paper that became *The National Enquirer*) named James A. Macdonald, also
known as Colonel John R. Stingo, a classic American hustler. "I have three
rules for keeping in condition," says Stingo. "I will not let guileful women
move in on me, I decline all responsibility, and above all, I avoid all heckling
work. Also, I shun exactious luxuries, lest I become their slave."

Again and again, well before and after publishing the 1952 series of articles that form the core of *The Honest Rainmaker*, Liebling adverted to Stingo—as if the old man embodied talismanic power, like the hunchbacked Belmont Park shoeshine genius, Mike the Bite, who pemitted "women turf speculators" to rub his hump, but never for less than ten dollars a pop. Colonel Stingo first turned up in a "Wayward Press" column in the *New Yorker* in 1947, and he was there in the issue of January 11, 1964, which contained both Liebling's final piece of reportage and his obituary. (That Liebling seems to have had Stingo all to himself is an astonishing thought today; in our era, the Colonel would have been a regular on the talk show circuit and had a contract for a book of his own.) "A Long Rider's most precious resource is a well-cataloged mental file of acquaintances," Stingo said. "A good friend should not be lightly used, but put away in a drawer like a good pair of pajamas, for use on a special occasion." Among his friends were the rainmakers Professor George Ambrosius Immanuel Morrison Sykes of the "U.S. Weather Control Bureau" and Professor Joseph Canfield Hatfield; Dr. Orlando Edgar Miller, the tent-revivalist and advocate of deep-breathing and the spiritual life; the multitalented swindler George Graham Rice (*né* Jacob Simon Herzig); and Harry Brolaski ("a free-booting Barbary corsair of horrendous background, but a good fellow withal"), the brawn and part of the brains behind the Great American Hog Syndicate, all in this book, along with Steve L'Hommedieu, the Prince of Handicappers; Bonehead Barry and Sad Sam Jackson and their search for The White Robin; and the famous horserace Stingo describes as "a competition in stimulative medication."

Liebling made his living as a reporter, at the *Providence Journal* and the *New York World-Telegram* and finally at the *New Yorker*, a man who, by his own admission, could write faster than anyone who could write better and write better than anyone who could write faster. He wrote superbly about New York City, war, boxing, gourmandizing, France, and journalism, always under immense pressure of deadlines and personal debt. When he started out in the thirties, New York, not Washington, was the mecca of American journalism, the perpetual boomtown that provincial newspapermen aimed for; government was a good deal less fascinating to them than the living American mythology of crime, show business, sport, the world of big money, big names, and sudden chances. The touts and sharps and small-time crooks who worked around Times Square, especially Colonel Stingo, interested Liebling more than the President of the United States. He thought they were more fun to write about and would no more have gone to Washington to cover the New Deal than he would have moved to Middletown and become a Congregationalist.

The Colonel resided at the Hotel Dixie on Forty-third Street, west of Seventh Avenue, an establishment that nobody ever mistook for the Ritz, but it was all right by Colonel Stingo, who for forty years called it home. (Like a lot of the old neighborhood, it has fallen on unspeakable times, and more than a decade ago the name was changed to the Hotel Carter, which did nothing to arrest its decline.) "Up there in my retreat I feel the city calling to me," he said. "It winks at me with its myriad eyes, and I go out and get stiff as a board.

I seek out companionship, and if I do not find friends I make them. A wonderful grand old Babylon."

The Honest Rainmaker is a romance and its subject matter is romance—the romance of newspapering, of city life and city speech, of everyday citizenship in a world populated primarily by con men and their pigeons (what Colonel Stingo preferred to call "boobs"). It makes the simple demand that is indispensable to all romance: the suspension of disbelief. Liebling, grandiloquent, invites the reader to become an accomplice, just as he and the Colonel have enlisted each other: "I was to find in all my experiences with Colonel Stingo that where he diverges from recorded history, he improves on it." The reader may swoon at some of the Colonel's palmy, scented, rococo sentences—"On the direction of Madame, the tonneau's side door swung ajar, revealing a vista of rich and ravishing splendor;—upon her Golden Barge in the simmering moonlight of a sheening night on the Nile, I am sure Cleopatra never looked more completely devastating than does dear Mrs. Harriman as she reclines her elongated figure lissomely strewn, lengthwise upon the satin-cushioned coach seat while smoking a costly heaven-scented Carolina Perfecto, a la Panatela . . . "—but whether Stingo's "damascened style" embroiders upon fact or fiction is ultimately "a matter of taxonomy, and immaterial." While the colonel expatiates, Liebling supplies the quotation marks, the alcoholic lubricant, and the deadpan assurances that Stingo's "reminiscences are not meant to be edited, but enjoyed."

Like virtually everything Liebling collected between hardcovers, *The Honest Rainmaker*, reread with fresh wonder and gratitude, reinfects us with what was romantic about Liebling himself. At the *New Yorker*, Liebling's neighbors, nodding off in their thin-walled beige cubicles, were regularly jolted back to consciousness by the sound of Liebling laughing aloud as he read pages he had just pulled from his own typewriter. When he bluntly proclaimed Colonel Stingo "my favorite writer," no more than the usual irony was intended. What he really meant was that Colonel Stingo was his *second* favorite writer. He was Liebling's Liebling.

Liebling died December 28, 1963. His last reporting piece, published two weeks later, a brief memoir titled "Le Paysage Crepuscule" (The Twilight Landscape), concludes with the author in his office at the *New Yorker*, writing at night, gazing at the Dixie, thinking of Stingo, pleased "mightily to know that the Colonel is still there." The Colonel was at that point either eighty-nine (according to Liebling) or ninety-one (according to the imaginative Stingo, who, Liebling wrote, seemed to have "run his last nineteen years in seventeen flat"). He outlived his Boswell, though of course it is Liebling who survives.

In the obituary that followed "Le Paysage Crepuscule," William Shawn wrote, in his characteristic understated way, that the journalism Liebling "was ostensibly doing somehow turned into the kind of writing that endures," but the subtext of his elegy was what Liebling, a few pages earlier, had written of Stingo: "His sentences soar like laminated boomerangs, luring the reader's eye until they swoop and dart across the mind like bright-eyed hummingbirds, for a clean strike every time."

The Legend

There was once a sheik, the richest and most puissant in all Arabia, and he owned thousands of swift dromedaries, the best in all Arabia, and thousands of thoroughbred Arabian steeds, the fastest in all Arabia, and his years were four score and nineteen, and his sons long since had reconciled themselves to his demise. So when, one eve, as the sun sank sad on the west side of the Euphrates, the old sheik summoned his eldest son to the side of his couch, the son sensed that it was the finish, although the word "official" had not yet flashed on the odds board.

"Draw near, my son," the old man croaked, "for my voice is feeble with years, and I would have you hear me."

The son, who was himself a green three score and ten, inclined obediently above his sire, and placed his right ear near the old sheik's mouth.

"You know, my son, that I own thousands of swift dromedaries," the old man said, "the best in all Arabia."

"Yes, Father," the eldest son said, "I know."

"And you know I own thousands of fat-tailed sheep, the fattest in all Arabia."

"Yes, Father," the eldest son said, "I know."

"And you know I own thousands of thoroughbred Arabian horses, the fastest in all Arabia."

"Yes, Father," said the eldest son, "I know."

"Well, Son," the old sheik said, "I bet on those horses.

"And now the First National Bank of Mecca holds a mortgage on the thousands of swift dromedaries, the best in all Arabia.

"And the First National Bank of Medina holds a mortgage on the thousands of fat-tailed sheep, the fattest in all Arabia.

"And the First National Bank of Trans-Jordan has foreclosed on the horses, and they are to be sold at auction in the paddock at Babylon tomorrow.

"So I have no material goods to leave to you."

The eldest son's heart was heavy within his breast, but he was a dead-game sport.

"It is well, Father," he said.

Then the old man, with a last mighty effort, sat up straight on his couch of gazelle skins and said:

"But I have something more precious to bequeath to you, my counsel."

"Yes, Father," the eldest son said, "I hear."

"My son," the old man said. "Never work a day. And NEVER, NEVER, take an honest dollar."

—Favorite barroom recitation of
Colonel John R. Stingo

1 / The Plug in the Door

WHEN THE New York *Times* published the news a while back that 169 towns and individuals upstate had filed damage claims against New York City for $2,138,510 and no odd cents, Colonel John R. Stingo was politely amused. The claims rested upon the city's efforts to produce rain from clouds over its Catskill Mountain reservoirs during a water shortage in 1950. These involved seeding clouds with dry ice, and were carried out by a meteorologist named Dr. Wallace E. Howell, who had a contract from February, 1950, until February, 1951, to help it rain. The upstaters accused Dr. Howell of drowning them out, even charging him with the tornado which swept the whole Atlantic coast on November 25. It seemed to be up to the city to prove Dr. Howell's experiments hadn't worked, although at the time they were made it had intimated they were at least partially successful.

Colonel Stingo sometimes refers to himself as the Honest Rainmaker, as in the phrase, "the Honest Rainmaker, who is among those with the Prattle of a Babe and the soul of Jimmy Hope the Bank Robber." When he read the story in the *Times* he said, "I'm astonished that these modern professionals, men of authenticated science, wind up with damage suits and hard feelings. When my rain-inductive colleagues and I concluded a campaign, we were invariably the guests of the benefited community at a banquet where *sec* and *brut* flowed like the showers in the dressing room of the St. Louis Cardinals after a sixteen-inning game on a day of record heat. We would all get stiff as boards and they would invite us to come back next season."

Colonel Stingo is a nom de plume, but hardly anybody calls the Colonel anything else, and not many of his casual acquaintances know he has another name. He has been a newspaperman, off and on, for sixty-five years by his own count, and is now, for that matter, but he has never seen a future in it. The Colonel has always believed that fortune swims, not with the main stream of letters, but in the shallows where the suckers moon. In pursuance of this theory, he has acquired a varied experience, which he willingly shares with his friends.

Colonel Stingo's real name is James A. Macdonald, and half a century ago, when he was writing about horse races for the New York *Evening Journal,* he used to sign it J.S.A. Macdonald, which led critical colleagues to call him Alphabet. The S stood for Stuart, a name he has since discarded, because, he says, it made him seem a Young Pretender. In that dawn age of Hearst journalism in New York he was a favorite of Arthur Brisbane, who saw in his damascened style the making of a Hearst editorial writer. "But I stuck to the turf," Colonel Stingo says. "I knew the money was in the side lines." Reminded that Brisbane died with around twenty million dollars, the Colonel comes up with a correction. "Thirty-nine million," he says. "But it was a fluke." The Colonel himself lives in what he terms a "one-room suite" in a hotel built over a bus terminal.

During the Hearst days a competitor, outraged by the Colonel's exclusive report of a projected hundred-thousand-dollar match race between Irish Lad and a kangaroo backed by a millionaire Australian, wrote: "Alphabet Macdonald never permits facts to interfere with the exercise of his imagination." The Colonel rightly considered this a tribute to his mastery of his material.

"The sculptor," he says, "imposes his design on the Parian marble." But in most of his tales there is an element of truth which passes through the finest filter, so it is impossible to class them as fiction.

It is a matter of taxonomy, and immaterial.

The Colonel is a small, lively man with a back as straight as the wide part precisely in the middle of his hair, which becomes wider but no less precise with the passage of the years. His straightness, his neatness, and a certain old-fashioned formality of diction befit an old military man, and there are a good many impressionable bartenders on Broadway who believe he is. He wears bow ties, clothes that have an archaic dash, even when they are a trifle worn, and pointed shoes that show off his elegantly diminutive feet.

"When I was young," he sometimes says, harking back to what he calls "the days of halcyon, before Charles Evans Hughes leveled a deathblow at gracious living in America—I wore shiny patent-leather shoes with sharp points, and if I didn't like you I'd kick you and you'd bleed to death." This is by some of his acquaintance considered an allegorical allusion to the power of the press. But the Colonel has not elucidated it.

Hughes, while Governor of New York, signed a bill abolishing betting on race tracks here. A few years later the bookmakers found a way around it which tided them over until track bets were again legalized in 1934. But the Colonel still thinks of the late Chief Justice of the United States Supreme Court as the man who ushered in the Dark Ages of Hypocrisy. "Prohibition was an inevitable sequelae," he says, "and so was the sordid pari mutuel." Hughes was also indirectly responsible for the Colonel's withdrawal from the New York scene. When the unplucked statesman was elected Governor in 1906 he was already pledged to stop racing. There didn't seem to be any future for a racing writer in New York, and so the Colonel snapped at a chance to go out to Los Angeles as sporting editor of Hearst's *Examiner*, in that then distinctly minor-league city. He didn't get back for twenty-three years, and it is in this period of *wanderung* that he places many of his most picturesque and least checkable anecdotes.

There is usually a white carnation in the Colonel's buttonhole, and almost invariably, when he is seen in public, a beer glass in his right hand. For a period before lunch, which is customarily his first meal of the day, he devotes himself to gold gin fizzes, which are made with the yolk of the egg. During this process of remedial imbibition he is morose and does not appreciate company. "I met a villain last night," he will say in explanation of his mood, "and he led me down the path of dalliance Gambrinian." If the bartender in setting down the shaker bangs it against the wood, the jangled Colonel will say, "Doctor, don't cut too deep! I have been riding the magic carpet." But he eats his lunch with good appetite. He often says he is a "good doer." On surveying the menu he says, "The entry list seems to have filled well," and then he goes down the line with few scratches. After lunch he makes what he calls "the Great Transition," switching from hard liquor to beer, which he continues to drink from then until he goes to bed, unless he meets a villain who induces him to deviate.

In periods when Colonel Stingo is what he describes as "non-holding," or financially straitened, he spends a large part of his time in the reading room of the New York Public Library, seeding the clouds of printed erudition above his already overflowing reservoir of odd information. Such knowledge he refers to verbally as "esatoric," although he can spell the word all right. When he ceases to be non-holding, and has an adequate amount of what he refers to as "Tease," he makes his *rentrée*, usually telling his favorite bartenders in detail about conditions in some place he has been reading up on in the Public Library. "Glad to get back," he says. "There's no place like New York."

He doesn't like to be in bars when he can't buy his share of the drinks or undergo an occasional small bite. "I am a man of money," he likes to say when he has any at all. "The next round is on me."

Since the Kefauver committee began its revival of the Hughes Inquisition, the Colonel has had time to do a record amount of reading. His job, writing a column for a newspaper called the New York *Enquirer*, is irreproachably legitimate, but carries no salary. His income has been derived from its perquisites, which are commissions on the ads he attracts to the paper's sports pages. Nearly all of these are from turf analysts, which means tipsters. Their profession too is irreproachably legitimate, since freedom of opinion is guaranteed by the Bill of Rights. But nobody is going to pay for a tip when he can't find a bookmaker to play it with. The harder things get for the bookies, the more nearly impossible they become for the purveyors of purported information. As the latter drop their ads, the Colonel's absences from his Gambrinian haunts become longer and more frequent, until at one time they threatened to merge in one long continuous hiatus, like that induced by the Hughes Law. Some of his friends, making an erroneous inference from his age and the protraction of his nonappearance, began to refer to him in the past tense.

At the moment of his remark about the decline of good feeling in the rainmaking business, I knew by a sure sign he was non-holding: he asked me how he could earn some money. I have known Colonel Stingo for five years, during which I had occasionally heard him allude to his career as a rainmaker, but I had never heard him tell the full story. I therefore suggested that he set it forth.

"If you write it," I told him, "you might be able to sell it."

"It's a strange idea, Joe," he said, "but I'll try it."

Before he would begin, though, he insisted that I promise to stand by to help.

We took rendezvous for that day week at Gough's, a bar on West Forty-third Street where there is a life-size oil portrait of John L. Sullivan wearing a frock coat. The Colonel was to bring with him a rough draft of at least a substantial part of the story of the Honest Rainmaker.

"While I am about it," he said, "I might as well write my autobiography, of which this is only one of the episodia minora. I shall call it *The Plug in the Door*."

"It is an ominous title, Colonel," I said.

"It is indeed," he said. "A phrase fraught with fear for hundreds of thousands of habitual hotel inhabiters. What mockery lies in the word 'guest' as employed by the average flinthearted hotelier! His so-called hospitality is limited by the visible extent of the inmate's liquid assets. He has a memory as short as a man who borrows five dollars; the months of faithful acquitment of obligations by the patron avail him nothing,—the hotel man's recollection extends back only as far as the last presentation of the bill. The sealed keyhole," he said, in his emotion mixing metaphors as smoothly as a bartender blends gin and vermouth, "is the sword of Damocles suspended by an economic hair over a large proportion of the American people.

"And yet," he added, a gentler light suffusing his rugged countenance, for the Colonel is a man of everchanging mood, "I have known the plug in the door once to save a friend of mine from trancelike despair. It was a snowy night in January, and he had just descended from an office where he had been trying for hours to write a story that seemed to him of less moment every time he looked at it. Ultimately he had thrown it into the wastebasket. He had bet on fourteen consecutive losers at Hialeah, his wife had left him to run off with an advertising man, and from a vertiginous pounding in his ears he felt himself due for a coronary occlusion. Proceeding but a few yards, he found himself at the corner of Forty-fourth Street and Times Square, the southeast one. He had had some idea of seeking out a place to eat, but he had no appetite and he could not decide where to go. Then it began to seem to him that it wasn't worth the trouble to go anywhere. The snow continued to fall, and he began to assume the aspect of a well-powdered Christmas tree.

"The discordant laughter of a party of revelers, outward bound from some dispensatorium of cheer, recalled him to a sense of his situation. He cringed at the thought of being accosted by a copper solicitous of his compos mentis, and the hilarity suggested to him a possible source of assuagement. So he entered the bar of the old Hotel Cadillac, which at that time still stood at Forty-third Street.

"The Cadillac was a hotel harboring a most Bohemian motley, particularly in the last phase of its existence; it was the last stand of many old show people fallen from high estate, and also of elements more riffraffian. My friend entered the bar. A mere partition set it off from the lobby. It was thronged with raucousness; the atmosphere was most convivial. He wedged his way between two blondes to attain contact with the mahogany; they evinced no indignation, although he ignored them. He drank one, two short scotches before he even began to look about him. By the seventh he was on terms of pleasant familiarity with his neighbors adjacent; he took them out to dinner and had a hell of an evening, winding up by inviting them to visit his apartment, solitary since his wife's defection. When he awoke next morning they were both still there. They had returned to their room at the Cadillac on the previous evening only to find their door plugged, they explained, and had adjourned to the bar, the habitat of wisdom and inspiration, to reflect upon their situation, when they made the happy encounter. Had the management not locked them out, my friend might have succumbed to despair and self-destruction, which would have been a pity because his wife left the advertising man and came back to him three days later. They lived happily ever after, until she ran away with the night manager of an automat."

We shook hands and parted.

2 / The Pasha Strikes Out

GOUGH'S IS a saloon which has been on Forty-third Street for only five or six years, but the portrait of Sullivan gives it an air of maturity. One item of *décor* like that can make a place. I remember when a man I know opened a speakeasy in 1925 and put a suit of armor in it. As soon as you saw the armor you knew the proprietor had confidence he would last, investing in such superfluous elegance. And it couldn't be a clip joint, or they would never have anything around that a drunk who got rolled could come back and identify. The armor established the place. A lot of saloons are open for years without getting established.

A life-size portrait of Sullivan is of necessity a big thing. He was six feet tall and the artist naturally had to leave something for him to stand on and something over the head so you can see he isn't wearing a hat. This is a very dark portrait, so it is hard to see in places whether the black is frock coat or background. The picture looks as if it had been painted in the nineties, after Sullivan had lost the title and gone on the wagon. His face is fat, he is wearing a fine moustache, and his right hand is on his belly, as if he is going to begin a temperance lecture. There is a light at the top of the frame and a little sign at the lower right-hand corner of the picture which says, "John Lawrence Sullivan, Heavyweight Champion of the United States, Born, Boston, Mass., 1858—Died, 1918."

The sign was put there a couple of months ago, after a stranger had come in and looked at the portrait for a while and then burst out laughing. The stranger had walked over to the bar and said to the bartender: "I know who that is, it's John L. Sullivan."

"Who else would it be?" the bartender had asked.

"Well, I'm from Naval Intelligence," the stranger had said, and he had a card to prove it, "and some fool reserve officer was in here and reported to us that there was a bar on Forty-third Street with a life-size portrait of Stalin and a votive light over it."

The sign went on next day.

The portrait is signed by somebody named Daunton, but the Colonel, who has a scheme to sell it to a millionaire Texan with an Irish name for a quarter of a million, believes that this is a case of wrong attribution.

"Daunton may have been some dauber engaged to clean the picture," he once told me. "I never heard of him. I believe the painter to be Copley. Much better price." When I reminded him that Copley had lived in the eighteenth century, he said, "I meant Copley the grandson." He has an answer for everything.

The Colonel, by his own account, was born in 1874 in New Orleans, and there is no reason to quibble over the date. He has no trace of southern accent, and this has led certain friends to the assertion that his true birthplace was considerably north of Louisiana, in Montreal or Brooklyn, and that his present version of his origin was suggested by the name of the hotel where he now lives, the Dixie. But if his cradle was not bowered by magnolias, it should have been. He is a true romantic.

Personally, I believe the New Orleans story, even though one of the Montreal-theory men who knew the Colonel fifty years ago insists that from the day of his arrival here the Colonel was a good ice skater. "There were no artificial rinks in the nineteenth century," he says. The way I figure it, what the man really remembers is that the Colonel *told* him he was a good ice skater, which is not the same thing.

The Colonel himself has spoken to me of his regret at losing his Louisianian accent, by a process he describes as slow attrition. "It got rubbed off, Joe, like pollen off the bee, by contact with a thousand charming flowers," he said. "In the speech of each I left some trace of my native music. From each I received in return some nasal diphthong or harsh consonant. It was a heavy price." In a more practical vein he added, "The accent would have been of great assistance if I had wished to set up on my own as a turf adviser. A southern accent is an invaluable asset to a tout.

"Also," he said, "it would have aided me in religious work. The great Dr. Orlando Edgar Miller, an evangelist who took in more money at Carnegie Hall than Paderewski, used to say to me, 'Jim, if you were a taller man and you hadn't lost your southern twang, you'd be a hell of a revivalist.'" Religion has played a large part in the Colonel's life. I once heard him say, "It's the strongest thing man ever invented, with the possible exception of the Standard Oil Company."

As in journalism, Colonel Stingo believes, the real money is in the side lines. "The immediate collection is of little import," he says. "The Rev. Dr. Hall, with whom I was once associated, had a self-exegetic Bible, which he sold for a hundred dollars a copy, but only on the written agreement of the subscriber that it would remain in his personal possession until transmitted to his heir. It was a masterwork superb. I wrote a chapter myself. To be eligible to buy a copy you had to be a graduate of the salon classes for ladies, six lessons for fifty dollars; or of the esatoric course for men, twelve sessions for two hundred and fifty. We sold 412 Bibles in the first month of one race meeting at Seattle. The bookmakers made us a proposition to leave town because we were getting all the Tease. That was before the Reverend Doctor began betting on the horses. After that they offered to pay the rent on a hall if we would stay."

The Colonel's habitual expression is that of a stud-poker player with one ace showing who wants to give the impression that he has another in the hole. He looks as if he knew something amusing that he didn't have the right to say. In poker this may be either a bluff or fake bluff, designed to induce other players to get into the two aces. In the Colonel's case, however, the expression means only that he finds the world a funny place.

When he showed at Gough's with the first section of his manuscript, he made me think he was a veritable Georges Simenon or Edgar Wallace, or that in the manner of the elder Dumas or Henry Luce he had placed himself at the head of a literary factory, for he produced from the diagonal slash pockets of his nubbly blue jacket two long manila envelopes bulging with manuscript.

"I suggest that you have a look at the autobiography first," he said, handing one of the envelopes across the table to me.

On the first sheet, under a neat row of asterisks, he had typed the title:

PLUG IN THE DOOR

and then, after four blank lines:

```
  Projected Story in Book Form of Everyday
People in Everyday Life.
```

On the next page it said:

```
            Characters in the Story Play
              The Duchess
              The Millionaire Kid
              Dynamite Jack Thornby
              "Wild Bill" Lyons
              Harry the Coupon King
              Mike The Bite
              Senator Casey
              Mary The Martyr
              The Singing Kid
              Madame Alda
                   &
              Colonel John Adams Howard,
                 Circle C Ranch
                 Cheyenne, Wyoming
```

On the third page, a memorandum on procedure, it said:

```
            Establish Personal Basis.
Developing Story to Bring in Alluring Events Over the
Chronological Sequence.
```

The fourth page said just:

```
            Chapterial Outline
```

and led to twelve pages each headed by a chapter subject but otherwise bare. On the page following the Colonel had taken a fresh start.

```
            Plug In The Door
```

This one said:

```
        A Story of a Life Variegated
```

Finally, on about the twentieth page, the Colonel had apparently taken his spring.

```
     The Stories and Rhymes heard at Mother's knee in
the prattling days of childhood persist and live to
the end of the recipient's tenure here below.
```

```
    The inclining influence there exerted upon the
delicate tendril of babydays shapes and directs the
Fate and Destiny of all men, of all women, no matter
who or what they may be; as illustrious as a Caesar,
as squalid as the Thief of Bagdad.
    But, strange as it may be, it is of my
Grandmother and my Great Grandmother that, perforce, I
must talk in getting along with the Story of A Life,
my life, we've, you and I, thought up under the
aforementioned titleage of Plug In The Door, a
circumstance and a terror uncounted multitudes of
ordinary mortals know so well.
```

All the remaining pages were blank.

"I couldn't go on after that," the Colonel said. "I was overcome by emotion. But the lead is the main thing, Joe. Everything will follow along nicely after I once barge into the episodia."

I was, quite truthfully, not much disappointed. What I had wanted him to write was a story about rainmaking. To set down his life from its beginning, I felt, might be a valuable spiritual exercise for my friend, but the years stretching from his great-grandmother's knee to early manhood could have only a limited popular appeal. They wouldn't help much to keep the plug out of his door at the Dixie.

"It reads very well, what there is of it, Colonel," I said. "But how about *The Honest Rainmaker?*"

The Colonel smiled and handed over the second well-stuffed envelope. The pages in this one were covered with typescript. The first began:

"Rain,—it's abundance, it's paucity,—meant Life and Death to the Ancients for from the lands and the flocks, herds, the fish of the sea, the birds of the air, the deer and mountain goat they found sustenance and energized being. All the elements depended upon the Fall of Rain, ample but not in ruinous overplus, for very existence.

"Through all human history the plenitude of Rain or its lack constituted the difference between Life and Death, the Joy of Rain or existence and misery."

"That's the first part of a speech I used to deliver to chapters of the Farmers' Guild in California when I was clinching deals for Professor Joseph Canfield Hatfield," the Colonel explained, gesturing to the waitress to bring him a second bottle of delight Gambrinian. "The next ten pages are on the same high level, but I would not suggest they are of the highest interest to our potential readers. Anyway, it will give you an idea of what I can do when the Ark of the Covenant falls upon me.

"Rain has always made the difference between plenty of Tease and non-holding for those farmers in the California valleys, a circumstance of which I was made much aware in July, 1908, when I was one of three hundred guests of a rich man named Captain James McKittrick on his stupendous estate, the Rancho del McKittrick, twenty miles from Bakersfield, at a party to celebrate the advent of Sudi Witte Pasha, a rainmaker the Captain had imported at vast expense from the Sudan. The episode begins on page ten."

I found the place and read:

"This enormous Rancho comprised 212,000 acres, an area so large that it required a Cowhand, with many pinto relays, two days and two nights to cross it, West to East or North to South.

"But the world's prime essential, golden Wheat, remained the prime crop. With rain precipitation at the very right moment the year for Rancho del McKittrick, with its 62,000 acres to Wheat, would be beneficently happy. Otherwise, no Rain no joy in Mudville, mighty Casey, he struck out. So the expansive Capt. McKittrick had brought on Sudi Witte Pasha, the World's Heavyweight Champion Rainmaker, to see what he could do about the anguishing situation in the Lower San Joaquin Valley, —no rain and ruin around the corner.

"The old Pasha had twenty-two Professors and Holy Men in his Mob and a whole mobile Library of Books with imploring Cantors, bewhiskered Priests, Bell Ringers, Soothsayers and Pricemakers,—all quartered in the lap of luxury in the Santa Clara Villa, an adjunct of the Manor House, with a retinue of Chefs, Servitors and Body Guardsmen at command. We all understood that the Captain agreed to pay Pasha and his lads the sum of $150,000 and all expenses, to and from Cairo, Egypt, for a three months' service and demonstration of his magic Bag O'Tricks.

"In the middle of July, 1908, with $2,000,000 worth of Wheat just beginning to ripen off in the field, the Egyptian Rainmaker went to work to bring on the aqueous dispensation. His chatty Camp Followers first greeted the Morning Sun and took a dip in the cold waters of Cherry Creek before going into the big Two-Day Fast, touched off by a little body lashing, and a sort of an ear piercing Indian War Dance, much like those you see done by the Indians in Arizona.

"The real Kick-Off came the third day with a series of Incantations and the throwing about of quite a deal of reddish colored powder and sweet smelling myrrh. The pretty Samia never swung such belly convulsions in her Royal Court Dance at Hotel Mecca, beneath the Pyramids, as did little Miss Matti, the Pasha's apple of eye, towards the end of the Exhortation to the Spirits of Rain. We were told by Interpreters what the dance meant.

"The fourth day was given over to the throwing upon the Runways, surrounding the miles of Wheat Fields a brownish sort of little nut, known as the Kofu Bean from the Eufrates Country in ancient Persia,— all ground up fine. It was done en masse, the Pasha in command, and with his impressed Rancho help of about 200 cowboys, cowgirls, and field workers going down the furrows ladling out the seeds, right and left, one might recall the ancients sowing their fields in biblical times out of shoulder bags with a blessing and hope of a fruitful harvest in the months to follow.

"That night in the Great Hall of the Manor House was staged a feast of Food, Fun and Frivol, the likes of which I had never seen before or since. It was for about 300 persons, and lasted until sundown the following day. Chefs down from San Francisco "curried" everything within sight,—even Sherry's ice cream, rushed through by special train from New York. Choice vintage of Paul Masson, one of California's choicest, flowed like water. The Feast of Belshazzar was pikish compared to this Orgy in Imploration for Rain; yet dire was the choleric ranchero's reaction when nothing happened.

"After 56 hours we were to see results, affirmed the Pasha; meantime, to engage in supplication and reverent prayer. Well, we waited and waited for exactly nine days but not a sign of rain; then came the Blow Off. The jolly Captain,—the Show had cost him an additional $40,000—came to a sudden and drastic decision; "Enough is enough," he said while forthwithedly ordering prepared at once his two special railroad cars, the 'Erma' and the 'Sally Jane,' lying in the Southern Pacific Railroad siding, a mile down Cherry Creek, for an immediate emergency itinerary,—to take the whole caboodle of Oriental scientists and rainmakers to the nearest station on the Sunset Route, the Old Santa Fe town of Barstow, where arrangements had been made to attach the cars to the outgrowing Pelican Express for Phoenix, Fort Worth and New Orleans; with a stop over for a resumpton of egress by Cromwell Line steamer from the Crescent City through the Straits of Gibraltar to the palm-waving beaches of dear old Cairo and the verandah at Shepherd's Hotel."

So it ended. I went back and reread that one tremendous climactic sentence, in which the irate millionaire sweeps the whole caboodle from the shores of the Pacific to the palm-waving beaches of old Cairo, with glimpses in transit of Barstow, Phoenix, Fort Worth, New Orleans, and the Straits of Gibraltar. Eight thousand miles or so in a few seconds. It made me visualize the soothsayers, price makers, and dancing girls picking themselves up off their rumps on the beaches and waving *their* palms in astonishment, as if they had been dropped by a Djinn, or Genius. The genius in this case is the Colonel's.

"It must have been quite a party," I said. Colonel Stingo gave the barmaid a sign of the hand to bring on another round for both of us, and when he had seen this signal honored, he acknowledged that I was right. "It was a stupendous quaffery," he said. "Of course, my interest in the proceedings was purely cultural and Belshazzarian. I was engaged in the promotion of race tracks, and our mutual interest in the turf, rather than agriculture, had brought me into contact with Captain McKittrick, a grand fellow. But I could see the strength of the Pasha's racket immediately. If the Fates had been kind enough to vouchsafe a normal rainfall, he could have parlayed it into an empire like Pizarro's. Where there is a need, someone will arise to fill it. I didn't think his presentation was particularly adapted to the American market, though. The exotic inspires distrust. A display of cold science, with impressive paraphernalia, is more effective, especially if combined with a spiritual note."

The Colonel had by now emptied a third bottle of the Gambrinian amber. "The subsidization of the Pasha was not the first attempt to influence the rain gods in California," he said. "For years wheat growers had been bringing in bands of Apaches from a reservation at Douglas, Arizona, to do rain dances. It didn't cost much and they figured it couldn't do any harm. That's why I was intrigued by this clipping,"—and he handed me a paragraph that looked as if it had been cut from a Sunday magazine section:

"OLD ORDER CHANGETH: Navajo Indians near Gallup, N.M., have become skeptical of—or just plain bored with—their ancient rain-making rites. During a recent drought, they hired professional rainmakers to seed the clouds over their reservation. Result: one-and-a-half inches of rain."

3 / Toad in Spring

"MY OWN ENTRY into the rainmaking arena did not immediately follow my perception of its potentialities," the Colonel said. "I followed after false gods. I started a race track at Salt Lake City in 1909; had to do business with the elders of the Mormon Church to get the green light. Our track was out at a place called Lagoon. After we got our track going nicely an outraged husband, an old-time Mormon, shot our track manager for the usual reason. The Mormons, although sub roseately polygamous, were monopolistic in their conjugal views. This caused a scandal, and the elders shut down our track and opened one of their own. Afterward I got a heavyweight prize fighter named Tommy Burns, who is now a faith healer in Coalinga, California. We are still dear friends and correspond incessantly."

As if in evidence, the Colonel displayed a calling card which read:

Compliments of
TOMMY BURNS

FORMER WORLD'S HEAVYWEIGHT BOXING CHAMPION

A demonstrator of Universal Love

PHONE 442   BOX 566

Coalinga, California, U.S.A.

Scrawled over the print was a line in handwriting: *God is Life & God is Love & not a human being up in the sky.* On the back of the card was a printed message, headed: THINKING KINDLY MAKES PERFECTION.

"He's a dear old Tommy," the Colonel said. "We severed our professional connection in Reno, Nevada, the day after the fight between Jim Jeffries and Jack Johnson on July 4, 1910. Jeffries never hit Johnson a punch. Burns and I had previously agreed he should retire, but Tex Rickard, the promoter of the Jeffries–Johnson fight, offered us twenty-five thousand dollars to fight Stanley Ketchel, the Michigan Assassin. I put it up to Tommy. 'You fight him,' he said. 'I'm going fishing.'"

The Colonel sighed. "We could have beaten Ketchel, too," he said. "After that I engaged in a variety of promotional ventures too multifarious to recount now. I would see an enterprise that needed the services of a good public relations man, and I would talk myself in, always for a piece. It was in that manner I encountered Professor Joseph Canfield Hatfield, in about 1912. I was in a town called Modesto, California, where the chief attraction of the particular evening was a cocking main, to be held in the auditorium of the Salvation Army Temple following a meeting of the Modesto local of the Farmers' Guild.

"Cockfighting is not my idea of the sport supreme, but having nothing better to do I attended, and for the same reason I got there early. Here this tall angular individual, Professor Joseph Canfield Hatfield, a squinty-eyed old fellow around fifty or so—was up on the platform lecturing about 'the induction of rainfall by vibratory detonation.' He had already been around for perhaps fifteen years with his theory, but had never yet made a major score.

"The first wheat growers in California had been the owners of huge ranches, but after the introduction of Turkey Red wheat to California between 1875 and '90, a variety that could grow on poor and semi-arid lands, there got to be more and more 'small' wheat growers with ranches of about twenty-five hundred acres. These made up the membership of the Farmers' Guild."

This was a field on which the Colonel had me completely at his mercy, since it was impossible to check his statements by reference to the American Racing Manual or Nat Fleischer's Ring Record Book, my usual editorial resources.

I ordered up a replenishment of the Gambrinian, and Colonel Stingo continued.

"Always the dread of the wheat grower in California in the valleys of the San Joaquin and the Sacramento River and further north in the terrain of the Columbia River and the tortuous Fraser River is lack of rain precipitation. But the Professor didn't quite know how to transmute their apprehension into auriferous deposit."

I cite, from his manuscript:

"In all sincerity this old Prof. Hatfield believed that Cannon Detonation at certain times under certain conditions would induce Rainfall; he said he had been successful in South Africa, round about Pretoria and Ladysmith and along the Tugela River bottoms in creating Rain Precipitation at the very precise time when the downpour saved the Boers vast crops of grain and fodder. He claimed credit for prolonging the Boer War a whole year.

"This incongruous Hatfield, a highly religious man, continuously bespoke the Deities in his exhortations as though his Gatling Gun would more surely serve scientific expectations through the kindly office of the Occult. He availed fasting and a wing and buck salute to the Morning Sun as a means to further favorable propituary. At the same time, I would remark at this juncture, recollection suggests the Professor knew the practical difference between the Net and the Gross and the possibilities thereof.

"Marco Polo returned from Cathay with an explosive yellow powder to the Savants Salon in Venice with the story of the first known attempts at Rain Precipitation through chemical action or physical impact according to Prof. Hatfield.

"Before not fewer than 4,000 curious long-haired gentry in Angelus Temple, Los Angeles, Calif., in his first days in the Golden State the mystic Prof. Hatfield, put to it by a Platform Barnyard Committee on Science, stated that it was his understanding that the Ancients exploded the powder by centralizing the sun's actinic rays but that he, 'the master,' used a more effective modern device,—'the awful Gatling Gun with it's discharge of pure dynamite: the gun which had won the Battle of San Juan Hill in the Spanish-American War and elected a Rough Rider to the appalling office of President of the United States of America.'

"The yokelic audience evocated in unison 'Amen, crack again.'

"I did the spade work and brought the situation to a near climax by assembling two representatives from each of the 80 Locals of the Guild with power to sign up on the Professor's neatly contrived contract of service and payment. We signed the contract at Tulare.

"The proposition was for each Local to guarantee Prof. Hatfield just $1,000, to be deposited at the Title Guarantee Trust Company in Tulare in advance. On the part of the Hatfield Rain Precipitation Corporation, through device and services of our scientific Detonationary Method, we were to assume all expenses and full direction. The official Gauges, Containers and Measuring Paddles were approved and the centrifical point of test and calculation to be the Roof of the Court House at Visalia, Calif., in heart of the Drought Wheat Lands with crops, in case of Rain, worth at least $2,000,000 in jeopardy.

"We, the Rainmakers, the Party of the First Part, always Innocents Abroad and Unsuspecting, had 32 days and nights in which to deliver 4.10 (four decimal ten) inches' depth of rain water. Rainmakers were to receive $10,000 an inch for every inch from 3 inches and below, up to 4.10 inches. If 'the can' ever showed as much as 4 inches we, the Rainmakers, were to receive the sum of $20,000 an inch for the whole amount of precipitation. We could win $80,000 and the Professor's expenses for the 30 days' Preliminary Campaign had been just $6,120: we got $1,200 of this back from the Sunny Jim Breakfast Food Co.'s advertising campaign, —so that our Nut was about $5,000.

"There was not one of the Delegates, and not a Wheat Grower in the Valley but wished heartily for the Rainmakers' success; they did not begrudge the money and wished us well. The women prayed in the churches for our success and a score or more Barn Dances and Picnics were given in our behalf, for the Professor was a natural friend maker and great alround wonderful old thief and grand good fellow. I wore off the O'Sullivan rubber heels from French, Shriner & Urner twenty-dollar shoes that month of July dancing with the buxom farm girls. And what hoedowns they were,—from sunset to sunrise. Their homemade whiskey and kitchen beer would cure cancer first time at bat.

"They say all first-class Boob Traps must contain a real smart Ace-In-The-Hole. The Rainmakers on this occasion, as well as on all other similar occasions, possessed that desideratum to a high degree.

"It was just the Meteorological Tables and Rain Precipitations for Central California issued by the Weather Bureau of the United States and the Analytical Charts and Study Averages issued by the Department of Agriculture, Washington, D.C. Then there were the Tables on Rain Precipitation from Sacramento and the Merchants Exchange, San Francisco. Many the long-hour midnight vigil I spent over those masses of demonical figures and equations in collaboration with Mr. 'Kid' Bloggs, a mighty man with Horse Figures, who was, and is, a smart Handicapper of the Gees at home and abroad.

"Without going into a labyrinth of meaningless Figures to the layman it may suffice to state the Rundown showed that for the 32-Day Period it was 55 per cent in the Rainmakers favor, viz., that 4 inches of Rain would fall regardless of Prof. Hatfield and his Gatling Guns and stores of 'pure' dynamite.

"Before an immense gathering on the North Slope of Mount Meadows, a sort of junior mountain, foregathered State, Civic and Departmental officials and the Locals turned out to a man,—about 5,000 persons on a hot dry afternoon beneath a burning Mid-California 'desert' sun. After the speeches and the Band had droned its last brassy blare Prof. Hatfield announced his retirement with Staff and ascent, not to heaven, but to the mountain's apex and bade the crowds retire to safe distance on the lower slopes. The double Battery of Gatlings went off like the Clap of Doom with a repeat, every five hours under Director of Ordnance Dr. G.A.I.M. Sykes.

"Just about midnight a perfect deluge suddenly engulfed the country-side causing Prof. Hatfield to swell his chest and bleat his salutations like a toad in springtime. The old boy thought in his inner soul that he had something on the ball but was not thoroughly convinced the Occult Powers had not framed up on him by staging a Show for his benefit and especial delight; perhaps he deserved the indulgence of the Fates, he thought. The Precipitation was 1⅛ inches, which is a lot of rain in any-body's country. Next day all the newspapers were full of the story and the Professor became slightly deified; the whole Valley stood enraptured and the fields and the ripening grain bloomed forth in gentle freshness won-derful to behold. The farmers were so happy, and even the banks began to loan money.

"Three times more during the thirty-odd days and nights we had real heavy downpours. We made a Gross Total of 3⅝ inches;—just under the full 4 inches. The overjoyed Locals held a Special Meeting and voted us the full $80,000 and invited Prof. Hatfield to return next season. The crop came in most beautifully. It was a bumper. That winter many a California wheat grower spent Christmas at New York and the childhood home in New England.

"We were paid all O.K. My cut was about $22,000. On the strength of our success the Hatfield Outfit was invited by the Farmers of the Colum-bia River in Oregon to a conference the following year in Salem. Meanwhile the puffed up Prof. Hatfield had received overtures from in-terests in the Sudan in Egypt and accepted the offers but he left us all behind.

"It was a great opportunity for Dr. Sykes and myself to go ahead on our own hook. Overnight the Doctor became the Miracle Man and I the Chief Salesman. We kept on our Staff of nine people and a Battery of Cannon used in the Civil War. Same old deal and once again we are hoping for good luck with the lay of the cards all in our favor or com-paratively so based on the Rain Precipitation Figures covering the Oregon Territory. To make a long long story short we win again and the world is ours. My take is $9,200. Paid off the Boys and Girls and disband for further orders.

"But we never did come together again for the reason that the Guilds-men found out they could do just as well themselves provided they had the right sort of Cannon.

"While shooting off their Cannon one Guildsman lost his leg and several Farmers were chewed up a bit. The rain fell just the same and the jig was up. The idea cooled off to a whisper and a story of the yesteryear."

The rain, the cold November rain, beat down on Forty-third Street as I finished reading the Colonel's story.

"In this climate," I said, forgetting 1950, "they ought to pay somebody to prevent rain."

"I was in that business too," Colonel Stingo said.

4/ The Third Palace

THE PALACE BAR and Grill, on Forty-fifth Street off Longacre Square, has not, like Gough's, the air of a shrine. It is a salon. Sophie Braun, who presides over it, suggests a collaboration between Vigée-Lebrun and Rubens, with soft white hair, pink skin, and substantial proportions. She is a woman whose quiet courtesy inspires courteous quiet in a potentially obstreperous clientele, and it was this power of Mrs. Braun's that first attracted Colonel Stingo to the place.

Joe Braun, her consort, has an equally restful personality. A sallow, stocky man of fixed habits, he goes to the races on each of the 198 afternoons of the New York season and bets five dollars on every horse Ted Atkinson rides. This is in addition to his otherwise-motivated betting, —a sort of left-hand bass to his play on the other side of the piano. He also places much faith in the advice of a friend who sells pari-mutuel tickets at a hundred-dollar window. It is impossible to tell from Joe's expression at the moment of encounter, however, whether Atkinson is on a winning or a losing streak, or whether the hundred-dollar bettors are doing any better than the herd. He smokes cigars and removes them from his mouth for only brief lapses into speech. Once an unfortunate fellow player, who had borrowed a considerable sum from Joe, paid him off with a number of plots in a Jewish cemetery. "I thought I might as well take them before he bet them on some pig," Joe said.

This left Mr. Braun with several surplus resting places, as he and Sophie had no children. So he presented one to Colonel Stingo, who accepted. "I couldn't be in better company," the Colonel declared, with feeling.

It was at the Palace that I awaited the arrival of the Colonel with the second installment of his story.

He arrived, smiling as he showed off an envelope as rounded on the sides as a rye loaf.

"Joe," he said, "if I say so myself this is a *pisseur*." The Colonel frequently lends elegance to an old-fashioned turn of speech by Frenchifying it. Thus he will sometimes refer to a figurator, or man who sells ratings on horses, as a *rateur*. "A touch of French here and there challenges the reader," he says. He often speaks of a rich man as a member of the *bourgeoisie*, pronouncing the *s* as a second *g*. "A rich man, a powerful man, plain as an old shoe, and as sweet a fellow as you would ever want to meet," he will say describing some prestigious figure of his youth. "A member of the *bourgeoigie*, and a great old thief." *Pisseur* is reserved for objects of his highest approval, like P. T. Barnum's Jumbo or the swindler George Graham Rice.

We took possession of one of the Palace booths, and the Colonel said, "I would suggest, if I might, a libation to the Goddess Pluviosa, synonymous, in the life of the Honest Rainmaker, with Fortune. In the summer of 1930, having transferred my pursuit of the Golden Fleece back to the eastern theatre of operations, I was decidedly non-holding. Old Dr. Orlando Edgar Miller, my principal in a campaign of religious education, had been laid by the heels in California. He was in durance vile, as a result of persecution by the American Medical Association, which contended he could not prolong people's lives by swinging them in a hammock, thus extending their vertebrae. An ice-skating rink which I promoted in San Francisco had been eclipsed by the subsequent erection of a larger rival, and it was too late to arrange a comeback for Tommy Burns, even had he been willing, because he was by now on the half-century mark. A storm cloud lowered over the American economy, and the moment seemed inauspicious for any kind of a score.

"Hearing of my lack of immediate projects, an old California friend of mine who had himself scored handily in New York had written to me, urging me to challenge the big city once again. I recalled a phrase I had once heard from the lips of Elbert Hubbard, also about New York. 'It's a hard place to live, Little Mac, but the money's there.' I had a house near Golden Gate Park, in San Francisco, staffed by a Chinese couple, man and wife, whose stipendia were somewhat in arrears. I presented them with the house and came on like the Argonauts, by a slow ship through the Panama Canal. But venture capital had apparently taken refuge. The depression of October, 1929 refused to rescind itself, and the old town had changed. I had a room at the old Hotel Imperial and office space in the Knickerbocker Building at Forty-second and Broadway, but I was beginning to worry about the plug in the door.

"When without specific objective, I have often found it rewarding to go to the race track. I have made it a lifelong rule, since the age of fifteen, never to bet on horses. Freed of this vulgar preoccupation, a man at the track can sometimes see opportunity beckon."

"Didn't you ever bet a horse?" I asked, incredulous.

"At an early age I learned the futility of the practice," the Colonel said, reminding me, as he spoke, of another friend, Izzy Yereshevsky, the proprietor of the I & Y Cigar Store, which remains open twenty-four hours a day except on Yom Kippur at Forty-ninth Street and Seventh Avenue. There is a cigar box on the counter which also remains open twenty-four hours a day, into which customers drop contributions toward the burial expenses of old horse players. "Don't any of the boys win?" I once asked Izzy, who is, like the Colonel, a non-player.

"How did you think them horses gets feed?" Mr. Yereshevsky asked me.

"I have just finished a section of my autobiography," the Colonel said, "which will shed light on what you seem to regard as an eccentricity." Before I could steer him back onto the story of the Honest Rainmaker, he had planted in front of me a chapter of *The Plug in the Door*, and since he then turned all his attention to a *delice Gambrinienne*, I had nothing to do but read.

5 / Baptism of Fire

"IT WAS 1888. Back home in New Orleans my destiny became the live subject of commentation at all family gatherings. What to do with him? In those times Springfield Lodge, my ancestral home, filled me with delight always. It cost my Grand Father a great deal of money and was regarded as one of the most typical and palatial in the whole South.

"My dear Mother finally announced that she had achieved the brave heights by securing 'James Aloysius,'—that's me, a job with a weekly Irish Catholic newspaper. A fine kindly gentleman was Father John Quinn, the Editor of the New Orleans *Catholic Register*. I'm assigned the task of securing Data and writing pieces about the 'dear departed' of St. Jerome's Parish and collecting sales returns from the news stands based upon the prior week's sales. I would have been much more at home keeping score of the Southern League games at Heinneman Park for the Pelicans.

"After writing a few dandy pieces about prominent decedents of the Parish, and after aggrandizing $20 or so from the downtown news stands and top carriers, a comforting discovery came to me,—I learned, much to my surprise and delight, that a perfectly adorable spot to rest the body and cool the fetid brow from much deep-sea thinking and unremitting pave-pounding, was 'Sitting Bull' Bush's barnlike Poolroom, where business was done on five different Fields of Horses in five different cities. Also, the newly established Young Men's Gymnastic Club's tremendous Training Quarters for Pugilists, Wrestlers & Chicken Fighters provided elegant and restful surcease for a young and aspiring journalist who, after all, liked the finer and higher things of life.

"But one day Fate stepped in. On this occasion a prominent Parishioner had gone on to his paradisical reward. He was big, he was top news. To acquire the facts and picture necessitated a trudge away out Canal Street and here I was some $60 winner on the horses in Mr. Bush's cool-off Poolroom. All based on the 'monetary leverage' for I was utilizing the News Stand collections to sustain my speculative moves. To tear myself away from such idyllic environment and engaging occupation would be unthinkable to most mortals, and it certainly appealed to me in that direction. I figurated there was justifiable cause.

"So a way out popped from the box.[1] I consulted the Town Oracle who stood at my right side where he could get a clearer view of the chalked-up prices on the First Three of the last heat at Latonia. 'Why Mr. John Sidney White, the guy you say has kicked off, I knew him well. I can and will tell you all you wish to know about him.' This was comforting and everything I might hope for in realization. Said I, hastily getting Pad and Pencil together, 'That is fine. You have saved my neck. Please let me have it in gobs.' And the considerate Horse Player just did that little thing. 'The late Mr. White,' said he, 'was cut down in the very prime of life. He was one of the most athletic and herculean types of men our city had ever known. He could beat 10 flat in the hundred and put the 16-pound shot at Yale in his Sophomore Year no fewer than 59 feet. And how those women in the Rotunda of the French Opera went for White, a walking Adonis. And you say it was Heart Disease. Well, well I so regret to hear the sad intelligence.'

"After close of the Poolroom operations, and, bye the way, I may say my speculation turned out to be a stalemate,—quit even,—I repaired to McConkey's marble-tabled short-order Bazaar in Commercial Alley and transposed the above facts as related by the Town Oracle into a right nice piece for the *Catholic Register*, wherein it duly appeared the next Sunday. Recently, the dear Father had complimented me by suggesting I should take the Junior Class at Sunday School next week. Looked like I am standing high in his estimation.

"Rather early on the succeeding Monday the Reverend Father sends for me.

"So I look into the eye of Father Quinn wonderingly. What wrong had I done anyway? You could see he intended to be stern. So here goes. Here is what he said to me. 'Mr. Macdonald you have been doing very nicely on our *Register*' said the Editor, 'but in reference to that glowing symposium on the late Mr. White's physical perfection, I recall you said he was the modern Adonis, I must call to your attention that Mr. White had lost his left leg at the siege of Port Hudson and the absence of his

[1] The Colonel is fond of figures of speech taken from the game of faro (originally *pharaon*, another example of his Gallic predilection). He will bet this game or bank it whenever he gets a chance. "The percentage is almost nil," he says, "unlike the pari-mutuels with their fearful sixteen-per-cent bite. The complexity of the game and its equality, however, militate against its survival. Gambling houses, even in Nevada, are full of slot machines now. It is an age debased and mechanical."

nose was due to the ravage of malignant cancer. Now, Mr. Macdonald we who have the destiny of the *Register* in hand do not claim to rank in journalistic brilliance with "Marse" Henry Watterson, Horace Greeley, or Charles A. Dana, but we are sticklers for authenticity. We're very aggrieved Mr. Macdonald.'

"Some time went on and I'm a regular at Bush's Poolroom. Somehow I'm never much loser, never much winner. But one Saturday night when the Deadline for News Stands Collections is at hand I'm short $18, current exchange, and no fussing around. Like a brave bull in the afternoon, I walk into Father Quinn's study with the salutation: 'Father Quinn may I ask an indulgence please sir. I find myself incommoded in the sum of $20.00 which I extracted from Collections this very day. Shall come in with it next Monday noon. Is that all O.K., Father?' This kindly man and fine Editor looked at me with his two saucer-shaped blue eyes, rejoining: 'My boy, worry no further. Mr. Bush sent for it and I've paid him the $18.00. I'm busy, I'll be seeing you later.'

"But one day this very human and monumental spirit of goodness said, 'My boy don't you know this is no paper for you to be working on. I've gotten a new position for you this coming Monday on Mr. O'Malley's very sedate New Orleans daily *Item*. I'm sorry to see you go but destiny for you beckons to other and larger fields of newspaper endeavor.'

"And, so it was that I reported to the *Item* front boss and was assigned a desk and utensils. No sooner had I gotten well set in my work than two belligerent Editors began shooting at the visiting Chief of Police, the slugs skimming over my head but some of them bouncing merrily off'n a steel pictorial cut extended in front of me for final check up and O.K.

"And that was my beginning in a chosen field of Destiny, the newspaper business, a story of a Lifetime in the pursuit of the Fourth Estate."

6 / A Day with Dominick O'Malley

"You see what race-track betting brought me to," the Colonel said when he perceived I had finished. "Do you blame me for refraining in the intervening years?"

"On the contrary, I admire you," I said. "But what brought you into the line of fire?"

"Mr. O'Malley had abandoned his desk at the usual hour of twelve and betaken himself for prandial relaxation first to the bar of the St. Charles Hotel, where he had a three-bagger of Sazeracs, then to Hymen's bar on Common Street, where he increased his *apéritif* by four silver gin fizzes and after that over to Farbacher's saloon on Royal where he had a schooner or two of Boston Club punch. O'Malley was not of that *sang-pur* elegance which would have got him past the portal of the august Boston Club, the most revered in New Orleans, but he had bribed a fancy girl to wheedle the formula from the Boston Club bartender. It consisted of twelve bottles of champagne, eight bottles of white wine, one and one half bottles raspberry syrup, one half bottle brandy, one half bottle kirschwasser, one quarter bottle Jamaica rum, one quarter bottle Curacao, two pineapples, two dozen oranges, two and one half lbs. sugar, seltzer and ice. This was enough to serve several persons.

"When he had finished his preparations bacchanalic he strolled over to Antoine's, where he had four dozen freshly shucked oysters without any muck on them, a red snapper flambée in absinthe, a salmis of three woodcock and four snipe, a chateaubriand, *bleu*, six bottles of Bass's ale, and a magnum of La Mission Haut Brion of the comet year. After that he smoked a made-to-measure cigar, as long as his arm from the inside of the elbow to the tip of the middle finger, and drank a dipper of Calvados from a cask that had been brought to Louisiana from Normandy with the first cargo of sparkle-eyed Cyprians in 1721. Not more than one quart had been drawn from the cask in any one year since, and it had been carefully replenished each time. Having effectuated the *trou normand*, O'Malley consumed an *omelette au kirsch* and a small baked alaska, followed by a *caffè espresso* for which he sent the maître d'hôtel to a dive operated by the Maffia. 'The hardest thing to get in New Orleans,' he always said, 'is a decent cup of coffee.' He then started to walk back toward the office, which was on Camp Street, with some vague notion of pausing on the way to drape a beautiful octoroon's ivory throat with pearls, and would have arrived at his usual hour, after half-past four, had he not met with an unforeseen vicissitude."

The Colonel paused and looked about him with an expression that approximated distaste. When he is in such moods his current Gambrinian haunts seem to him to lack éclat.

"I'll settle for another beer," he said, and when it had been brought continued.

"I, a mere kid, had been entranced from the moment of Mr. O'Malley's exit by the notion of seating myself in his swivel chair and cocking my feet on his desk," he said. "Expecting momentarily his return, for I had heard that secular newspaper men ate, so to speak, *sur le pouce*, I refrained for the first four hours and fifteen minutes. Then, deciding that he might not be back at all, I yielded. I made my way furtively to his desk, sat down, swung my legs up, and encouraged by the smiles of the older men, even took the boss's green eyeshade off the blotter and placed it on my towish potato. I then raised a steel line cut from the desk and, pretending to inspect it, held it in front of my face, thus veiling my identity. I did not know it was the habit of Mr. David Hennessy, the Chief of Police of New Orleans, to arrive at the *Item* office each afternoon at four thirty-five to shoot at Mr. O'Malley. The fellows in the composing room set their watches by it and sent the second edition to press.

"It was a tryst. O'Malley would arrive at four-thirty, hang up his frock coat, lay out his revolvers on the desk in front of him, and start to write a leader taking the skin off Hennessy. He would indite daily a virulent editorial charging the Chief with official dereliction by permitting the poolrooms, policy bazars, brothels and bagnios, the stews and knocking shops, to run wide open every day including Sunday, a day of extreme reverence south of the Tennessee River. Mr. O'Malley was in political control of the city and figured that any madame who wanted a Sunday turn at bat should apply to him personally. At four thirty-five the Chief, who had been steaming up on Creole coffee laced with contraband Cuban rum at McConkey's in Commercial Alley, would proceed across Camp Street and ascend to the first landing in the *Item* building. He gave Mr. O'Malley five minutes to get set. With little knowledge of trigonometry, but with natural copperial intuition, Mr. Hennessy would select a likely angle of trajectory through the wooden partition screening the city room and the corner where Mr. O'Malley sat in pontifical augustity.

"These first shots were a long price to wing Mr. O'Malley but a good bet to drive him under his desk in search of cover, a position from which he could not efficiently retaliate. Advancing behind the barrage, Mr. Hennessy would reach a spot from which he could survey the city room. But there he would be caught in a cross fire between the sports editor and the editor of the religious page, and after emptying both revolvers would be impelled to retreat. It was a lesson in logistics which I have never forgotten.

"But do not think that Mr. O'Malley had not his troops in elegant *élan* and precise readiness for these manoeuvres. At the first muffled roar and crackling sound of timber rendered, all hands except the enfilading pair, from the city editor to the meekest copy boy,—would secure shotguns conveniently placed for the purpose and rush to the front windows looking out on the street below, knowing full well that the miscreant Hennessy must, perforce, make egress and present briefly a target. After I had survived my first payday I was initiated into the routine. But on this first day of employment I was completely unprepared when a bullet from a Smith and Wesson whammed into the steel plate I held in front of me, knocking it from my hands and me *derrière dessus* behind Mr. O'Malley's desk. I learned afterward that it was the most accurate opening shot Mr. Hennessy had ever fired. 'A perfect carom,' the religious editor said. 'He played it off that new machine, the typewriter. I always said they had no place in a newspaper office.'

"After Mr. Hennessy had retreated, shrinking up close to the front of the *Item* building so as not to give the boys with the fowling pieces a clean shot, all my seniors apologized profusely for not having tipped me off. They hadn't thought I was in any real danger, they explained, and had just wanted to see some of the cockiness taken out of me when the first missile whistled overhead. 'It is ceasing to be fun,' the sports editor said. 'Also, I suspect the Chief of wearing the cover of a wash boiler inside the seat of his pants. The man in the slot had what looked like a clean hit on him day before yesterday and the only result was a loud clang. What worries me, though, is what has happened to the boss? He is either in the clink or some panelworker has stolen his trousers again.'"

The Colonel's wide, generous nose is slightly retroussé, and when he looks up at me his nostrils form a deeply indented M. They have a look of unshakeable sincerity.

"The first surmise was correct," he said. "Mr. O'Malley, returning to the office from his last mysterious port of call, had been hurrying through Commercial Alley, a narrow lane between St. Charles and Camp Streets, in order to arrive at the rendezvous before Mr. Hennessy. Had Hennessy got there first, Mr. O'Malley would have found himself cut off from his base. But in making his way through the alley, the editor, a man of generous girth, came into abrupt collision, like a crack flyer of the Southern Railroad meeting a freight train of the Louisville & Nashville, with the editor of a rival newspaper, the New Orleans *States*, headed in the opposite direction. The two had exchanged acrimonious ink about a suggestion, publicized by Mr. O'Malley, that a bank of which his fellow editor was a director was on the point of failure. Mr. O'Malley had been refused a loan. The bank was the Hibernia National, known in New Orleans of the epoch as the Irish Rock.

"The editor of the *States*, whose name, as I recollect it, was Ewing, invariably carried an umbrella with a sharp ferrule, vouchsafing it served him as a sunshade in the summer. He thrust it immediately at Mr. O'Malley's left eye, being resigned to an exchange of shots and thinking that by this preliminary he might impair Mr. O'Malley's aim. He missed the eyeball, however, although he put a nice hole in Mr. O'Malley's brow, and forthwith the fusillade began. Of course down there in those days there was so much shooting the general public knew just what to do. The patrolmen on St. Charles and Camp detoured all traffic headed past the ends of the alley, and a number of shopkeepers on Commercial reached out from their doorways and grabbed the right hands of the contestants, an efficacious method of terminating hostilities. Sometimes they made a mistake; one of the duelists was left-handed. The effect of the error could prove lethal. Both Mr. O'Malley and Mr. Ewing, however, were conventionally orientated, and there were no casualties beyond the effusion of gore from Mr. O'Malley's punctured pumpkin.

"The police escorted both men before a magistrate, and from the clutches of these Dogberries O'Malley would soon have talked himself free, had not Ewing, himself a political power, sworn out a warrant against him for impairing the credit of the Hibernia National and causing a run on the Irish Rock. The judge happened to own stock in that institution. O'Malley was therefore immured, soon to be joined by a Mr. Kiernan who published the New Orleans *News*, and who had joined in his campaign of retribution against the Hibernia. A swift messenger informed us at the *Item* office of their predicament."

"What happened to Ewing?" I asked. "He started the fight, didn't he?"

"He was released," the Colonel said. "In those days a mere felonious assault was considered of no moment."

I found this easier to believe because of a conversation I once had with a leading member of the Bar in Nevada, where the law still has a decent respect for human combustibility. We were talking about a friend of ours in Reno who had got shot in an argument about something or other a couple of years previously. "Harry got it in the liver," the jurist said. "They were laying five to one against recovery in the morning line at the Nevada Turf Club. But there happened to be an ace surgeon in town who still had a couple of days to wait for his decree, and he got the slug out without hurting him."

"What happened to the other fellow?" I had asked then, and the legal light had answered:

"He's fine, just fine. Saw him down at the Golden Hotel bar last week."

"Did they arrest him?" I asked.

Eminent counsel looked at me with some astonishment. "Why, no," he said. "If Harry had *died* we would have arrested him, though."

"A high bail had been set," the Colonel said, unaware how far west my thoughts had strayed, "and while the senior members of the staff sought bond for the captives, I was despatched to the St. Charles Parish Prison, where they were incarcerated, in a hired hack with a case of vintage Irroy *brut*, and Mr. O'Malley's English bulldog, Mike, whom he had left tied to the umbrella stand when he went out to lunch. I found the prisoners in good spirits and left them in better after they had emptied the first three bottles, kindly inviting me and the turnkey to have a glass with them. I went out thinking I had landed in the pearl of professions. And so it was, in those days of halcyon, the very cap and zenith of American journalism."

The Colonel appeared to ruminate for a while, and I thought I could visualize the procession of eminent zenithians, like Marse Henry Watterson and the youthful William Randolph Hearst, that must be passing behind his eyelids. But he was thinking of something else.

"I have never ceased to regret, Joe," he said, "that on my first day at the *Item* I was the indirect though innocent cause of Chief Hennessy's death. The bullet that struck the plate in my hand ricocheted through the flimsy ceiling and hit an old-style southern gentleman in the business office in the calf of the leg. His name, as I remember it, was Mr. Troup Sessams, and he had withheld his fire previously because he considered the shooting downstairs a strictly editorial matter. When the bullet arrived, Mr. Sessams said, 'This is no damn joke.'

"He closed up his roll-top desk, hung his alpaca office coat on a hook, put on his long-tailed frock coat and a hat with a five-inch brim, and withdrew from the lower drawer of the desk a rosewood case containing two long-barreled dueling pistols with which he had eliminated all ante-bellum rivals for the hand of his wife, at that time heiress to a plantation Faulknerian, but since, like so many of us, non-holding. He loaded the pistols and placed one inside each breast of his frock coat, in the long pockets provided for that purpose by antebellum tailors. He then walked downstairs, limping a little,—the shot had only grazed him,—and followed Hennessy out into the night. It was the end of the Chief. His perforated body was discovered next morning. The year was 1889; the precise date eludes me."

"But wasn't Hennessy the New Orleans police chief who was killed by the Maffia?" I exclaimed, beginning to think I remembered something I had once read.

"That was the common theory, Joe," the Colonel said, "and the citizens of New Orleans acted upon it to the extent of shooting eleven Italians and then hanging them to trees. But those foreigners were desperate characters anyway, and doubtless deserved their fate."

In the course of a recent visit to New Orleans, I sought corroboration of Colonel Stingo's recollections. My research there seems to indicate that while the years may have blurred his memory in regard to some of the facts and caused it to embellish, if not invent, others, there is a certain hard core of veracity in what he remembers and no doubt at all that at least some of his cast of characters did exist in roles more or less akin to those he ascribes to them. There is the matter of Mr. O'Malley's *embonpoint*, for instance; I learned of one editorial fracas in which it served him ill and rather more gravely so than in the one recounted by Colonel Stingo. This was a duel between Mr. O'Malley and Colonel Harrison Parker, editor of the *Picayune*. Mr. O'Malley had published in the *Item* a cartoon representing Colonel Parker as a dog led on a string by the governor of Louisiana, whom Mr. O'Malley disliked. The newspaper offices were on opposite sides of Camp Street. One day, both editors emerged into the street at the same time, bound for lunch—apparently the lunch hour was reserved for shootings in that miraculous city. "O'Malley fired first and winged Colonel Parker, crippling his accustomed pistol arm," a local historian who described the incident to me said. "Colonel Parker took his pistol in his left hand, but knowing he could not shoot accurately with it, walked across the street to get close to O'Malley before pulling the trigger. Colonel Parker had commanded a regiment in the Confederate Army, and the pistol was a Tranter .52, a monstrous weapon throwing a slug as big as a heavy machine gun. Mr. O'Malley, not caring to confront his fire, tried to scrounge himself up behind a telegraph pole, of which we then had many in the downtown section. But he was so big and fat his belly protruded beyond the defilade furnished by that im-

provised position of defense, and Colonel Parker, advancing to the opposite side of the telephone pole, leaving a trail of sanguinary testimony to
his courage as he walked, took careful aim and shot his man right through
the protuberance, the bullet entering under one end of his watch chain
and emerging from under the other. Both men were seriously dis-
commoded."

As for Mr. O'Malley's connection with the *Item*, it appears that he did
not become proprietor of that newspaper until 1894 or '95, half a dozen
years after Chief Hennessy's death. A police reporter emeritus, almost as
old as the Colonel, told me that there was a New Orleans Chief of Police
who sometimes used to shoot O'Malley (although you couldn't set your
watch by it), but his name was Ed Whitaker, and he didn't become chief
until 1906, when Stingo was thirty-two years old. However, Whitaker was
a recorder, or police magistrate, during the nineties, and he may have
started shooting O'Malley then. Hennessy and O'Malley were deadly
enemies during the Maffia days, but at that time O'Malley was a private
detective, not yet an editor. It is suspected that O'Malley bribed a juror
during a trial of the eleven Italians for Hennessy's murder, and so secured
a hung jury and a mistrial. The lynching followed. O'Malley's fee is said
to have provided the capital with which, when things had quieted down,
he bought the *Item* and set up as a reforming editor. O'Malley lisped. He
had an old iron safe in his editorial office which he used to say contained
dossiers on every outwardly respectable citizen of New Orleans, accumulated during his days as a private detective. "You see that safe?" he used
to say to callers when he was premeditating a front-page attack on some
particularly saintly target. "It's full of that sonofabits."

It would seem that the Colonel has intertwined elements of the
Hennessy-O'Malley cycle with others of the O'Malley-Whitaker cycle, to
produce a result artistically superior to either. The Tristan legend under-
went an analogous development. The roles, and even the identities, of the
two Iseuts are inextricably confused, like those of Hennessy and Whitaker.
Only the hero, O'Malley-Tristan, remains a constant.

7 / Reunion at Belmont

"THIS HAS BEEN a labyrinthian digression," Colonel Stingo said, with a
handkerchief dabbing the Gambrinian foam from beneath his nostrils,
and signaling his readiness for a refill. "But here I am, this fine though
overcast early afternoon in September, 1930, if memory serves, the
Wednesday following the opening on Monday, Labor Day, when the Fall
Highweight Handicap had been won by that marvelous sprinter, Balko,

under a hundred and thirty-six pounds. The second day's racing had been marred by a torrential downpour beginning after the second race, and the question of weather for the rest of the short meeting, only twelve more days, but including the Grande Semaine of American racing, was naturally a subject of managerial preoccupation. The Westchester Racing Association was offering a generous stake list,—the purses had been announced at a period when the country looked financially impregnable, —but for the first time since the end of the First World War attendances at all sporting events had fallen off, a circumstance imputable to the quasi-disappearance of Tease from public circulation. The pari-mutuels were not yet grinding out their vast gist of vulgar gelt for the New York tracks, though they were in operation in other regions, and not even bookmaking had been formally legalized, as it was in a few years to be. The hand of Charles Evans Hughes still lay heavy on the state that had gifted him with its highest office.

"The tolerated bookies, who discreetly received bets on the track, presumably only from members of their acquaintance, bought their operating franchises from the Association by paying a high rent, nominally for boxes in the grandstand. But the income from this source was limited. So the gate money was vital if Belmont was to meet the nut, and the directors of the Association, although all millionaires, had not got that way by losing money, an ordeal to which they were still painfully unaccustomed although in many cases recently initiated. The president, Mr. Joseph E. Widener of Philadelphia, was even less accustomed than the lesser millionaires who surrounded him. He was a Prince of Good Fellows, attired in atelier-like clothes, and possessed of the divine inflatus for money-getting. I knew him from the happy days preceding the advent of Charles Evans Hughes, when I had frequently chronicled the triumph of his racing colors, the red and white stripes.

"From here on, Joe, you may as well read my account of the sequelae." And the Colonel, leafing through his manuscript, found a jump-off spot for me, passed the bundle across the table, and signaled to Louie, the lunch-counter man who doubles as waiter, to bring him another Gambrinian libation.

"Upon arrival at the Park," I read, "I made my way to Mike the Bite's lucky Shoe Shine Stand just in off the Betting Ring, the scourge of the Pari-Mutuels not having descended upon the tranquil scene of the Oralist, as yet, in 1930, in fact, it was not to be for 10 years later. The proprietor, a slightly colored man, perhaps an octoroon, was of true name William Beeson, but styled Mike the Bite because he was such an easy fellow to promote for a loan. This was because of native generosity, not lack of business acumen, for Willie had built up for himself a considerable fortune by his occult activities. The stand provided but a small portion of his revenues. He paid $300 a month rental for the two-seated stand and charged 25 cents for a slap-dash polish with quick brush-off. But he also sold, to customers both male and female, a daily rabbit's foot for $2 and an agreement to bet $2 for him on his third-race selection. He must have been quite a figurator, or else quite a salesman, because he put out around 50 rabbits' feet per diem. Not all the rabbits' feet customers took shines.

"On two long hanger racks in the rear the Bite undertook to care safely your overcoat or umbrella; his way of assuring himself the customer's return and, above all, payoff. If the Bite's selection came down in front in the third, it requires no great computation to see he was a sure thing to become rich.

"The second dodge of the Bite was quite classic. Early in life his back was broken during a Tornado at his place of nativity down South, notoriously the home of high winds, viz., Gainesville, Georgia. Nobody ever had such a magnificently large Hunch as the Bite believe me.

"And be assured the Bite made the Hunchback Business pay him better than it had Lon Chaney, who played Quasimodo in the silent films. He made a play for the lady Horseplayers only. He bought two suits a year, one for the summer and one for the chilly days of autumn, generally at $35 each. But he paid $5.00 extra for a very special alteration. Where the coat rested plumb atop the Hunch this mastermind contrived a large Patch Pocket that opened and closed on a shiny zipper about six inches long.

"For years, the Bite held to the psychic fixation, in effect, experience had shown him, that only women could enjoy good luck in playing the horses by the laying on of the hands upon the prodigious Hump. He would say oftentimes that under no circumstance would he sell 'a tough,' as he termed the merchandise, to a man, only to a woman, and never less than $10.

"As the years went by the Bite built up a large and steady patronage among the women turf speculators. They would come sidling up quietly to the Shoe Shine Stand and back in the rear of the hanger racks. The Bite would follow, tip toeish like, and in a flash a tug on the zipper would bring exposure of the Hump. By a quick and dexterous move the lady Horseplayer reached down a 'pinky' and 'the touch' became achieved.

"I climbed up on Mike's stand not because I was a candidate for the eleemosynary department, still less to get a horse in the third, but because it provided a perch from which I might survey briefly the hurrying throng, all panting with greed, intent on the accumulation of unearned increment. Also I liked to exchange a greeting with the Bite, who had a particular esteem for me because I always addressed him as Willie, his real given name. And from my perch I perceived a friend of olden times, the tall, gaunt, Professor George Ambrosius Immanuel Morrison Sykes, D.D. (Zoroastrian), whom I had known first as assistant to Dr. Joseph Canfield Hatfield, the father of artificially induced precipitation, and later as my own partner in the Honest Rainmaking business.

"He was hurrying with long strides, but not in the direction of the betting ring, from which I judged he was on some tryst intent. Since he was not given to extra-conjugal romance I took it that his appointment was with a solvent boob. I followed with my eyes his progress across the clubhouse lawn, and to my astonishment recognized the resplendent form encountering his as that of Mr. Widener, who was accompanied by the Racing Secretary of the meeting, a Mr. Schaumberg, since, like his boss, gone under the wire.

"The incongruous three joined in colloquy and shortly moved away to a tree surrounded by benches, where they seated themselves. I, having by now felt the tug at my trouser-leg which was the Bite's signalization of the completion of his onceover, descended from the chair and followed them. It was a cinch, I had already estimated, that Mr. Widener would not wish Dr. Sykes to bring on *more* rain, so I wondered if the good Doctor had found a method of keeping it away.

"The gentlemen had selected for the talk the Joyner Oak, set within a richly verdured parkway enclosed by four brightly striped benches of heavy hickory wood and spiked in the supporting headpieces by wooden stanchions, instead of modern steel clavers.

"The benches had been presented to the Westchester club by the late Pierre Lorillard, the Master of Rancocas Farms, Jobstown, N.J., as an ornament to Belmont Park when it was first opened.[1]

"Across the Lawn stood the entrance to the private elevator which would take Mr. Widener to his offices in the upper reaches in the Club Preserves within the huge grand stand, and quite apart from the expensive Turf and Field Club in the ancient Manice Mansion further along and across the green swarded Paddock with it's celebrated group of Old English Trees and Rose Bushes in hedge formation. Suddenly, the knot of earnestly conferring men became restive, and Mr. Widener made his adieu with a gentle move towards the elevator entrance. Messers. Sykes and Schaumberg would be obliged to cross my path if they directed their way to the Racing Secretary's Office.

"Sure enough, that was the direction they took. Almost abreast of me, Dr. Sykes suddenly saw and recognized me. An effusive greeting followed.

"Suddenly, from here, there and everywhere, occurred a rush of persons from beneath the Paddock trees, from underneath the grandstand and out of the recesses of the Racing Administrative Building, all towards the trackside rail, all in answer to the thrilling alarum, 'They're off.' Like a red coon dog catching high scent, the Secretary broke into a run and was gone.

"That was the cue for me to isolate Dr. Sykes from the mass of possible interference round about; I edged him away to Mike the Bite's stand and manoeuvred him back behind the hanger racks, where we could talk

[1] This is the kind of thing on which I never know how far the Colonel is spoofing, if at all.

unobserved. He came quickly to the point; he had been doing business in late years as the Weather Control Bureau, of Burbank, Cal. Out there, he said, he had received a letter from a lady in New York with a name fragrant of millions, asking whether he could prevent as well as cause rainfall. If so, she said, she would be willing to defray the expense of a conference here in New York. On arrival here he was to report to the offices of the Westchester Racing Association, when a meeting would be arranged between him and Mr. Widener. The good Doctor had come on speedily.

" 'My latest apparatus has proved as efficacious in driving away rain as in inducing it,' he said with a perfectly straight face. 'But I would appreciate your assistance with the meteorological data. It's a good thing to know what you have to contend against.' He had reported on arrival, and Mr. Schaumberg had made the appointment for him with Mr. Widener.

" 'Funny thing about him, though,' the Doctor said, 'He said he couldn't make up his mind on the deal until we'd both talked it over with the lady. Said he had great confidence in her intuition. So we made another appointment for tomorrow, same time, but out at the Widener barn, where the lady's car will be parked. These rich Easterners are very suspicious. He seemed to doubt my good faith.'

" 'That's because he has never done business with an Honest Rainmaker,' I said, and we both laughed. 'I have known Mr. Widener for many years,' I added, 'and I am prepared to corroborate whatever assertions you may make, within reason, about your past accomplishments. Also, as you may recollect, I have an adroitness in handling the feminine component, a way with the ladies, and I suspect that Mrs. Harriman,'— that was the fair one's name,—'will have the determining voice.' So I was in like Flynn, for 45 percent of the whole deal, which like a promising but untried mining claim we did not yet know the full value of, yet it bore a Bonanza aspect. The old Doc stipulated 10 percent for Mrs. Sykes, who he said had accompanied him to New York, and 45 percent for himself. I contributed my office facilities, desk space and mail service at the Knickerbocker Building, so that the Weather Control Bureau could offer a New York address, always a denotation of substantiality. I was to be the outside man, or talker, and old Doc was to profess the zealot, unapproachable and hard to understand.

" 'Now,' I said, 'I would suggest that Mr. Widener, who has in his life drag-netted a vast accumulation of profits, is more attracted by the possibility of making money than of guaranteeing against loss. I would therefore suggest that we offer him a forfeit for non-fulfillment of our promise, —something like double his money back if it rains.' I had in the back of my mind that it rains less than once a week on the average in early September, a hot, sultry time in the vicinity of New York usually, but I was going to check it before I made the price.

"So the Good Doctor and myself left Mike the Bite with his Lares &

Snares; making headway to the Doctor's brand new Buick we soon found ourselves speeding along the Boulevard en route to New York; we felt no desire to see the rest of the races, having matters more emergent on our minds. I for one had to see what Weather reports for the Long Island district in past years were available at the New York Public Library, my source of avail in an endless variety of situations. The appearance of the Doctor's vehicle did not deceive me; I was acquainted with the liberal credit arrangements available in a time of increasing automotive merchandising difficulty.

"'Are you holding, Doctor?' I asked him. He shook his head. 'Just enough to live nice for a couple of weeks,' he said. My resources were similarly limited. I thought that some small capital might be necessary to launch the enterprise. But I had already fixed in my mind a potential source for such collateral. 'Semper Paratus' is the motto of the Long Riders."

"The Long Riders" is a term the Colonel likes to apply to himself and all his associates, past and present, in allusion to the train robbers who used to ride out of the Indian Territory of Oklahoma with Al Jennings, a character Colonel Stingo claims as a boyhood friend. The analogy is purely poetic, however. The only gun point at which the Colonel has ever taken money is the muzzle of Professor Hatfield's cannon.

"Doctor and Mrs. Sykes had taken a month's lease on an old brownstone house in the West Eighties," the manuscript went on. "There I joined them in the late evening, after a long afternoon profitably spent in meteorological figuration. We could afford to lay Mr. Widener 2 to 1 and still have a percentage of .7499 in our favor, I had discovered, while the greediest bookmakers content themselves with .15 and .20, and the remorseless parimutuel as at present constituted but .16. But by a subtlety in the wording of our wager I could bring the real odds down still further for the Grande Semaine, beginning with Saturday, Sept. 6, the date of the Lawrence Realization and Champagne Stakes, and running through Saturday the 13, Futurity Day, on which the best two-year-olds in the country were to vie for the championship and a prize of more than $100,000. It turned out to be $121,670. We had an edge in our favor beyond the dreams of avarice.

"But this old joker Sykes maintained the pretext that his manipulations were in fact capable of affecting the result, and that my calculation of probabilities was only supplemental. 'A lot of things have developed in our profession since your time, Little Mac,' he told me, 'including radio.'

"That night we dined with fine gusto, and remained at table for hours at Café Conte on Astor Place recalling old times and old friends. Mrs. Sykes was a big woman with a blarney and a swagger that would have been useful in a sideshow of Adam Forepaugh's Three-Ring Circus of ancient time. In the Rainmakers' Campaigns in the Far West it had been her specialty to attend gatherings of the women of the Farmers in their churches and Meeting Houses where she would lead the exercises and the prayers. This time, she said, she would exercise another talent. She could mix drinks as expertly and diabolically as any leering Night Club Bartender I ever knew. 'It should help with public relations,' she said.

"With a freshening shower and spanking breakfast, I was in fine fettle as Dr. Sykes and myself stepped into his car for the long ride to Belmont Park next morning.

"And now the Bugle Call for the opening race of this drizzling murky day here at Belmont Park clarioned through the Paddock and across the vast stretches of the Queen of All Racing Courses in the New World.

"We knew that within ten minutes we would be at Mrs. Harriman's side, along with Messrs. Widener and Schaumberg."

8 / "Long, Lissome, Lucreferous"

"PRECISELY on the dot, we kept our appointment with Mrs. Harriman at the Turf & Field Club. A very gracious lady and one of the real beautiful women of her day and time, she chose to receive us upon the Driveway leading up to the Clubhouse verandah while seated in a handsome custom built, 8-cylinder, imported Hispano-Suiza.

"I afterwards learned this motor car cost, laid down in New York from Toledo, Spain, the surprising sum of $22,000, one of the most luxurious and expensive jobs in the United States in 1930. On the direction of Madame, the tonneau's side door swung ajar, revealing a vista of rich and ravishing splendor;—upon her Golden Barge in the simmering moonlight of a sheening night on the Nile, I am sure Cleopatra never looked more completely devastating than does dear Mrs. Harriman as she reclines her elongated figure lissomely strewn, lengthwise upon the satin-cushioned coach seat while smoking a costly heaven-scented Carolina Perfecto, à la Panatela, with the poise of a Winston Churchill tweezing a Wheeling stogie.

"In quiet souciance, a quick glance measured Dr. Sykes and myself for her Ladyship, and we were evidently satisfactory for she said, 'Now boys what may be your first name,—yes you blue eyes—yours?' Timidly abashed, I squeaked up,—'Jim.' Dr. Sykes merely suggested, 'Just call me Doc.' Then came the first imperial command from the Royal Divan's purpled folds to a Club attendant,—'Please, immediately, chairs for the gentlemen from the Clubhouse.'

"Now, all of us are nicely grouped about Mrs. Harriman and her Throne Room in commodious club chairs awaiting the opening phases of the impending Grand Symposium.

"Tall, slim and elongated she was, and her wide wondering eyes were in shade the color of sea shells along the Caribbean beachway at sunrise; her honey-tone-colored hair, bunched in braids after the affectation of Elizabeth Barrett Browning, generally matched up with a single California pink rose in long tendril, while her every physical movement bespoke the Della Sarte motif in its fullest synchronization,—albeit she appeared languorously and coquettishly lazy."

I paused in my reading to congratulate the Colonel on his descriptive powers.

"It reads like Dr. Faustus casing Helen," I said. "Mrs. Harriman must have been a remarkable woman."

"She had a weakness, however, Joe," he answered,—"an inquiring mind. She was curious of the occult, and had landed on the mailing list of every peddler of the esatoric, from Father Divine to the Omnipotent Oom and the Rosicrucians. It was through one of her yogi cronies, no doubt, if not through a Bahai, that she had learned of Doctor Sykes's prowess, for the old boy ranked high in the mystic confraternity. She was therefore predisposed in our favor."

The Colonel is a strong rooter for the opposite sex, whom he considers it impossible to buck.

"Since you cannot defeat them," he sometimes says, "it is necessary to win them over to your side. There is not a man, however intelligent, who is one half as smart as any woman."

The Colonel's ideal of feminine beauty remains constant.

In this he resembles an old wartime friend of mine named Count Prziswieski, a minor figure in the exiled Polish government.

"All my life I have been faithful to one woman," the Count once said to me,—"a fragile blonde with a morbid expression."

He found this woman in every country, and she never aged, although the Count did. The fragile blonde with a morbid expression, wherever she turned up, was in her twenties.

My knowledge of the Count's predilection saved us both embarrassment one week end when I was away from my London hotel and returned to find he had been a guest there during my absence.

"Do you know the Count Ginwiski?" the night porter, an inquisitive sort, asked me. "Said 'e knew you. Rum cove."

"I certainly do know him," I said. "One of the county families of Poland."

"And do you know the Countess?" the porter asked artfully.

"Very well," I answered. "Thin blonde woman, much younger than he is, speaks English perfectly."

"Good night, sir," the porter said in a disappointed tone.

The Colonel's ideal is a dashing woman, tall, lissome, understanding, and, above all, loaded down with Tease. He represents her in a prototype called the Duchess, who appears throughout his writings columnistic and his reminiscences, but who is not permanently identified with any individual. Like the fragile blonde, she stays the same age, but the Colonel's ideal is thirty-five rather than twenty, for at thirty-five a woman has at once more dash and more understanding. The Colonel's affair with the Duchess began, he says, when he was getting out a weekly paper called the *Referee* in San Francisco, in the period following the retirement of his pugilistic meal ticket. The *Referee* dealt largely with night life,—"which was in those days variegated," the Colonel says. It was his sharp, shiny-shoe period. He wrote a column of night-spot notes under the signature of the Duchess, "a woman of the world, well heeled and a hell of a good fellow, who visited the resorts both advertising and non-advertising and commentated on the personalities she encountered there. There soon ceased almost totally to be non-advertisers." He has revived the Duchess many times,—she was the only woman present at the Gans-Nelson fight in 1906, according to one of his columns for example, and also the most beautiful spectator of the finish of Middleground's Kentucky Derby in 1950, not a grayed-eyelash older.

His description of Mrs. Harriman conforms to this type, and possibly Mrs. Harriman did. I have not looked her up in a picture morgue.

The *Referee*, with many enterprises of vaster commercial import, was submerged, the Colonel says, in a reform wave which swamped San Francisco just previous to the Panama-Pacific exposition. There was a conflict of maelstrom proportions before the reformers won out, he says, with a slight shudder at the recollection, but in the end they shut the town tighter'n a drum.

"And what was the editorial policy of the *Referee* during this struggle for righteousness?" I once asked him.

" 'Let Paris be gay!' " he answered.

But this is what the Colonel himself would call a labyrinthian digression.

9 / "*The Detonatory Compound*"

I RETURNED to the manuscript. Mrs. Harriman was speaking.

" 'Here at Belmont Park this season we're confronted by a severe Depression and a continued period of rain would ruin us,' explained Mrs. Harriman, 'and I thought you California experts might be able to prevent it. What may be your reaction?'

"The nudge that Dr. Sykes trained into my ribs was quite unnecessary for I realized my time at bat had come to hand. Slowly from my brief case emerged the Syllabus which I had prepared the night before on Rain

Prevention and what we could do for the panicky top people at Belmont Park.

" 'The new and most modern method of meteorological control and precipitation engenderment will be utilized, the Silver Iodine Spray based on Canalized Wave Vibration,' I intoned. 'The cost of installation for the term of ten racing days or less will not exceed $5,000 and it is our firm belief, after many years in the ancient and honorable profession of the Rainmaker, you will not have more than two days with a perceptible rainfall.'

"Syllabus explained that our Proposition is based solely upon an ability to prevent rain. It is *not* a bet, like rain insurance as offered by Lloyds of London, but a measure designed to insure good racing conditions as well as protect the sportsmen backing the meet from loss. However, as a guarantee of our seriousness, we included an indemnity provision.

"Then came the all-important Denouement: 'the terms.' They embraced simply this: 'We, the U. S. Weather Control Bureau, hereinafter to be styled party of the first part, agree to induct, maintain and operate the Iodine Silvery-Spray and Gamma-Ray-Radio system, the cost to us not to exceed $5,000, cost of buildings and labor to be defrayed by the Westchester Racing Association. The party of the second part agrees to pay party of the first part $2,500 on Saturdays, Sept. 6 and Sept. 13, and $1,000 on each intervening weekday for its services in preventing rain. Party of the first part agrees to pay to party of the second part $2,000 on any day on which United States Weather Bureau reports rain, even a trace, within purlieus of Belmont Park between 11 A.M and 5:30 P.M. Payment to be made each day at 6 P.M. at the Office of the Westchester Racing Association, Belmont Park.'

"This looked like a two-to-one bet but it wasn't. It was even money on weekdays and we couldn't lose if we tried on Saturdays.

"When I read off, 'cost of buildings and labor to be defrayed by the party of the second part,' the Good Doctor Sykes shifted nervously while his face assumed the ghastly aspect of an Egyptian mummy. If we had had to get up that Tease we would have been in trouble. But Mr. Widener acceded. He said though that he thought we should get up a certified check for $2,000, the amount of our forfeit in case we failed on the first Saturday, as earnest of our corporate responsibility. It was up to me to find the two grand, as I was handling the business side of the enterprise.

"Mr. Widener still hesitated, as one who feared a trap. The sum involved could to him be of no consequence, a fleabite, but he fancied himself a sharp guy.

"Sharply sudden came a lull in the negotiative colloquy with all eyes and attention veered upon Mrs. Harriman; her brow bore a knitted texture just for a fleeting second or two, then came a faraway look evidently penetrating the distant realm of occult portent, for with beatific transition she suddenly exclaimed: 'Joe, my boy, it comes to me as clear as crystal, the augury is for you and fine success. Close the Deal with the gentlemen.'

"That was a lucky trance for us Rainmakers I may assure you. Without further ado, Mr. Widener accepted terms, extended a handshake to me along the diameter of the friendly little circle. The deal was a bet and was on as sure as you live. On Mrs. Harriman's suggestion we adjourned to the Turf & Field Club for a snack and a service of illicit but authentic Irroy *brut*.

"With laughter and banter the gathering broke up, Mrs. Harriman, womanlike, having the last word. She expressed the thought to Dr. Sykes; —said she, 'Well Doc, your partner, Jim, is quite a lawyer fellow, isn't he?' The Good Doctor said I was not a man of the law.

" 'What has he ever done?' the lady inquired.

"Replying, Dr. Sykes rejoined,—'Well, up in the Lehigh Valley once he talked a mocking bird out of a tree.'

"With an all around expression of good luck and high hope for keeping that rain away from the door we all went our various ways. We the Rainmakers stood to make $10,000 if every day was clear, or lose $4,000 if it rained every day.

"But where would I get that $2,000 in those Hooverized days of tight money? Why, sure enough, there he was—dear old Mike the Bite, a real natural. 'Fade my four for the Lord's sake,' as Dr. Orlando Edgar Miller would say on occasion.

"Making my way from the haunts of the Haute Bourgeoisie in the Turf & Field to the moiling fringe of the betting ring, I braced him.

"I found him in good spirits; his tip for the third race, Baba Kenny, had won, although paying only even money. That had meant fifty-three-times-two-dollars profit to him, however, as well as satisfaction, and he had bet it back on a filly named Chalice in the fifth, which was just coming up. Our conversation and the jollification in the clubhouse had consumed considerable time. 'I got it right from Ollie Thomas, the clocker,' he said to me, 'and she is 25 to 1 in the ring.' That was one occasion on which my adherence to non-speculation proved costly, for the filly came down in front, a gray by Stefan the Great, she took the lead from the first jump and increased it with every stride, a *pisseuse*.

"Availing of the auspicious moment, I said, 'Willie, I have an opportunity to make a good score, but I need the use of two grand until Futurity Day.' And I explained to him as much of the project as I thought necessary.

" 'When I see you two buzzing Mr. Widener and Mr. Schaumberg yesterday out there on the lawn I wondered what you could be up to now,' he said.

"I averred abiding faith in Dr. Sykes's powers, but Willie was a man of occult intuition himself. 'It looks like the Racing Association made a dutch book,' he said. 'You got a good bet there.'

" 'I will pay you $2,200 next Saturday,' I promised him. 'If you wish, I will give you a note.'

" 'No need of that,' the Bite said. And he got his checkbook out of the drawer of the oldfashioned cash register and wrote out a check, telling me I could have it certified at his bank next morning, but it wasn't necessary, —Mr. Widener knew him. I heard tell afterward that when Mike the Bite died, in 1946, he was worth $600,000 in securities and property.

"And that was our last major obstacle overcome. We were turning into the stretch, with a clear field in front of us and in a contending position. Such loans could be negotiated only on the Race Track, where there was to be found a breed of men and a business method, together with an instinct, found nowhere else. But the noisome breath of the mechanical maw of the mutuels has changed all that, and the Old Breed is dying out.

"I carried the check back to the Racing Secretary's office. Mr. Schaumberg smiled when he saw the signature. 'You couldn't have a better man on your side,' he said.

"Now we were set to go, but we had only about 36 hours left to install all our apparatus, for the Good Doctor declaimed he needed a start of a few hours to dispel rain clouds that might converge upon the track Saturday noon. 'It is not an instantaneous process,' he said. 'There are some types of clouds I can dispel with one punch, but others require a couple of hours of softening up before I shoot it to them.'

"My role changed. Instead of a silver-tongued advocate I now became a construction superintendent."

At this point in my reading I became a trifle boorish. "Colonel," I said to my old friend, "do you mean to say this really happened?"

A pained expression contracted the Colonel's nostrils, but he recovered quickly.

"I expected you'd ask that sooner or later, Joe," he said. "Anybody would. And so I brought along a few old clippings from New York newspapers of that period that I happen to have preserved at the Dixie. There are more in the newspaper collection of the New York Public Library."

I had not attended any race meetings in the summer of 1930 myself,—I had been working out of town,—and I had assumed as I read along that the Colonel was writing about a scheme that had abutted in fiasco. I was waiting for the point in the manuscript at which the plan of the Rainmakers would go sour.

"Allow me to introduce my exhibits at the proper place in the narration," the Colonel said. "The points at which they are appropriate are marked in the manuscript."

So I read on.

"It was agreed we, the Rain Preventers, were to have at disposal every possible facility available at trackside, including the fine old disused clubhouse at the head of the stretch, abandoned when the finish line was moved in 1926 and a constricted area of about one-half acre at the head of the Widener Course, the straightaway down which the celebrated Futurity is run off annually. Sweeping down past the long grandstand, on the afternoon of Friday, Sept. 5, 1930, the observer arriving by the old clubhouse would have seen piles of our paraphernalia and materials with workmen and installators standing about awaiting our instructions.

"Inside the old Clubhouse on the top floor, busy as the proverbial bees, Dr. Sykes and his Mrs. were directing workmen in the setting up of the two heavy Vibrator Units and the Chemicalized Repository; I am not adept in machinery so I cannot describe their aspect more technically than to say they looked ominous. The lady, noisy as a steam tea kettle, had just issued orders that no person might enter 'the laboratory' from this moment on except by presentation of a Permit Card.

"The weird-looking Detonatory Compound at the head of the Widener Course had been completed during the morning and its equipment completely installed. Under the experienced eye of the Doctor and my urgings, vehement rather than initiate, all matters had progressed as per schedule and we would open on the morrow.

"There was little architectural ingenuity employed in the design of the Compound thus established out in deep right field; it was a one-room structure made of plain lumber, a pentagon 16 feet high in height and 12 feet on a side, with an earth floor and no doors and no windows, an important point counter-espionage-wise. A veritable packing box. Entrance was made through a tunnel of 9½ feet from an entrance immediately to the north of the layout,—you had to bend down to get in.

"Sprouting from the Roof were two Vibratory Rods of shiny steel and within an evil looking contraption best described as suggesting an abandoned oldtime Refrigerator with an electric charged battery, quite concealed, and a washtub full of the most noxious-smelling chemicals outside a slaughter house."

The Colonel had next pasted up a clipping from Audax Minor's department in *The New Yorker* of that September 13, 1930.

"The rain control machine is very hush-hush. Both the negative and positive actions, which are interchangeable, are under guard. The five-sided shack in the hollow near the training track interested us most. There is something cabalistic about it, with planks and two-by-fours laid out in curious designs around it, and the five scantlings nailed to the sides of the shed that shelters the remote radio control with a spider web of wires. Then, too, there's the big five-pointed star strung with radio aerial wire and festooned with ornaments from discarded brass beds and springs from box mattresses. The star always faces the way the wind blows. I'm quite sure Dr. Sykes has read *Rootabaga Stories* and how, 'on a high stool, in a high tower, on a high hill, sits the Head Spotter of the Weather

Makers,' for he has a platform like a starter's box, several feet higher than the shed, from which he may direct the magnetic impulses—or he may be practicing to be a starter."

The Colonel's manuscript continued:

"Audax was never in a position to describe the interior. Mr. Widener himself was admitted only once to the Holy of Holies, and in negotiating the low tunnel suffered the sacrification of a $250 imported English suit draped by Carabis of 3 Creechurch Lane, London, and the wreckage of a solid gold wrist watch presented to him by Lord Derby, another racetrack promoter. Once in he looked around in amazement but received a convincer when the Good Doctor coyly edged him into contact with the rusty steel shell of the Detonatory Giant; old man John Franzel, the Lord High Executioner in the Death House at Sing Sing, never was more facile in the feathering of a switch than Dr. Sykes, for the tall Mr. Widener received an electric shock that left no further doubt in his mind but that the occult forces of nature and the Detonatory Pulsations of Higher Physics were at work in the Grand Cosmic Order.

"As a survivor, he afterwards expressed to the panting Newspapermen, a week later, that he felt lucky to escape the lair and snare of Dr. Faustus with his life. Yes sir, it's true; it's facts and history.

"The only Scribe to make the tunneled passage and live to tell the tale was Mr. Ned Brown, then the Sporting Editor, New York *World*, and he became teetotally bald within five days and has remained denuded ever since, complete and totally, yea verily.[1]

"Between the Compound and the Laboratory, a distance of a good Yorkshire Mile, ran the Ethereal Conduit upon which traveled with the speed of Light augmented 30,000-fold the initiatory Pulsations to the Vibrator, and thence, via the antennae, to the natural Air Waves and channeled Coaxial Appendixtum.

"Without the permission of Consolidated Edison, the devious Sykes pair diverted from the blue ambient some 32,400 kilowatts of electric energy daily to the Ethereal Conduit, thereby greatly annoying, and in some remote instances, totally frustrating, the good House Wives of Hempstead Plains busy with their can openers and electric stoves in the preparation of the evening meal for the lowly husbandman plodding his

---

[1] This is a house joke. Ned Brown, an old friend of the Colonel's, who is at present editor of the sterling publication *Official Wrestling*, was bald before he ever heard of Dr. Sykes, and denies that he ever penetrated into the Paracelsian Dungeon. He was in 1930 not sporting editor, but boxing columnist of the *World* (his column was called "Pardon My Glove") and spent most of his summer afternoons at the race track, since, as he explains, he did not have to go to work until evening and he always had a badge. As a spectator he remembers full well the Colonel's surface activities at the racecourse in behalf of the Weather Control Bureau, he says, but he did not enter into the subterranean.

"When I was a cub reporter," says Mr. Brown, recalling an era virtually Triassic, "Jimmy Macdonald was already a top turf writer. So when I ran across him at Belmont, we used to chew over the rainmaking business, in which he was then engaged."

weary way homeward at day's end. From that day to this, Edison has not even filed a bill let alone received compensation for service rendered.[2]

"But, ah, back to the good old Clubhouse. The scene suggested the gauze and tinsel of the Bazaar of Baghdad, for here in long rows stood bright-colored glass jars, containing the various elemental chemicals used in explosive composition which in turn discharged upon the Air Currents the silver-crested Eidems which dispelled aqueous concentrations on contact, thus lessening the incidence of rain precipitation. From the top of the Vibrator, similar in grotesque appearance to the one set up at the Compound, ran an insulative tubing to the Ethereal Conduit jutting out from the building's rooftop to the skies above."

"What was really in those jars?" I asked the Colonel.

"I think it was colored water," he said, "but the good Doctor never told me." I returned to my reading:

"Hours after the running of the last race the General Staff of the Rain Preventers and a numerous detail of workmen remained at the Laboratory and the Compound. Every last item had been perfected in readiness for the great scientific enterprise of the morrow.

"Lights twinkled in the clubhouse and away across midfield under the rising Harvest Moon the eerie structure of the Compound loomed in ghostly outline; across on the backstretch the Recreation Centre, where foregather nightly the Trainers, Grooms, Swipes and Gallop Boys, stood out in full glow, and a bonfire at the entrance to the main track which nightly incinerates the trashy odds and ends engendered during the busy daytime hours shone its red fire while its illuminant rays disclosed a circle of men and boys busily engaged in what appeared to the trained eye of the old Frontiersman, peering through the lenses of Mrs. Sykes's imported French Lemaire binoculars, a roaring oldtime Crap Game in full locomotion.

"The yawning Grand Stand stood out against the night skies like a hulking Naval Aircraft Carrier, stranded, silent and menacing, against the background of sentient silence, a fearsome suggestion of what might happen should it rain ten hours hence; here and there over the vast expanse the searching lights of the night patrol of Pinkertons in protectory guard of the giant plant twinkled their assurance of an undeviating maintenance of their faithful Watch. Gallant Fox and Questionnaire, entered to contend in the Lawrence Realization Stakes, worth $50,000 to the winner, next day at one mile and five furlongs, were wound up no tighter than we."

---

[2] I hope this passage does not bring down upon the Colonel a posse of collectors from the Edison Company. He is still non-holding.

10 / "La Grande Semaine"

"This is the day of days. At eight o'clock in the morning a cold gray mist came in off Jamaica Bay and overcast the whole backstretch area but only for a brief moment, for as the last batch of horses working out with their Trainers and Swipes had departed the quarter-stretch, the mists disappeared with them and a golden sweep of sunshine overspread the scene, bringing much joy and hope to the inwardly sweating coterie of Rain Preventers.

"All that happened was it cleared up, but naturally we took full credit for it. We had engaged a publicity man, at $200 for the week, and he invited all interested newspapermen to drop in at the Sykes' town house, any time after hours, and sample Mrs. Sykes' Pisco Punch, a drink whereof she professed to have the ancient Peruvian formula, delivered to her by a medium who had wheedled it from the ghost of the Inca High Priest during a séance in Riverview, California. Naturally the press was not unfavorably disposed toward us, and we were away running.

"The funny thing about it is that a lot of the other people around the track began to believe there was something in it as soon as they read it in the newspapers. Racetrack habitués are in any case given to superstition, as the Bite daily demonstrated, and I sometimes encounter old-time turfites even today who will asseverate with conviction that Professor Sykes must have had something.

"The day was a success *extraordinaire*. Twenty-five thousand persons paid admission, an excellent attendance for those depressed days, and William Woodward's mighty three-year-old colt, Gallant Fox, prevailed by a mere nose over James Butler's Questionnaire, his keenest rival. Gallant Fox had been beaten only once in his career,—in the Travers at Saratoga, on a muddy track. We of the Weather Control Bureau could flatter ourselves that we had preserved him from a second such disaster. We received, however, no token of recognition from Mr. Woodward, which saddened us, for his horse had won $29,160, no meagre increment. I shall always remember a sentence written by George Daley, of the *World*, recounting Gallant Fox's victory:

"'One hundred yards from the wire the Fox appeared to hang and looked beaten, but just when a sob went up from the throats of many, he again settled to his bitter, grinding task and he prevailed.' In the secondary feature, the Champagne Stakes for two-year-olds, Mate, a horse destined to win the Preakness Stakes the following spring, defeated the immortal Equipoise by a head.

"But the most pleasing feature of the day for us, the Rain Preventers, occurred at 6 P.M. when, without demurrer and amid general acclaim, we collected our first check for $2,500. 'Weather Clear; track fast,' the chart said.

"After cooling out we decided to pay Willie Beeson, the Bite, his $2,000 forthwith, and the $200 interest on the following Saturday as promised. So, after the proper endorsement by Dr. Sykes as President and myself as Treasurer of the Weather Control Bureau I scampered over to the stand where the Bite was making all secure for the night.

"The Bite seemed as tickled as I was at our success. He said, 'You boys just forget that $200. Getting the big chunk back is good enough for me.'

"The next five racing days were like a dream. Weather clear; track fast. We collected $1,000 every night. The newspaper men and women were our chief trouble. We wanted to avoid too detailed disclosure, because the Good Doctor and I felt that if we went through this one undefeated, we might get more racing contracts. In the middle of the week the feature editor of the *Telegram*; it hadn't become the *World-Telegram* yet,—had a brainstorm. Home radios, as the mind of man runneth not to the contrary, had not achieved perfection in 1930. People were wont to exchange remedies for static, as for horse lumbago in days of bucolic old. Dr. Sykes, unfortunately, had let it be bruited about that we had one of the most powerful radio installations in the Western Hemisphere, and the editor sent a reporter out to ask the Good Doctor if that might not be responsible for the radio interference now so prevalent in Queens and Nassau counties on both sides of Belmont Park, where the *Telegram* was trying to build circulation. The Doctor, although denying him ingress to the sanctum sanctorium, oracled that it might. The *Telegram* published the story, with one of those playful leads about how 'householders who have been wondering why their pet radio programs sound like jabberwocky can blame it all on Dr. G.A.I.M. Sykes.'

"In a couple of days two inspectors from the Federal Communications Commission appeared at Belmont and insisted on examining our installation. After looking it over they exonerated us, naurally. But some revengeful Hildy Johnson who had overindulged in our Pisco punch, a skull-popper, got wind of their visit and interviewed them. The result was a first-page story in the *World* saying that the inspectors had minimized the efficacy of our equipment, maintaining its radiaction was imperceptible.

"We chose to ignore it as a canard, standing upon results for the authentification of our claims. The beautiful Indian summer weather brought on a track lightning-fast with a dusty cushion flying at all times. Belief in the efficacy of our manipulations even caused us some embarrassment when an associate of Dutch Schultz propositioned the Good Doctor to bring on a heavy rain overnight because the boys had a good spot for a mudder in the fifth race on the morrow. 'Mud brings this mule up thirty pounds,' the emissary enlightened us. 'We been running him on the fastest tracks we could find and he hasn't finished better than next to last since Christmas. He'll go away at 40 to 1.' They offered us ten thousand down and a bet of another ten going for us. The Good Doctor wanted to take him up. It was then I began to look askance at the old boy, wondering if perchance he had begun to believe he was genuine. I talked him out of it, saying that if we failed to produce good weather for the Association we would forfeit only two thousand dollars, but if we failed to produce a deluge for the mob we would die the death horrible. 'And there is always a chance of a slipup, Doc,' I told him. So we told the hood we would do our best, but could promise nothing. When the next day dawned clear, as usual, they scratched the horse, and I breathed as with a sense of calamity averted.

"The situation was complicated by the intervention presently of another mugg, who represented himself as a friend of Al Capone, requesting assurance of a fast track for the sixth on the same day his competitor had asked mud for the fifth. They had a speed horse going and would bet a couple of thousand for us. 'We will do our best,' I said, 'but promise nothing.' The horse come in at four to one but the hoods would give us only four thousand dollars, pretexting they had been unable to get down all the money they had intended to bet. We professed indignation but pocketed the four thousand. 'You will pay us the balance the next time you come here to get any weather,' I told the plenipotentiary, 'or no dice. The Honest Rainmaker hath spoken.'

"Coming up to Saturday, Futurity Day, the last inning, it begins to look like Dr. Sykes, with good support from the Rainmakers' infield, is on the way to a No Hitter victory over the elements, and the Rainmakers could afford to sit back and enjoy the hubbub their advent had engendered on the Race Track, in Society, and within the Mystic Circles of the Town. We had banked six checks in succession, one for $2,500 and five for a grand each and were $7,500 in hand and in front at the Night & Day Bank at Broadway and Fortieth, Manhattan, beside the four-thousand-dollar bonus legitimately acquired from the Speedhorse Boys. I will note here that of the first five days of the meeting, without the intervention of the Ethereal Conduit and the Giant Detonator, on only one had there been rain. Sceptics continued to suggest we were riding with the season.

"Certainly the old Ford Model T engine in the Vibrator at the Laboratory had been servicing us just dandy, while the Galaxy of Varicolored Bottles and their chemical content had played a role in noble inspiration. There were 16 of these Bottles of all manner of shade and tint suggesting the oldtime Drug Store with its window display of tiger fat, snake serum, and good luck potion in huge glass demijohns. The ancient Cigar Store highbred wooden Indian, could he come to life, might have had a good snicker at the spectacle.

"We could win $2,500 on the last day, if the weather remained fair, enabling us to pocket our fee intact, or take only $500 if it rained and we had to cough up our $2,000 forfeit. In any case the campaign averred itself a glorious victory, and Mrs. Sykes decided to throw herself around socially and hospitably by giving a soiree at the Red Room of the Hotel Imperial, Herald Square, Manhattan, the night after the Futurity, and 330 invitations were sent out, saying bring your friends.

"On the last day there was a precipitation no more substantial than that from an atomizer, but we accepted our responsibilities, however we might have felt, inwardly, about the Bourgeoisie exacting its Pound of Flesh on such a technicality. The races drew 25,000 paid admissions, as they had the previous Saturday, and the great Jamestown, owned by George D. Widener, the President's brother, won the Futurity by a nose from the great Equipoise, with Mate third. The total stakes were $121,760, of which the victor's share was $99,600. The Grande Semaine thus ended pleasantly for all concerned: the Westchester Racing Association, which had maintained its attendance; the Widener family, and even the general public, which had heavily backed Jamestown, a favorite at odds of 11 to 5.

"But most especially was it a victory for the United States Weather Control Bureau, which showed a net profit of $8,000 in eight days including a non-profitable Sunday, not bad on an investment of zero capital, and in addition to the unofficial supplementary income of four grand from the Mob.

"Mr. Widener, in handing over the final $500 check, thanked us for our satisfactory services, and said he hoped to see us back again the following season. I understand that to the end of his days he deprecated derision of Dr. Sykes and his theories. He maintained that the United States Weather Bureau, whose meteorologist ridiculed the Good Doctor, had little cause to carp, when its own predictions for the New York area were notoriously inaccurate."

I looked up from the last page of the story of the Honest Rainmaker.

"Did you ever work the dodge again?" I asked.

The Colonel shook his head. "The newspapers killed it," he said. "But poor old Dr. Sykes assisted them. He walked right into a haymaker. I should have kept him incommunicado with his arcane impedimenta. It seems that right at the top of his success some Park Row wag had accused him of ineffectuality and taking a free ride. The old boy, incensed, had said that he would show he *could* control weather, by producing rain as soon as his contract was finished. Monday, September 15, the next racing day after the Futurity, was set for the test. The old boy, who was really pretty weatherwise, the result of long speculative observation, may have believed that with the approach of the September equinox the weather was in fact due to change. The clouds on Futurity Day bore out in a general way this prognostication. But he overweened himself.

"He promised these reporters that he would produce torrents of rain on the track between two-thirty and four-thirty on Monday afternoon. The next day's papers chronicled the event. I was not even out at the track myself, for the Doctor had purposely neglected to inform me of his fool-hardy undertaking. If he had pulled it off it would have been a great publicity stunt. But when you are sitting pretty you should refrain from endangering your position; it is like breaking up a full house to draw for four of a kind.

"The day dawned bright and sunshiny, the papers reported. The mock-ers assembled just before post time for the first race, when the good Doctor strode out to his cavern and interred himself. Almost immediately clouds began to gather. At three he emerged from the depths and in-formed observers that there would be a whale of a storm at four. He explained that he needed the intervening time to assemble more clouds. It was cloudy and threatening all afternoon, but the deadline came and passed without an obedient drop, and the old Doc looked mighty chap-fallen.

"Colonel Matt Winn, who had made us a tentative offer to prevent rain at the Churchill Downs meeting in Kentucky, dropped the proposi-tion like an option on a horse that proves unsound, and the deluge of derision breaking upon our heads deterred Mr. Widener himself from extending another contract. So, as once before in California, the rain-maker's art died the death, not to be revived for a score of years. You have to have an airplane now to practice it, and I am too old to qualify for a pilot's license."

"And what happened to old Doc Sykes?" I asked.

"I don't know," the Colonel said. "I haven't heard from or of him in many a year, and if he's still alive he must be near ninety." (Dr. Sykes still is alive, or was as late as September 1952, I learned subsequently. And he is, or was, only about as old as the Colonel. But they had apparently lost contact during the biographical interstice.)

He appeared to find insufficient solace in his beer. Then a recollection cheered him.

"Joe," he said, "you should have had a snort of Mrs. Sykes's pisco punch. It was a grand party. Sherry did the catering and the Philhar-monic Chamber Music Quartet entertained the guests playing everything from *Wozzeck* to 'Turkey in the Straw.' The Banjo-Eyed Kid, Coon-Can Artie, and Commodore Dutch lent their arms to the season's debutantes preferred for the grand march. But the pisco punch constituted the standout.

"It was said New York had not before ever seen or heard of the insidi-ous concoction which in its time had caused the unseating of South American governments and women to set world's records in various and interesting fields of activity. In early San Francisco, where the punch first made its North American appearance in 1856, the police allowed but one drink per person in twenty-four hours, it's that propulsive. But Mrs. Sykes served them up like *pain, à discrétion,* as the signs used to say in front of the little restaurants in Paris, meaning you could have all the bread you wanted. As a consequence, discretion vanished.

"Two hours after the salon had gotten underway even the oldest gals were still hunting the bartenders. Many of the old-time veteran Cellini, who hadn't scaled a garden wall in forty years, made a double score for themselves that evening, a memorable amoristic occasion. It was a famous victory, said little Peterkin. What I tell you about it now will be little noted and soon forgotten, but what those women did will be long remembered."

Daylight died in Forty-fifth Street outside the Palace Bar and Grill, and the Honest Rainmaker, who seldom feels in form before electric-light-time, continued to perk up.

"Joe," Colonel Stingo said, "last summer a tout introduced me to an Argentine trainer who knows a lot of people who own cattle ranches down there. Anyplace there are ranches they must need rain. If I had the courage of my convictions I'd go out and buy myself a Spanish grammar."

11 / The Life Spiritual

WHEN I first worked upon Colonel Stingo to set down his memoirs, he said, "You don't know what you're getting into, Joe. I am not the fine man you take me to be."

My effort to set him right on that score resulted in an estrangement, but we became friends again.

At another time he appeared to believe I was giving him too much of the worst of it, for he said:

"It is only a boob that conducts an enterprise in such a manner that it leads to embroilment with the law. I myself have never collided with it head on. But I have had many associates less wise or fortunate. One was Dr. Orlando Edgar Miller, a Doctor of Philosophy of the University of the Everglades, Rushton, Florida. Dr. Miller, when I first met him, was of appearance pre-eminent. Sixty years old, straight as an arrow, with snow-white hair and black eyelashes. He affected a Panama hat, Palm Beach suit and white buckskin shoes even in the dead of a New York winter. He presented an undeviating outward semblance of sanctity, but he was a deviator, a dear old fellow. Having drawn the multitude toward him, first thing you know he had his hands in all their pockets.

"During the course of the revivals he conducted, frequently lasting for weeks if the supply of boobs held out, he professed a diet of one orange a day, but he was a practiced voluptuary. He did not like oranges, but he ingested plenty other comestibles. 'We eat too much and no mentality can be alert when the body is overfed,' he used to proclaim in Carnegie Hall, where he lectured to throngs, and then he would take a taxi to a speak-easy called the Pennwick and eat a steak with a coverture of mushrooms like the blanket of roses they put on the winner of the Kentucky Derby.

"After that he would plunge his fine features in eight or nine seidels of needled beer, about forty proof, a beverage worthy of revival, for it combined the pleasant Gambrinian taste with an alcoholic inducement to continue beyond the point of assuagement. Or he would decimate a black bottle of Sandy Macdonald scotch landed at Rockaway Point and conveyed fresh to the table by courtesy of Big Bill Dwyer. Scotch, like the lobster, tastes best when fresh from the ocean, a truth which we have forgotten since repeal.

"But let him, in the lobby of Carnegie Hall after one of his meetings, be introduced to a man with upwards of fifty thousand dollars and he would ostentatiously gnaw an orange peel. It was my duty to keep him informed of the financial status of the potentially regenerate, a task for which I was well qualified by my experience as credit man for Tex Rickard's old Northern gambling house at Goldfield, Nevada, and in a similar capacity for Canary Cottage at Del Monte, California, and the late Colonel Edward Riley Bradley at his Casino, Palm Beach, Florida. Many a man rife with money makes no outward flaunt. His habiliments, even, may be poor. But, Joe, when it comes to rich men, I am equipped with a kind of radar. The houses I worked for collected on ninety-five per cent of markers, an unchallenged record.

" 'Not the mythical bacilli but improper breathing causes tuberculosis,' this old Dr. Miller would hold forth in public. 'Among the ancient races who understood proper breathing there was no such disease.' The cure he espoused was by the laying on of hands, calisthenics and giving the right heart, and the women flocked to be laid hands on, even the most buxom averring a fear of dormant maladies. In his pulpit appearances he stressed spiritual values,—Biblical exegesis, personality and love. He advised women to pull their husbands' hair to prevent baldness. He was a regular cure-all.

"He was accompanied on his forays by the Countess Bonizello, a lady born in Davenport, Iowa, but who had married, she recounted, an impoverished member of the Italian nobility, since deceased. She had at any rate been long enough on the Continent to acquire that little froufrou, and spoke a certain *patois*,—French and English. She gave evidence of having been in early life a beauty, and she was full of guile and could handle men and was a real good fellow. When they hit a town she would take a suite at the best hotel and he would assume a simple lodging in accord with his ascetic pose. She would play the role of a wealthy devotee who had followed him from Europe, platonically, of course, and she would organize the social side of the revival.

"She had in fact met him in England, so they said. There, in 1914 just before the First World War, he had conducted revivals in the Albert Hall. He induced the Duke of Manchester to put the O.K. on a line of credit for him, and was going to build a sanatorium for the cure of tuberculosis by his methods when unfortunately a woman died under his ministrations, and the British Medical Association, 'captious without a point of criticism,' the old Doctor used to say, had him haled before a Court. 'As if other practitioners never lost patients,' he said. 'Why, an Austrian prince named Hohenlohe paid me a thousand quid, when the pound was worth $4.86 and several mils, because he was so pleased with the way I treated him. That was what inflamed Harley Street against me.' The Court let him off with a reprimand, but the publicity queered his act in England, and he came home. Here he emphasized the spiritual shots in his bag, preaching that right living is the road to health, but the American Medical Association suspected he was laying hands in private, and he had to put up with persecution which seldom affected his monetary success."

A look of reminiscent admiration suffused the old Colonel's countenance.

"Of my adventures with Dr. Miller I could speak endlessly," he said, "but my purpose is only to illustrate the fine line between *fas* and *nefas*. There was no need for him to transgress that line. He was a man of great animal magnetism, reminding me of the appellation by Max Lerner of General Dwight D. Eisenhower,—'the charismatic leader,' which Mr. Lerner says means one you follow because he seems to have a kind of halo around him. Dr. Miller once said he was good for $250,000 a year on a purely spiritual plane. He drew Tease from the repentant like soda through a straw.

"But eventually the day came when the old Doctor overweened himself. Some Hollywood sharks sold him the idea of becoming a movie star. The old ham could fancy himself and the Countess bedazzling unseen multitudes. There seemed to him nothing ludicrous in the proposition. Essentially he was a boob too. The idea was to form an independent producing company and sell stock to people who came to his revivals. The way of separating the sheep from the goats, to wit the holding from the non-holding, at these meetings was to distribute envelopes among the multitude, specifying that only contributions of a dollar or more were to be enclosed, and the donors were to write their addresses on the envelope if they wished free literature.

"The Doctor was not interested in the addresses of people with less than a buck. Such were requested to drop their coins in the velvet-lined collection box, where they wouldn't jingle. The jingle has a bad effect on suggestible people who might otherwise give folding money.

"We had a follow-up system on the names. Paid workers followed up each prospect. If, as occasionally occurred, they encountered a scoffer who had invested a buck just to see what would happen, the name was scratched from the mailing list. Incidentally they were pretty good estimators of a chump's net wealth. I went to one of a series of meetings an exegizer held at Carnegie Hall this winter, and the old operating procedure is still standard. We left no room for improvement.

"When we swapped towns with another big preacher, like Dr. Hall the hundred-dollar-Bible man, we sometimes swapped mailing lists. But we would always keep out a few selected prospects, and so, I suspect, would the other prophet. The ready-made list helped in the beginning, but the one you could trust was the one you made yourself. The purpose of this labyrinthian digression is to indicate that after ten years of listmaking, old Dr. Miller had a mighty lever to place in the hands of a stock salesman.

"I was assigned to write the scenario and it was unique, indisputably. It was the only one I had ever written. It was called the *Bowery Bishop* and was based on what I remembered reading about Jerry McCauley's Bowery Mission. Dr. Miller, of course, was to play the saintly missionary, and there were two young lovers. It had been intended that the Countess should play half the love interest, though her bloom was no longer of the first blush pristine, but at the last minute she backed out. She said there were reasons why she did not want her photograph too widely distributed. This was of good augury for the enterprise, the promoters said, as the film would be surer to click if the Doctor had the support of some well-known movie names.

"We engaged two great stars of the silent films to play the young lovers. With a scenario, stars and a sucker list, the promoters were all set to go. The stock salesmen were getting twenty-five per cent commission. The nature of the promotion literature was such, however, that I felt sure trouble impended. Purchasers were not only assured of a large profit, but guaranteed against loss. I declined office in the company. I went out to Honolulu to arrange a great Miller revival there, which was to begin simultaneously with the release of the picture, and when I returned to California, the inevitable had ensued.

"Stock had been sold to the amount of $320,000, of which $240,000 had been turned in to the treasury. With part of the $240,000 a picture had been made. But only a handful of theatres were available to show the film, which was, as one might expect, a turkey. The old Doctor, seized by foreboding, had hit the booze and played away the rest of the money on horses and the stock market, deluding himself that he might thus recoup solvency. I advised him to lam before the inauguration of the uproar, and he sought sanctuary in Australia, where I commended him to the good offices of some friends I had in the fight game there. The Countess Bonizello left by the same boat. I had one or two letters from him after he got out to Sydney saying he was making plenty Tease. The revival business in the Antipodes had been in a crude stage before he arrived, he wrote. The surpliced choir with which he embellished his performances and the social éclat imparted by the Countess had remedied all that.

"But such peripheral triumphs did not content him. In 1926 or so I had a letter from him dated Calgary, Alberta, and so I knew he had ventured back to the outskirts of the battlefield, and he was contemplating a new campaign. The next tidings were bad. He was under arrest, and California authorities were trying to extradite him. They did, and he got six.

"We disappeared from the surfaces of each other's conscious lives, like two submarines, interrupted in a mission of destruction, which submerge without the formalities of parting.

"Now," Colonel Stingo said, "we do a fade-out and pick up the thread of our narrative again in the winter of 1936. The place is New York and my condition is distinctly non-holding. I am inhabiting a rendezvous of the discomfited known ironically as the Little Ritz, on West Forty-seventh Street, in New York, and in the period subsequent to Dr. Miller's misfortune I have known many ups and downs, but now I am for the nonce down. I have the price of a meal, though not in a restaurant such as the Voisin, the Colony or Shine's, and I am heading for the Automat. But before eating I decide to take a walk to increase my appetite, for I may not be able to raise the price of another repast that day. Chicken today, feathers tomorrow, and dear old Dr. Miller is far from my mind.

"It is snowing, and I cannot help regretting the climate of California, and perhaps conceding the foolhardiness of my renewed challenge to the metropolis. But as I pass the Union Church on West Forty-eighth Street I see a message of hope: the Rev. Orlando Edgar Miller is conducting a service there. I enter and there he is in the pulpit, as straight as ever. The ten years, including six with time off for good conduct, have touched him but lightly. I tried to make my advent unobtrusive, secreting myself in a side pew, but the dear old rascal made me immediately.

" 'I see among us a dear good friend, Mr. James Macdonald of California,' " he said. 'I am sure he has a Message for us. Will you come forward, Jim?' So I walked down the center aisle.

"Were you abashed?" I asked the Colonel. "Or were you prepared to speak after such a long spiritual layoff?"

"I have an invaluable precept for public speech," the Colonel said. "It is to think of five topics, one for each finger of the hand. On this occasion, I remember, I thought of the Christmas season, which it was, the miracle of the loaves and fishes, the Poor Little Match Girl, Oliver Twist, and Tiny Tim. I began by saying that as I gazed upon the countenance of my reverend friend, Dr. Miller, the Ark of the Covenant of the Lord had fallen upon me, and that I was moved beyond expression to find here, at this Christmas season, when so many were in want, a living reminder of the miracle of the loaves and fishes, whereby the Lord had provided for many although the supply of comestibles looked limited. My prospects for spiritual nourishment had looked bleak as I wandered down the cold street, I said, and then I saw the name of Orlando Edgar Miller and knew my hunger would be satisfied. These were the times when multitudes, like the Poor Little Match Girl, were expiring of hunger, spiritual hunger, and cold, not knowing that just around the corner was a man who might warm them and stoke them to Divine Grace. He was not angry when, like Oliver Twist in the story, they turned to him again and asked for More, evermore,—and like Tiny Tim——

"'We shall have to let Tiny Tim go until some other time,' that dear old rascal Doctor said, 'for we have so many other beautiful features of our services to complete before six o'clock, when we must vacate the premises according to the terms of our lease. This church is not ours alone, though I would willingly remain far into the night to hear the conclusion of Brother Macdonald's beautiful train of thought.'

"I could tell from his dear old face that he had a hard time restraining hilarity, knowing full well the purport of my parablism. He motioned me to a seat on the front bench until the end of the service. The collection, I was glad to see, was of comfortable proportions, including many envelopes. When he came down from the platform I went up and shook hands with him and he gave me the address in the West Seventies where he was living and told me to go on ahead up there and he would come along as soon as he had finished his routine of benevolent adieux. 'I must clinch my sales for God,' he said.

"I went on along up to the address, which was an old brownstone house that he had taken over *in toto*. The Countess was not in evidence but three hatchet-faced old secretaries, well past the mid-century, were. It was a ménage most circumspect, and I could sense that the field of the old scalawag's deviations had narrowed with the infirmities of age. The Florabels regarded me with some suspicion, as of an outwardly unsanctified appearance, but when the old boy arrived, he led me directly into his study.[1] There, having locked the door, he went to an old-fashioned wall safe and drew out of it a black bottle of unclerical demeanor and we went to it and had a fine time.

"We rode upon the flying carpet of reminiscence: for example how we had prevailed upon one of the leading oyster growers of the Pacific coast, a Scandinavian gentleman, to endow a two-week revival featuring hymns with special lyrics composed in his honor, as: 'Thank you, Mr. Snorensen,' to the tune of 'Onward Christian Soldiers.' The lyrics were thrown upon a screen, as those of popular songs were in movie theatres of that era. I had first used this device to publicize a fight between Burns and an Australian heavyweight named Bill Squires, at Colma, California, in 1906. After the revival proper Mr. Snorensen treated all the executives of his company and their wives to an esatoric course with graduation ceremonies in white robes and white mortarboard hats and presented them all with fountain pens. We beat that squarehead for forty grand, and he had starved hundreds of oyster shuckers to death.

"'Those were wonderful days, wonderful,' the dear old Doctor said. 'And by the way, Jim, we parted so hastily that I never did pay you the

---

[1] A Florabel, in the Colonel's idiom, is the antithesis of a Lissome, his highest term of aesthetic praise for a female. It had its origin in his reaction to the newspaper photograph of a woman so named.

last week's salary you had earned.' This was a bow to convention, simply the old man's way of offering aid without embarrassment to me, for he knew full well that I had held out an ample share of the Hawaiian contributions to the revival he had never held there. So he slipped me a hundred, which in those depression days was riches.

"When we had fortified ourselves enough to face those Gorgonic old spinsters we sallied forth and took them all out to a vegetarian restaurant where they stuffed themselves with nuttose and date pudding, and then the old Doctor put them in a taxi and said he and I would walk home together, since he had not completed his daily pedestrian exercise of fifteen miles. We went to Al Muller's bar north of Madison Square Garden and got stiff as boards, and finally the Ark of the Covenant of the Lord fell upon the old Doctor, and he spake.

"'Jim, there is just one thing I have never been able to understand,' he said.

"'Why did they leave you outside when they put me in?'"

12 / A Day with the Analysts

IN THE FALL of 1951, as the public prints have recorded, Congress passed a bill requiring bookmakers to buy a fifty-dollar tax stamp and then pay a mulct of ten per cent on their gross business, in addition to their ordinary income tax. Shortly thereafter, I received a mimeographed letter of valediction from a bookmaker who had me on his mailing list:

> It is my firm conviction that the bill recently passed is both discriminatory and unconstitutional. . . . What balloon-head figured this bill out?
>
> Sometime, sooner or later, an injunction will be granted. Until that time, I PREFER TO REMAIN INACTIVE!! I'll go on record as saying that no one, bookmaker or not, can be assessed 10% of his gross business and still pay an honest income tax!
>
> Most of you should be very happy that all this has come to pass. For the first time in years there will be money in your pockets around Christmas time. Think kindly of the old fellow in the Santa Claus suit as you pass by him on the corner. Reflect a minute, and if you have no change, toss him a bill or two.
>
> Because, judging from the look of things, that guy in the red suit will probably be me!

A lot of other bookmakers have followed the writer of the above letter
into a retirement they hope will be only temporary. Among the people in
whose pockets their defection didn't leave money is a friend of the Colonel's I met not long ago named Irwin Kaye, who uses as his registered
trade-mark the title "World's Master Analyst." Mr. Kaye is not one of the
Johnny-come-lately type of analysts who trace no farther back than Sig-
mund Freud. He is a turf analyst, or forecaster of equine probabilities, a
member of a brotherhood that probably derived profit from the horse
races in the Greek games of the seventh century B.C. and that was certainly well established in England when Charles J. Apperley, better
known as Nimrod, produced his one-and-sixpence volume *The Turf*
published in 1851. "What is it that guides the leading men in their betting?" Nimrod wrote, and answered himself, "Private information,
purchased at a high price—*at a price which ordinary virtue cannot with-
stand.*" Mr. Kaye, while withholding the price he pays for what he represents as private information, tries to sell it at one within the reach of a
large public. For forty years, the margin between what Mr. Kaye paid for
his information and what he sold it for kept him in comfortable circumstances. Now that bookmakers have become scarce, however, his clients,
unable to bet, have no use for his information. So they don't buy it. This
leaves Mr. Kaye as badly off as he would have been all these years if there
had been a law against telling a man the name of a horse that is likely to
win a race. He therefore suspended publication of his medium, known as
"the sheet," last winter. His only remaining service, for the time being,
was providing very special information by telephone. "Winners I 'got
plenty, but nobody to give them to," Mr. Kaye told me on the occasion of
our first meeting. "I got a guy at Miami and one at New Orleans, and they
ain't hardly making what to eat. They call up with good things, but
nobody to play them. I pass them on to a fellow what used to make a
good bet. What happens? He couldn't get the bet down. At least, he gives
you that story."

The would-have-been bettor's failure to find a taker starts a cycle of
destitution, because if he had made the bet and won it, he would have, in
accordance with a common arrangement between client and analyst, paid
Mr. Kaye the full profit from an accompanying wager—ten dollars, say,
or twenty, depending on previous stipulation—made on behalf of Mr.
Kaye. Mr. Kaye, in turn, would have remitted a percentage of his take
from the appreciative customer to the guy at Miami or the one at New
Orleans. The guy would then have bought white-on-white shirts, hand-
painted neckties, and neutral grain spirits adulterated with whiskey, and
the whole national economy would have profited, whereas it is a well-
known fact that if you let a sucker keep his money, he sits on it.

All this is an illustration of the principle formulated by Colonel Stingo:
"Disasters never run singly but always as an entry." The chain of disasters
started by the law aimed at the bookmakers had, in fact, reached the

Colonel himself. The Colonel continued to write his column "Yea, Verily" in the New York *Enquirer*, a newspaper that appears every Sunday afternoon dated the following Monday. The *Enquirer* also carried a column by Louis Bromfield, who was beaten off by lengths every time he and the Colonel came out of the starting gate together. But the Colonel depended for life's amenities principally upon commissions paid him on the advertisements he attracted to the paper. (Bromfield presumably has other assets.) The advertisers were for the most part turf analysts like Mr. Kaye and, until recently, Mr. Kaye's brother, Long Shot Murphy, now retired from the analytical field. Murphy was a nom de course, like Kentucky Colonel or the Masked Jockey or Si and Smudgie, to name a few Kaye competitors. The Kentucky Colonel is a partner in a candy store and newspaper route in Brooklyn, where he grew up amid the blue grass of Prospect Park. Mr. Kaye himself thinks the use of his genuine patronymic sounds more responsible.

When the analysts can't sell their information because the bettors can't bet, the analysts can't afford to advertise. This left Colonel Stingo nonholding, but he continued to compose his weekly column while awaiting a dawn that he believed could not be farther off than the opening of the New York racing season in April. Then the analysts would have potential customers among the crowds going out to the track, where betting is legal. Quite probably they would advertise again, to reach these customers. In the meantime, Colonel Stingo sometimes visited his accounts on a strictly social basis, to maintain contacts. One time he suggested I go with him on a tour of the devastated areas, and that is how I happened to meet Mr. Kaye.

I waited upon Colonel Stingo in his chambers in the Hotel Dixie at noon on the day set for our tour and found him just dressed and fixing in his lapel a slightly ivoried white carnation, which, he explained, he had bought on starting his prowl the night before and which still seemed too good to throw away. "It is a hang-over," he said. "The carnation, I mean." The only phase of inflation I ever heard the Colonel deplore is the rise in the price of these flowers. "A good carnation now will stand you forty cents," he said. The Colonel is seventy-nine years old, by his own declaration, but he still has a light foot and, when he has not been riding the magic carpet too hard, a clear eye. He is not an early riser, and attributes the short lives of most people with good habits to the inner tensions these set up.

As an example of the fatal consequences of restraint he likes to cite George Smith, the famous race-track plunger once nationally famous as Pittsburgh Phil, who was a great judge of horses and riders and sometimes bet a hundred thousand dollars on a race, usually on one of his own horses. Smith never smoked, drank, took tea or coffee. He never permitted his face to express any emotion during the running of a race or when the hole cards were turned up,—he was a heavy gambler on cards and dice too. "So naturally," the Colonel says, "he dropped dead,—the natural consequence of repression of the self-indulgent faculties."

Like most people of pronounced seniority he reads the obituary pages with attention, and had a morning of quiet triumph last winter when two insurance shamans, a past president of the Actuarial Society of America and the vice-president of a major company, died on the same day, aged sixty-two and fifty-four respectively. "I bet they avoided excitement, late hours, high blood pressure, tasty food and intoxicating liquors and had themselves periodically examined with stethoscopes, fluoroscopes, spectroscopes and high-powered lenses," the Colonel said. "The result was inevitable and to be expected, the result of a morbid preoccupation. The anxious fielder drops the ball."

I twitted him with the vigorous old age attained by Mrs. Ella Boole, past president of the Woman's Christian Temperance Union, who recently passed on in her ninety-fourth year, but the Colonel had a ready explanation of her survival.

"She must have been a secret tippler," he said.

On this particular noon, Colonel Stingo was in good form, attributable, he informed me, to his not having met with a villain on his excursion of the previous night. A villain is anybody who induces him to switch from beer to hard liquor when he is out late. Beer seems to preserve my friend like a beetle in amber. It affects his figure no more than it does Miss Rheingold's. Colonel Stingo's nose runs straight down from his forehead without indentation at the bridge—a contour characteristic, he says, not without pride, that has marked many great men of action, like Napoleon, Terry McGovern (the irresistible featherweight), and Al Jennings (the famous train robber), the two last having been friends of his. The Colonel himself, however, does not believe in what he calls "the life strenuous."

The Colonel proposed that we begin our day with a call on Mr. Kaye, whose office is in the Newsweek Building, at the corner of Broadway and Forty-second Street, hardly a block from the Dixie. The address brought back the vanished past to the Colonel. "This building used to be the Hotel Knickerbocker," he said as we entered it. "The bar was so elegant they had a printed menu for the free lunch." The door of the Kaye office, on the fourteenth floor, bore the legend: "Irwin Kaye, Publisher and Analyst." I paused with my hand on the knob to ask the Colonel what Mr. Kaye published. "A daily racing sheet," he said. "Graded selections. He had it on sale at about four big newsstands in the center of town and sent it out by mail to subscribers. But he isn't getting it out now, on account of this unfortunate situation."

The walls of the large office were decorated with framed photographs of race horses from Colin to Stymie, looking down upon the multigraphing machines and filing cabinets indispensable to any small direct-mail business. We found Mr. Kaye alone, seated at his desk and working over the past performances in the *Morning Telegraph*. He is a thin man, with a thin face that slants forward from the top of his head to the point of his long chin, the nose forming most of the incline. When we entered, he jumped up to greet the Colonel. The analyst proved to be shorter even than Stingo, by a couple of inches. "Colonel!" he shouted, pumping the Colonel's right hand. "You look six to five to live to be a hundred!"

The *Enquirer's* star columnist appeared flattered. "We just stopped by, Irwin, to ask your views of the situation," he said, after introducing me.

"It's dead," Mr. Kaye said. "I've got plenty of good things but nobody to play them. Sometimes old customers call up and ask *me* do I know a bookmaker. So what am I—a solicitor for bookmakers? Is it my business to look for bookmakers? Cops look for bookmakers. They don't find any, they pinch a ninnocent guy, what then? A salesman probily. They got to show a record, make a narrest."

Mr. Kaye's voice rose, indignant. "It's communism, that's what it is, communism!" he howled. "They think any guy in his right mind can give them ten per cent the gross? They going to drive the solid element out, the only fellow to take a bet will be a noutnout criminal, which if you win he won't pay you. Let that happen a couple times, the player is cured."

The voice dropped to the sweetly reasonable as Mr. Kaye continued: "Let them take two per cent and give a license to operate without ice fa the cops. Why not the guvvament get it, fa crying out loud, not some feller in a cellar on Twelf Aveny? If it was depriving a baby's milk, it's different. But every person is a sucker—you got to take it that way. So why should the sucker pay all the taxes, in *addition* to what he loses? The only way to save the sucker taxes is let the bookmaker pay taxes. But *let* him."

Mr. Kaye, emotionally exhausted, sat down, waving us with a limp left hand to chairs in front of his desk.

"There is much to what you say, Irwin, from the point of view of pure logic," the Colonel said. "But there is little hope, I fear, of legalized bookmaking forthwith. I see you performing a figuration on the *Telegraph*. Are you thinking of reviving your sheet?"

"What good?" Mr. Kaye asked. "I had two girls and my daughter getting out the sheets and mailing, but I let them all go. The sales didn't pay the girls' salary, and I told my daughter she might as well go home instead wasting her time around here. I'm figurating to kill time till what way the cat jumps."

"And what do you think of Senator Kefauver's announcement of his presidential candidacy?" the Colonel asked, like a little boy poking at an unexploded firecracker to make it go off.

"I'll lay forty to one against him if he runs!" Mr. Kaye shouted, coming up out of his chair. "He's got friends? Not here! He can't even speak English. Did you ever heard such a naccent? His wife is a nice woman." Mr. Kaye's voice grew heavily ironic. "She wants to be in the White House. You and I should have their worries, Colonel!" The Master

Analysts of the Democratic Party later concurred in Mr. Kaye's figuration of the senator, deciding not to start him.

The Colonel, perhaps sorry he had teased the Master Analyst, turned the talk down happier, reminiscent channels. "Irwin is one of the most talented figurators in the profession," he said to me. "I've known him since he was a boy."

Figuration, more commonly called handicapping, is the art of picking winners off the figures, or past performances, which may be interpreted in as divers ways as the entrails of the sacrificial sheep. A guy in New Orleans is not on the telephone with a good thing in every race, but the figures are always available. A consecrated figure man, in fact, scorns tips, even from a reliable source, as mere distractions beclouding his deductions with extraneous haze.

An analyst, Mr. Kaye kindly explained to me, does not disdain information, but he weighs it. He has to be a good figure man to start with. If the information concurs with his figures, or if his figures sustain the plausibility of the information, all, or almost all, is well. "I worked with the original Clocker Lawton, whose real name was George Garside, for five years—1910 to 1915—and the old man saw I had the makings of a second Steve L'Hommedieu," Mr. Kaye said. (Lawton was so famous a figurator that his name became a hereditary title. The present Clocker Lawton is his son.) "Who was Steve L'Hommedieu?" I asked, and the Colonel answered reprovingly, "The Prince of Handicappers." I could see that my ignorance had dropped my claiming price about fifteen hundred dollars in his estimation.

"I made hundreds long-price winners," Mr. Kaye said. "So I went into business for myself. I can go back as far as Baby Wolf, which he opened at two hundred to one, but when I made him he was played down to four to one. That's the kind reputation I had."

"What was the longest-priced winner you ever made?" I asked, adopting Mr. Kaye's idiom.

"A horse named Rock Candy, at Bowie," Mr. Kaye replied. "He paid $440.80 and I hardly took a buck. I gave him to my customers, but nobody played him. They thought I was crazy. A good thing is supposed to be two to one, three to one—not two hundred and twenty to one." He did not explain why the customers who had played Baby Wolf on his sayso had shied away from Rock Candy; perhaps in the interim he had had a string of losers.

Recalling past glories cheered Mr. Kaye up; I could see from his face that the thought of Senator Kefauver had receded. "Look at my scrapbook," he said to me, holding out a black-leather folder he had had within easy reach. "I am the only analyst that ever got sued for giving too many winners. The guy was a furniture salesman and spent all his money on broads, the wife sued *me* because she said if I hadn't given him the winners he wouldn't have had any money the broads would have let him alone he would of been home with her! So she sued me for alenation of her husband's affections, as if I would have been doing her favors to give him stiffs, she would of been the first one in to complain I was rooning her husband!"

This story, not easy to comprehend when delivered orally, was both clarified and substantiated by clippings in the scrapbook. On October 18, 1933, it seems, a woman in Brooklyn had sued Mr. Kaye for a hundred thousand dollars for alienating the affections of her husband, Louis, because Lou had won so much money that he spent it, and his time, with chorus girls.

"I told him go back to his wife," Mr. Kaye went on. "I said, 'Why give it to girls, they're only a passing fancy, why give it to strangers?' I told him. So he went back to his wife and she dropped the suit."

The scrapbook showed that at one time Mr. Kaye had exploited the incident in his advertising campaign. One of his ads read:

IRWIN KAYE

FAMOUS ANALYST

THE TALK OF THE COUNTRY.

Ask a Fellow Player

I AM BEING SUED BECAUSE YOU WIN!

Read it Yourself

Another ad I liked ran:

PROF. KAYE

World Famous Analyst

SAYS:

NOW LISTEN, PLAYERS—BE WISE!

If owners and trainers make mistakes,

and they make plenty

What chance have you got?

Do you still think you can dope out horses? No!
Follow the crowd, I will work for you also. You
also will save many a foolish wager, also thousands
of dollars. Subscribe now and you will be surprised.

All the ads included the names and prices of recent Kaye winners.

It appeared from the clippings that only after passing through the grades of Famous Analyst and World Famous Analyst had Mr. Kaye awarded himself the degree of World's Master Analyst, which he registered as his trade-mark in 1947.

I inquired of Mr. Kaye how an analyst differed from a figurator or a tipster. His answer reminded me of a passage in old Nimrod, who wrote that successful plunging must be based on "great knowledge of horseflesh and astute observation of public, running, deep calculation, or secret fraud."

"A tipster is a fellow what might know something or he might be guessing," Mr. Kaye said. "A figurator is a figure man. But some owners never try—and *that's* what I gotta analyze."

I asked him for his definition of the word "tout," but this proved injudicious. I gathered from his reaction that a turf analyst takes the same view of a tout that J.P. Morgan & Co. takes of a bucket shop. "In the first place, there ain't no such thing!" he said. "What do you mean, a tout?"

"The difference, I should suggest," Colonel Stingo said, "is that the legitimate turf consultant, adviser, counselor, analyst, or even tipster, acts in good faith. The tout is cynical."

After a few more commiserations, the Colonel and I took our leave. As we started for the door, Mr. Kaye settled down again to his calculations with the *Morning Telegraph.* "The funny part is I *like* to figurate," he said by way of farewell. "Maybe if business stays bad I'll become a horse player myself. Then I'll have to go look for a bookmaker."

Out on the street, the Colonel proposed that we walk downtown to call on a profound figurator named James Trombetta, who has an office on Seventh Avenue near the Pennsylvania Station. We might break our journey by taking lunch on the way, he said.

"The quality they all have in common is that they are impressed with their own science," Colonel Stingo declared as we set forth. "They overween themselves. They are Dr. Fausti." The Colonel, as I knew from previous conversations, hasn't bet on a horse since the administration of Benjamin Harrison, and thinks anybody who does is crazy. He prefers a flutter at faro or *chemin de fer*, games in which there are no jockeys.

"The occupational disease of figurators is betting on their own selections," the Colonel went on. "They all swear they don't, like the bartenders who say they never take a drink. But sooner or later, like the bartenders, they fall off the wagon, and the consequence is disaster. The slip may follow a string of good selections. They have given their customers two or three successive good-priced winners, and they begin to think brokerage is too slow a way of making money. ["Brokerage" is the trade term for the profit on the bet that the customer makes for his adviser.] Having been paid off by their grateful clients, they have a wad on hand. The percentage of pay-offs, I may add, is high, due less to the bettor's sense of honor, of which he boasts, than to the controlling passion—avarice. Simply stated, when a fellow has been let in on a winner at nine dollars or better, he wants to be let in on the next one. When he has been let in on two in succession, an anaconda wound around the mailbox would not prevent him slipping his check into it, correctly addressed to the tipster. Now the figurator thinks he really must have something on the ball. I have seen men of the cloth similarly affected when their prayers were answered, or so they imagined. So the figurator ventures his wad on what he considers an even more ingenious figuration than the last one—and the horse finishes down the course. His customers, who lose their money too, desert him, and next thing you know he is scratching around for his office rent, or trying to sell his list of boobs who will make a good bet if properly approached. The same recklessness may overtake a figurator when he has nothing to do but sit and brood." The Colonel sighed, and I suspected that he was worried about Mr. Kaye. "In ordinary times," he said, "a turf analyst, consultant, or adviser has no more readily convertible asset than his list. Now, however, no one would wish to buy a list of bettors who couldn't find bookmakers if you called them up."

As we approached Smith's chophouse, on West Thirty-sixth Street, where we had decided to eat, the Colonel discoursed further on the economics of the information business. "In times like these, the more names you have, the more money you waste on telephone calls, and if you make them collect, the clients refuse to accept them. I predict that the telephone company will find an unparalleled number of slugs in its coin boxes as a consequence of the situation. I once journeyed downtown to the company's executive offices to intercede as an intermediary for a handicapper who had been caught in a telephone booth by a company inspector. He had slugged the booth for $750, calling boobs as far away as Hawaii. To cap his misfortune, the horse lost, leaving him without any Tease he might make good with. Some friends, including myself, raised a total of $67.50, and I persuaded an executive of the company to accept it. It was a lucky thing, for I learned afterward that the fellow was under indictment for a mistake he had made in California. I wrote a paragraph about it in my column, and the result was a run on slugs in the one novelty store on Broadway that had the concession. It was impossible to buy a quarter-size slug for nearly a week—a striking demonstration of the power of the press."

The Colonel said that substantial analysts like Mr. Kaye and Mr. Trombetta, who have maintained offices, as well as accounts with the telephone company, for years, are not in the telephone-booth category. "But there is a disingenuous element in the business that does not advertise," he continued. "There have been occasions in the distant past when, in the fell clutch of circumstance, I have figurated a horse myself and sent him out as a special tip, gleaned from the slip of a drunken trainer's tongue. A horse like that in New Orleans once bought a gold mine for me. It came in at twenty-five to one and enough boobs paid off to net me fifteen hundred dollars. The gold mine was in Rawhide, Nevada, and a friend of mine who happened to be at the same meeting let me have it for an even thousand. But I never had an opportunity to develop it."

We strode on for a while in silence, and then the Colonel said, "My old friend George Graham Rice, the wizard of finance, used to say to me, 'All a man needs is one good gold mine west of the Missouri.' I'm still looking for it."

By the time we were at table and a waiter had brought us drinks, Colonel Stingo had apparently banished the memory of his mine. "In my youth, the great tipster—to employ a term not in favor with Irwin—was a man called Jack Sheehan. In time he sold his name and practice to a disciple whose square name was Boasberg," he said. "The original Jack Sheehan worked the Chicago tracks in summer and New Orleans in winter, and he always wore a plug hat and a wing collar and a cutaway coat, as though he owned a large stable. He stopped at the best hotels and he advertised freely—any paper would take tipster ads in those days. But he was ruled off making book against his own tips. Every once in a while, he would advise his clients to send him the money so he could get it down at the best price. They had bookmakers in those days, of course. Then he would pocket the money, having picked a horse that he figured to finish last. One of them ran in on him one day at sixty to one.

"Mark Boasberg, the second Jack Sheehan, as I have heard, migrated to New Orleans, where he became a mighty gambling man. But throughout his career he retained the Sheehan *nom de guerre*. When I last heard of him he was running easy, just off the pace, raising garden peas and broiling chickens in idyllic retirement by the banks of the Mississippi. Between you and me, I don't know how he stands it, having barely entered his ninth decade. He may be meditating a comeback.

"On the New York tracks around 1900, when I began to frequent them, the most prominent tipster was an old gentleman named Mr. Merry, who sported a long white beard in addition to formal attire. 'Get happy! Get happy!' he would cry. 'I have a winner today!' When they opened Belmont Park, they ruled that dear old man off, because they considered him undignified. I went to the Jockey Club myself and succeeded in having him reinstated. By that time, I was secretary of the New York Turf Writers' Association.

"Then, there was John W. Diestel, a very sterling figurator whose slogan was, 'I never advertise a winner I did not give.' And so many dear fellows who dabbled in the information business—the Singing Kid, the Swing-Door Kid, the Coon-Can Kid and the Banjo-Eyed Kid . . ." Moisture gleamed to windward and leeward of the Colonel's nose, and he had recourse to his bourbon-and-seltzer to steady his voice. He is very sentimental about old times. But after he had ingested a grandiose serving of lamb stew he became elucidative again.

"There is only one kind of horse player more incorrigible than a dyed-in-the-wool figurator and that is a system-player," he said. "The figurator is bewitched by his own intelligence, an empiricist. Each race is a problem that he is sure he can solve. But the system-player believes there must be some one underlying principle that will solve all races. He seeks the philosopher's stone. No salvation outside the church. There is a firm in Boston that stocks about a thousand systems, and you can buy them at from one to three dollars apiece, with fifty per cent off if you take ten or more. You can have your choice of the Getting Rich with the One-Bet-a-Day System, the Twelve Goldmine Longshot Angles, the French Marvel System, the Super Duper System, the Old Reliable System, the Logical Winning Horse Method, the Never-Die-Broke System, the Old Professor Longshot System, the Famous Movie Director's Million Dollar Racing Idea, the Mysterious Angle System, the Triple Dutch Winner, the Golden Win Producer, or the Supreme Advantage Method, to name but a few. The real system-player will go from one to another, like a fellow that used to be a communist and has to join something else to feel comfortable."

"Who invents systems?" I asked.

"System-players," the Colonel answered promptly. "The last stage of being a system-player is the invention of a system. I never knew a system-player who started out to discover a system and didn't come up with one. 'Eureka!' he cries. 'Play any horse that finished fourth in one of its last three races if he ran at a claiming price of at least a thousand dollars more than he is entered for today.' And catastrophe engulfs him."

"It is the old human need for certainty," I said. "You shouldn't be too hard on it."

"It isn't sportsmanlike," the Colonel said. "A system-player has the same mentality as the sucker who expects to be let in on a fixed race."

When we had had our coffee, we headed for Mr. Trombetta's. We found him hard at work behind his desk, in a fifth-floor office less ornate than Mr. Kaye's. "Jim Trombetta is an optimist," the Colonel had said on the way over. "He continues to advertise, although on a reduced scale." I knew this, having read in the *Enquirer* on the previous Sunday:

3 HOT HORSES A DAY
Genuine Last Minute Information
NOT FAVORITES—
FREE WITH TROMBETTA RATINGS
You'll Do Better With Trombetta
DAY'S PREFERENCE, DAY'S LONGSHOT
AT EACH OFFICE
Daily $1
Regular Mail
One Week $5
Five Weeks $20

This was followed by the customary list of recent winners picked by the figurator. Restraint was the keynote of Mr. Trombetta's copy. His advertised winners were all horses paying between $8 and $15.80—a nice, conservative return of from 300 to 690 per cent on your money.

The practitioner's appearance was consonant with his advertising—rich but conservative. A round-faced man in a dark double-breasted suit, he controlled with the right-hand corner of his mouth a long cigar. A black chesterfield on a hanger behind him and a derby on the hook over it indicated the dignity of his appearance when dressed for the street. He had evidently acquired his sense of style in the time of the late Jimmy Walker, which middle-aged New Yorkers recall with the same nostalgia Colonel Stingo reserves for the Edwardian era.

Admiration for Walker is his only point of agreement with Mr. Kaye, his bitter rival in figuration. "Walker was a crook," Mr. Kaye says, "but his motto was: 'Letchez all live!' Now we got crooks who want it all for themselves."

Mr. Trombetta was still getting out his ratings because, he informed us, he wanted to hold his organization together. It is a one-man organization. But business had fallen off drastically, he said. In a normal, pre-Kefauver winter, he used to send out about a hundred and fifty copies of his ratings every day, and things always got better in summer. Now he had only about thirty subscribers, producing a daily income that barely met the nut. "But I've been in this game for thirty years, and I'll stay until we see what happens," he said. "It ought to pick up during the New York season, anyway."

Spread out before Mr. Trombetta were the entries for the next day's races, together with each horse's biography, in the shape of a collection of race charts cut from *Daily Racing Form*, a tabloid that suspended publication in January, and from the *Morning Telegraph*. I asked Mr. Trombetta whether he missed the *Daily Racing Form*, and he said that its passing had increased his woes by one, because the *Telegraph* is a standard-sized paper, and the charts it publishes take up more room than the *Racing Form*'s did. The owner of the *Racing Form* was Triangle Publications, which also owns the *Telegraph*. One Broadway theory has it that the decline in betting and the consequently decreased demand for papers to pick horses from was what made Triangle decide to drop the *Form*. Another school of thought, more subtle, holds that Triangle was only waiting for an excuse, since the papers covered the same field and the survivor was sure to inherit the other's readers. The price of the *Telegraph*, these cynics point out, has risen from a quarter to thirty-five cents.

"The fomenters of this unfortunate legislation have made trouble for everybody, even legitimate newspapermen," the Colonel said. "I must say, however, that Frank Munsey did not await the appearance of a Senator Kefauver to scuttle the *Globe*, the *Mail*, the *Herald*, and the rest, nor the Pulitzers the *World*, nor the Dewarts the *Sun*. The march is ever toward monopoly."

Mr. Trombetta said things might wind up with everybody's having to move to California, where there is racing all year round. "Either that or build an indoor track in New York—a straightaway under glass, about five miles long," he said. "You could use the Third Avenue Elevated, which is broke. You could have mutuel-ticket sellers in the ticket booths on all the stations and sell clubhouse badges to get into them. They wouldn't be any more crowded than Jamaica on a Saturday."

"Are you getting many winners, Jim?" Colonel Stingo asked, and Mr. Trombetta said he was doing pretty well. "But I have long slumps, when if you played every one of my selections you would drop far behind," he conceded. "The trouble with daily ratings is that you have to name a horse in every race. If you wanted to hit a big percentage, you would play only six-furlong claiming races for horses over three years old. The claiming price brings them together. Two-year-old races and handicaps are too hard, and there are so few horses that can really go a distance that all long races are a gamble. And since the daily double started, racing secretaries try to make the first two races tough to pick, so there will be more double combinations. They card eight races, and the two that fill best are the ones they stick up top.

"Jack Campbell [the Jockey Club handicapper, who, incidentally, isn't a figurator but a racing official charged with imposing weights on handicap horses] once told me an important secret for beating the races," Mr. Trombetta continued. " 'Always take the last train from Penn Station,' he said. 'Then you'll miss the first race. And when you get to the track, don't hurry. Go into Harry Stevens' restaurant and have a bowl of clam chowder. Then, if you're lucky, you'll miss the second race.' But you can't tell the average player that. He wants to go out there and play eighteen dollars on the daily double, three horses and three horses, and then, if he is a small bettor, he has to play long shots to break even on the day. There aren't enough good long shots in the world."

A guilty grin turned up the corner of Mr. Trombetta's mouth that was not held down by the cigar. "Still," he said, "if you take the horses that figure fourth, fifth, and sixth in the first race and tie them up with the ones that figure the same way in the second, you can get a pretty good double sometimes."

Mr. Trombetta told me that as a figure man he followed the principles of the late John W. Diestel (here the Colonel glanced at me knowingly) —he "graphed" the horses. According to the Diestel method, the position in which a horse finishes is less important (for future reference, that is) than the rate of speed at which it runs the last portion of the race compared with the speed at which it runs the first part. "It is a tough concept to handle unless you've had a lot of experience," Mr. Trombetta said. "The idea is that a horse may have won all by himself and still have run a bad race if the others quit even faster. Horses like that become false favorites."

I was hoping to learn more, but we were interrupted by the advent of a female of most respectable appearance, whose accelerated breathing indicated a state of high tension. She wore a Persian lamb coat, which, hanging open, revealed a tailored suit, and her face, featuring a long, square-ended chin and tortoise-shell glasses, expressed the antithesis of frivolity. I thought Mr. Trombetta looked a trifle apprehensive, for the lady presented the outward aspect of a bettor's wife, and while all analysts advise their clients to play within their means, you never can tell what a boob will do.

"Mr. Pearlstein sent me," the caller said, allaying the figurator's anxiety. "Do you know Mr. Pearlstein?" Mr. Trombetta said he knew several, but he and the lady could not get together on which Mr. Pearlstein they both knew. "It doesn't matter," she said, after they had gone into the matter at some length. "This Mr. Pearlstein thought you might help me. I've been losing money."

This was one client, apparently, who still knew a bookmaker.

Mr. Trombetta, with the manner of an eminent consultant, leaned back in his chair and took the cigar out of his mouth.

"Why don't you cut down on your betting?" he suggested.

"Who can do that?" the woman asked.

"Play only one race a day, or if you go to the track, play only two or three."

"You call that action?" the woman said. "I'm too restless."

"In that case, you have a problem," said Mr. Trombetta. "I can't promise any miracles."

The woman looked disappointed and at the same time baffled. I fancied that she had come prepared to resist a sales talk.

"A flat play on all my selections over a stretch of years would show a profit," said Mr. Trombetta. "But you might run into a stretch of months when I had a lot of losers."

The woman looked resentful now, as if beginning to suspect that Mr. Trombetta didn't want to let her in on his secret. "How much is your service?" she asked. I was quite sure she knew.

"Five dollars a week, by regular mail," said Mr. Trombetta. "Where do you live?"

She gave the street number of a mammoth, mausolean apartment house in the West Seventies that I happened to be familiar with. (She probably placed her bets through the elevator boys.) "But I'm going to Hialeah next week," she added, sounding glad to have thought of a reason not to buy. "I wouldn't get your figures in time."

"We can send them by wire," Mr. Trombetta said, "but it's more expensive."

"I'll consider it," the visitor said, and departed.

"They're all a headache," Mr. Trombetta said when she had gone. "If you gave them six winners a day, they would kick because they heard from a woman friend she had a man who gave her seven."

"Nevertheless," said Colonel Stingo, "is it not a shame that a woman like that—a widow, no doubt, ill-equipped to draw the attention of the opposite sex, her children perhaps grown and married and having no time for her—should be harassed in the pursuit of her one remaining distraction? Should some detective knock off her present bookmaker, she would be in the same position as a diabetic deprived of insulin."

"She reminds me of a woman I knew, a friend of mine's mother," Mr. Trombetta said. "A wealthy widow eighty years old who spent her last years playing the horses. Fine days always found her in her box at Jamaica. When the weather was bad, she played by phone, through her bookmaker. Last fall, when her bookmaker went out of business, she had to go to the track every day. One raw afternoon, she caught a tough cold. It began a parlay of infections, and in six months she was dead."

"Kefauver killed her," the Colonel said sternly. "He should be indicted."

Just then the woman from uptown returned, still shorter of breath. She held a crumpled dollar bill, which she placed on Mr. Trombetta's desk. "Give me your sheet for today," she said. "I'll see how good you are."

The transaction was executed, and again the woman departed. "You can't cure them," Mr. Trombetta said.

The Colonel and I prepared to leave. "Well, Jim," the Colonel said. "In the words of the English poet Hutchinson: 'If winter comes, spring must be moving up to a position of contention.' And I project that when that bugle at Jamaica doth windily blow, the rush toward the mutuel windows will be like the Charge of the Light Brigade."

13 / Balmy Clime

As WE WALKED up Seventh Avenue after leaving Mr. Trombetta, the wind howled in our faces at a rate which, if it was blowing straight up the Widener chute, would stop a field of two-year-olds dead in their tracks.

When we stopped in the bar of Shine's restaurant to take shelter, the Colonel said, "Truly it is remarkable. Saul and the Witch of Endor. The faith of man in soothsayers is unquenchable. And his capacity for self-deception is infinite.

"Joe," he said, "I assure you that the Chatelaine, if she studied the matter for two or three weeks, could take a race card and a hatpin and pick winners as well as any tipster in the business. It is a snare and a delusion."

"The Chatelaine" is his name for my wife, who is tall and lissome, although not loaded down with Tease. The Colonel constantly avers a deep though paternal affection for her. She was born in Kentucky, a fact she is not averse from acknowledging, and when we find ourselves in disagreement in the Colonel's presence, he becomes a courtly mediator. "The Chatelaine is not really angry," he will say. "It is just that old Daniel Boone spirit."

The Colonel is not loquacious about his own domestic past, perhaps because he considers it unworthy of a Long Rider. He was married in 1903, to a Brooklyn girl, and he took her with him to California in his flight from the Hughes antibetting law. For nearly twenty years they had a house near Golden Gate Park in San Francisco, and the Colonel says there were two children who attained exemplary maturity, a son and a daughter. Like Pierce Egan, that embattled Regency journalist of London sporting life, the Colonel kept his family and professional lives on separate shelves. He recounts no domestic episodia.

When we had medicated ourselves against the hyperborean blasts—for the rule of the Great Transition allows exceptions for therapeutic purposes—he said, "Joe, if I were holding, I would be at this moment in Florida, the land of lime pie and short-priced favorites. But the spirit of adventure deteriorates, and I will not venture forth unheeled, as I did in prewar days."

"Pre what war?" I inquired undiplomatically.

"Pre World War II," he said. "Release from responsibility brings to the Long Rider a second blooming, and I may say that I never felt younger in my life than in what must have been about 1935, when I checked in at a small but pleasant hotel at Miami with just seven dollars in my right breech. I discovered from perusal of the local press that a political contest of sorts was in progress, and by attaching myself to the headquarters of one of the aspirants I quickly assured my sustainance while I enjoyed myself. I ghost-wrote radio campaign talks for this Huey Long in little, and he attained a summit of eloquence which much puzzled those intimately acquainted with his illiteracy. The climate was delightful.

"I adapted myself so well to my environment that I became at one point manager of the hotel," he said, "as well as senior resident. My tenure was transitionary but notable. Managements succeeded one another in that hotel with the rapidity of Roman emperors immediately after Nero. It was in a perpetual furor of reorganization, like the French government.

"From the beginning I learned to love the life there. Upon awaking in the morning I would lie abed in my room on the second floor, and through the wide-open window would come the song of the mocking bird and the voices of Flo and Jack, a couple on the fourth floor, by inclination disputatious. The colloquy, to say the least, was startling.

"This Flo was a Miss America emerita, but of not too old a vintage, tall and still lissome and a natural blonde. Her boy friend made book on the dog races at night, and that, naturally, left them the afternoons free to play the horses, a frequent cause of their recriminations.

"Her voice would assume a plaintive, irritating timbre, and his would become denunciatory, even menacing. But just as I would begin to apprehend the sounds of open violence, a member of the hotel personnel would shove the *Daily Racing Form* under their chamber door, and the exchange of strictures would lose audibility while they read it in bed.

They got only one copy, and naturally that would bring them together, and they would become reconciliated.

"By the time they reached the lobby, ready to drive out to the track, her demeanor would be imperturbable and her attire modish, and no one could imagine her vocabularial arsenal, or the asperity of which she was capable. Similarly her consort was the personification of affability, punctiliously allowing her to precede him and never permitting her to light her own cigarette.

"She had quite a wardrobe, including the tastefully renovated vestiges of the raiment bestowed upon her when she was a beauty-contest winner, and presented what Mayfair would term a smashing exterior. Sometimes of a morning I would hear Jack complain that she had so many suitcases and hatboxes in their room that he had no place except the bed for sedentation.

"We all became well acquainted, like travelers Chaucerian at some wayside inn, and in the evenings, while Jack was at the dogs, Flo and I would sometimes sit together playing gin or cribbage. Dogs had slight attraction for her; she said the greyhounds had faces that reminded her of a snoopy little old schoolteacher she disliked in her native Alabama. Her distrust was justified. Jack became afflicted by a couple of bettors who always seemed to know which dog would win. They took him good, and from the matutinal dialogues I learned that my friends' circumstances were stringent. This naturally placed a further strain upon their relations. Adversity sometimes brings people closer together, but not when they are of different sexes."

The Colonel and I had somehow found our way to a small table midway between the telephone and the head of the stairs that led to the men's room, and the medication was having a restorative effect, so we repeated the dosage, the Colonel this time enjoining the waiter to tell the bartender to leave off all the fruit except lemon and to omit sugar.

"While their star was declining," the Colonel said, "mine was in the ascendant. The hotel had fallen into the hands of a couple of young fellows from New York who had managed to extract a profit from it, but they became enamored of change. One got married and bought himself a couple of two-year-olds. They were not good enough to win at Hialeah so he acquired a horse-trailer which he hitched to his white De Soto convertible and headed for Oaklawn Park, Hot Springs, Arkansas, with his bride. His partner had a girl too, but he omitted to marry her, possibly because the union would have been of a bigamous nature. They too began a journey, but to New York. In departing, the two hoteliers appointed me locum tenens, or manager in their absentia.

"I had had time to study the problems of the Florida hotel business, which I had found largely psychological. Tenants who missed out on one week's room rent would become diffident about approaching the cashier with a payment next week lest they be demanded to shell out the bustle beyond their capacity to pay. With each successive rent day their recalcitrance would increase, and the hotel manager merged with the jungle tracker, ever pursuing and never catching up.

"On the day I assumed office I placed an imposing carnation in my buttonhole. I put on an expression of stern grandeur and assumed an early station behind the desk, from which I could see the various delinquents descend the stairs. I called them all over one by one and accosted the moratorium. 'Beginning today we tear everything off and start afresh,' I said, 'but from now on you will have to get it up.' The new policy was universally acclaimed; I felt I had been destined for the hotel business and had mistaken my vocation.

"In midafternoon I walked across the street to the House of Usher, a bar proprieted by a couple of ushers from Madison Square Garden who in the course of long service had hustled the price of a saloon. We started celebrating my accession to power, and all would have been well save for an accident unforeseeable. Mine host who had started north with his girl had incurred a certain amount of enmity in Miami. Some troublemaker had put the finger on him and he had been halted just after crossing the border between Florida and Georgia and arrested for intent to violate the Mann Act. After a night in a disagreeable jail he and his girl, bail furnished, had returned to Miami in a state of disgruntlement, and he had entered his own hotel demanding to be assigned to a room. The bellboy had signified to him my whereabouts, and members of the lobby gab circle had apprised him that I had torn up the tabs.

"With none of these preliminaries was I, of course, acquainted, when, hearing my name thunderously invoked, I looked up from a table in the House of Usher to see this man glaring from the doorway. On his face he wore a demoniacal expression. I had barely time to brush a buxom stranger from my knee when he was upon me. 'You are fired!' he detonated, like Professor Hatfield's Gatling gun. So I reverted to my status as a guest.

"Meanwhile," the Colonel said, "Jack has gotten what seems to be a break. The big booking syndicate which has the monopoly in the leading Miami Beach hotels is continually in search of new business. A representative, unaware that Jack is in dire straits, asks him why he doesn't give the syndicate book a bet. Jack is unable to believe his ears. He bets five hundred on a horse at eleven to five. It comes in, and he and Flo are in love and business again. He has his check next day and bets five hundred on another horse. This too wins, at eight to five, and all is well. Then he has three losers, and pays each time. He bets again, loses, and omits to pay off, hoping he can recoup at the dogs.

"A couple nights later I am sitting in the lobby with Flo, playing klabiash, when there irrupt two credit men for the syndicate. I can feel the vibration. They ask Jack's whereabouts, and Flo says he will not return until late. 'All right,' say the credit men, 'we will be around to see him in the morning. It is nothing of consequence, just a small tab he has neglected to discharge.' When Jack walked in half an hour later Flo told him what had happened and he kept right on walking, up to the room to pocket his shaving kit and then out into the night until he cools off.

"It leaves Flo in a position of difficulty, but she is resourceful, and I am there, an experienced Galahad. I get her a job with this political organization, running the women's committee for Yulch, my candidate for Governor, and this takes care of her feed bill amply. Her one insoluble problem is the arrearage in room rent. Jack has enjoyed the confidence of the management. An old guest of several seasons' standing he has frequently run long tabs and squared them. But now he has vanished into the empyrean, the boys demand payment instantly,—or it will be the plug in the door, and confiscation of Flo's extensive wardrobe. They have repudiated my moratorium, accusing me of conspiracy with my fellow beneficiaries.

"I will revert to the transitional, lest I lose the thread of my narration," Colonel Stingo said, calling for a bottle of Black Wolf Ale. The waiter asked if he meant Black Horse, and the Colonel, with grave mien, said, "Black Wolf is much superior. It is brewed in the Yellowknife country, two hundred miles within the Arctic Circle, the home of the world's richest unexploited gold deposits. I have frequently seen a bottle sold for one ounce of gold dust. But Black Horse will be all right.

"I got up one week's room rent in advance for Flo," he said, "gaining for her a brief respite from the hoteliers' fury. I urged on them consideration of the possibility Jack would raise some scratch in the interim and communicate with her, in which case she could discharge all. But the rent itself, fifty dollars a week, as I remember, was excessive for her current increment, particularly as the season was now virtually at a close, and you could get a room and bath for a dollar a day at many nearly empty hotels in other parts of town. I engaged one for Flo at a distance of several miles.

"We devised a pardonable stratagem," the Colonel said. "My room and hers fronted on a lot where hotel guests parked their cars. Rosebushes and other floral ornamenta were trained against the side of the hotel. Flo would pack a suitcase or hatbox with her finery, choosing consignments in order of cherishedness, and bring them down from her room to mine, without the necessity of passing laden through the lobby, which would have entailed interception. Then she would continue on down and walk around back of the hotel to the parking lot. I would drop the luggage into the bushes and she would retrieve it and convey it to her car, a battered but rakish vehicle.

"She would drive to her new lodgment and leave the stuff, then return. We got out all her feminine frippery in this manner, but there remained two problems,—her wardrobe trunk and her parrot. The ponderous trunk, of mighty dimensions, was insoluble. She could not carry it down the stairs in the first place, and in the second, if I had dropped it from the window the impact would have caused a detonation like that of a clap of thunder, the harbinger of a new hurricane. She therefore reconciled herself to its loss.

"But the parrot, Pat, was her companion of longest tenure, antedating Jack and a number of other human predecessors. His hawking and rawking in the mornings, similar to those of a middle-aged man with catarrh, had roiled and moiled me on occasion, conflicting as they did with the songs of the mocking birds. But when I had remonstrated with Flo she had said they were a perfect reproduction of Mr. Westmacott, a banker with whom she had been associated subsequent to her elevation to beauty queen. 'Pat is in a sense my diary,' she said, 'and besides, Cunnel, honey, those are not little old mocking birds you hear in the morning. Mocking birds sing at night. What you hear is just little old Pat imitating mocking birds.'

"I had been well aware of the nocturnal habits of the generality of mocking birds," the Colonel said, "but I had assumed this was a special strain imported from Las Vegas, Nevada, which is a twenty-four-hour town.

"At any rate she could not induce herself to relinquish Pat to his fate, possible reappearance on two blue plates as halves of a broiled spring chicken. So it was decided she would tie a pillowcase around the cage, with Pat inside, and I would drop it as gently as possible into the roses, where she would be as usual standing by."

The waiter had by this time delivered the Black Horse, and the Colonel sent him back for a garniture of bourbon. "It is a moment that I cannot recount without extraordinary stimulus," he said. "I find myself overcome by retroactive emotion."

When reinforcements had arrived and he had incorporated them he said:

"As I received the parcel from her hands I could hear poor Pat muttering imprecations, but I disregarded them, reminiscent as they were of many of the departed Jack's matutinal remarks. When Flo had had time to reach her appointed post I looked out to see if the coast was clear. Sure enough all was propitious. She was alone in the lot, and I leaned as far out the window as I could, dangled the muffled cage at arm's length and let go. It plummeted down, landed in the rosebush, a perfect hit, right on the target. But the pillowcase was torn off, and I must assume that a number of brambles had penetrated between the bars, also the cage came to rest upside down.

"Flo rushed, motherlike, to the retrieval, scratching her sun-lacquered arms as she dived into the shrubbery to rescue darling Pat. When she had placed the cage right side up, the bird of retentive memory spoke, in a voice of thunder:

" 'You sonofabitch, you do this to me?' "

We paid our check, and passed out into the night.

14/"In Deathless Resolve"

IT WAS in the summer of 1943, while in New York between a trip to North Africa and one to England, that I became aware of Colonel Stingo as a major literary enigma. The Colonel had been writing his weekly column "Yea Verily" in the weekly New York *Enquirer* for nearly ten years prior to that, but I suppose I had never before read him with attention on a day when he had all his stuff.

Curiosity about a writer, for me, depends upon some peculiar combination of personality and subject matter—Stendhal on Love, for example, or Philadelphia Jack O'Brien on "Instructions for Men Handling Big Boy on Night of September 23, 1926." The piece which first impressed me with the Colonel's quality, as I recall, was one in which he played Plutarch to a man who had built a race track in Camden, New Jersey. "Loined in nonchalant Palm Beach kalsomine white duck and tabbing his program with stubby lead pencil, he is watching handy field of sprinters trot postward in Fleetwing Handicap, 3 Y.O. & U. 6 furlongs, here this afternoon," the portrait began. "He is 53% owner of newest and best-paying Gold Mine in this America of our'n. And, his name is Eugene Tomaso Mori. Throw-off kid from Mori family that run quaint old Café Mori, Bleecker & West Broadway, New York, for years.

"This fabulous Gold Mine of aforesaid Mr. Mori is the Garden State Racing Association plant, Camden, N. J. May not be yielding quite the gross bullion of Porcupine's far-famed Hollinger, nor, the Empire shaft, Grass Valley, California, but Garden State has the rich veins and soft yellow stringers indicative of tremendous Bonanza output in years to come. Yes, Mr. Mori struck it rich when he made his strike on New Jersey's unbelievably treasure trove Mother Lode ledges only three years ago. . . . And this, despite most exasperating heartbreaks and setbacks in Construction Operation & Transportation in all Race Track history. . . .

"First, that powerful and bitterly narrow Reform Element which had defamed Jersey State since Dr. Lyman Samuel Beecher's bigoted day, brought Heaven and Earth to bear to squelch Mori's enterprises. Tax schedules were enacted and thrown like a Rick in middle of road. Then the wartime necessity killed off Motor Transportation. . . . Yet, today, this Camden racetrack is pretty snug and nice-away as any you wish to see. And all this time Mori just keeps on smiling while weeding out heavy Tease and plentee.

"I'm out here to Camden's miracle Raceway last week. And what spec-

tacle? Round about 85% attendance comes from Philadelphia. After
youse leave Philadelphia's subway terminal to Camden, then youse heel
and toe 2¼ miles to trackside. Or, perhaps, for a Buck hard, you can claw
onto one of the weird Horse drawn vehicles that transport the hungriest
Army of Straggling Fortune Hunters over on the March since 'Lucky'
Baldwin's Party went over Chilkoot Pass into Klondike in 1898. Like the
cavalcade in 'Jim' Cruise's pic,—*Covered Wagon*, leaving Platte River
in 1849, the Quaker City saffari of dyed in wool Horseplayers sinuously
winds down road far as eye could see. All ee samee Oklahoma's 'land
rush' on Cimmaron in Indian Territory days.

"Moiling and Sweating in Jersey's terrible midsummer's parching sun,
here they come, day after day. Women in run over heels, men in bare
feet, carrying their boots, sometimes. I've seen 75-year-old wooden
wheeled Bonecrackers in locomotion. Also, regular oldtime Hay Wagons,
daily Victorias, creaking Democrats, swaying Buckboards, and a collection of busses which must have seen service for Wells Fargo Express in
'Kit' Carson's heyday. But on they come in deathless resolve of a score
today. Perfectly oblivious to biblical admonitory suggestion,—'All Horseplayers must die broke.' Truly, this present day Pari Mutuel deleria begets
a human dementia comparable only to the grand old Bank player who
just had to go against Gaff for it was only game in town. And now, as I
join out this coolly fastidious Old Boy Mori, in liason with Col. 'Mat'
Winn, 'Herb' Swope, 'Packey' Lennon, and George Vanderbilt, to belly
Clubhouse Bar for further libation of that heather creamy John Begg
liquorial ecstacy, I'm told off a chunk of delectable news.

"Come devoutely wished Peace, this Pennsylvania Railroad, its line
between Philly and Atlantic City now running only 500 yards off Garden
State's front gates, will haul to Trackside that Philadelphia multitude.
Then, attendance will average close to 35,000 and the Handle will break
up to, perhaps, $1,500,000 every day. Today, Philadelphia is one of Amer-
ica's red hottest gambo towns in country. May be lot of proverbial Living
Dead in old Quaker City but it's surprising how quick come to life when
that Paddock Bugle gol darn doth blow."

I recognized this as notable prose. Shattering all frames of reference, as
the boys in the quarterlies would say, it ran off into multitudinous milieus
seldom simultaneously exploited by any one writer—gold mining, horse
racing, the history of American bigotry, and the *haut monde,* coolly
fastidious in white duck. The genres were similarly intertwined; parts of
the piece reminded me of Bernard de Voto, others of Horatio Alger, while
some passages were beyond the power of anybody since the anonymous
creators of the *Chansons de Geste.* The author knew the American past,
the parlance of the I & Y Cigar Store at Forty-ninth Street and Seventh
Avenue, and the Bible.[1] He had led a life variegated.

---

[1] I long thought "All horse players must die broke," was in one of the Lost Books,
whose contents have survived as oral tradition. But the Colonel says it is in "Apocalypse,
the Horsemen's Book."

The "Rick in middle of road" bespoke a bucolic, somewhat old-fashioned boyhood. To this the heavy Tease offered a piquant note of the incongruous, since Tease, for money, is the antithesis of a rusticism. "Soft yellow stringers indicative of tremendous Bonanza output in years to come," echoed an auriferous middle life, supported by the reference to far-famed Hollinger and the Chilkoot Pass. (It also echoed, as I later learned, the best mining-stock prospectuses of the Colonel's promotional years.) It was when the Colonel got out to that miracle raceway, though, I thought, that he drew a bead on the finish line and began to fly.

What he evoked was an irruption, like that Fourth Crusade that resulted in the sack of Constantinople. The profusion of image with which he illustrated this surge of human plankton carried forward by a tidal wave of avarice embellished but did not obscure his exposition of its motive. "But on they come in deathless resolve of a score today." And nevertheless he liked them, perfectly oblivious to admonitory suggestion as they were. They were like the old-time bank (faro) player who had to go against the gaff (the gimmick that put him at the dealer's mercy) because there was no other game. Sisyphus was out of the same mold. In instant contrast, he offered the superman, coolly fastidious, above the excitement of the crowd he mulcts, another major figure in the Stingo cosmology, I was in time to learn. Mr. Mori, smiling in the face of difficulty and weeding out that Tease, was a prototype of what the Colonel most admires and has never succeeded in being.

Above all, I could see, he was a stylist. "May be lot of proverbial Living Dead in old Quaker City but it's surprising how quick come to life when that Paddock Bugle gol darn doth blow," is a magic sentence. The "Dead" in the first clause is balanced against the "quick" in the third (the quick and the dead) and the "Living Dead" against the "quick come to life." "Quickly" would have spoiled everything. These first clauses are like the annual statement of the Guaranty Trust Company—in perfect balance. But the last clause changes the character of the whole structure. It is a Louis XV pleasure house added onto a double-spired Gothic cathedral. The sentence ends joyously like a dog wagging its tail. In fashioning this tail the author had shown his *maestria* once again. "The gol darn Paddock bugle" would have been less good. By displacing his adjective and using it as an adverb he had achieved an effect of sweet disorder, as in the phrase, "a hothouse bloody flower."[2]

I did not know, or course, whether Colonel Stingo achieved his effects deliberately or as the osprey builds its nest, but the result was there.

[2] It was Dai Dollings, a Welsh fight trainer, whom I first heard employ this phrase, in describing a brittle boxer entrusted to his care. The flower wilted in the fourth round. Horticultural similes are rare among fight handlers, but I knew another who always used to refer to Abe Attell as a honeydew melon. "He was a honeydew melon," this fellow used to say, meaning Attell was extraordinarily proficient. "Cauliflower ear" is a simile without verisimilitude. I have never seen a fighter's ear that looked like a cauliflower, save perhaps for a suggestion of *gratin* that could have been removed with a washrag.

His byline offered no more clue to the real identity of the author than the likeness which accompanied it in the *Enquirer*. This latter was a line cut of a conventional Old South gaffer with long sidehair, moustache and goatee, in working position behind a large square typewriter. In the background hovered a horse and jockey, evidently just emerged from a starting gate in the upper left-hand corner. The horse was a nose off the centered title of the column "Yea Verily," and to the right were three elbow benders gathered around a triangle of mahogany with a bartender inside it. One of the three was a soubrette. The easy symbolism, equine and convivial, failed to record the true range of the Colonel's interests, which, I could perceive, were as universal as the hand of the Clan Sullivan.[3]

I determined to seek Colonel Stingo out beneath this banal typographical mask, but in those days I had a habit of putting off all plans until after the war.

The *Enquirer*, as I have said earlier, is the only newspaper published in New York on Sunday afternoon. For the irreclaimable newspaper addict, therefore, it is "the only game in town," but although it costs ten cents there are not enough such hopheads to support a paper by themselves. To augment its chances of survival it bears a Monday dateline, so that it may carry legal notices, a class of business New York State law denies to Sunday papers that are dated Sunday. Since the Sabbatical appetite for reading matter is pretty well satisfied by the *News, Mirror, Times, Journal-American, Herald Tribune, Morning Telegraph* and *Daily Worker*, with a combined circulation of around nine million, there is not much left for the *Enquirer* except when some news story breaks too late for the last editions of the morning papers. John D. Rockefeller died for the *Enquirer*; Mussolini's executioners were similarly considerate in their timing of the Duce's departure. The Ward Liner Morro Castle burned on a Saturday back in 1934, and details were still pouring in on Sunday afternoon. Colonel Stingo, the only man in the office as the stuff came over the United Press ticker, added to the appeal of the story by filling the sea around the sinking ship with man-eating sharks, which as he said later, he penciled in because they seemed to be well suited by the conditions.

The paper hit its peak circulation, one hundred and twenty thousand copies, the Sunday of the attack on Pearl Harbor, and since it has become a fashion to start wars on week ends, it probably will have a scoop on World War III, if there is one. On less fortunate afternoons, the *Enquirer* has to use artificial respiration.

In its early days its founder, a former Hearst advertising man named William Griffin, used to assemble packs of ruffians and send them into the streets howling "Murder! Horrible Crime! Throwed a Baby Offa Bus!"

---

[3] *"Nulla manus tam liberalis atque generalis atque universalis quam Sullivanis."*

The horrible crimes, when you read the paper, turned out to be in three-line United Press despatches from places like Hankow or Ljubljana, but the headlines were as big as if they had happened in Columbus Circle. The vendors traveled in packs and kept the full price of the papers they sold. Griffin believed in the Hearst maxim: "There is no substitute for circulation." The wolf-pack scheme worked well through the depressed thirties, but hit a snag when the approach of war brought full employment. The supply of wolves failed.

Once the United States was comfortably in the war, however, circulation took care of itself. Something genuinely exciting was likely to happen on any Sunday afternoon. Besides, there was a boom in horse-race betting which brought the *Enquirer* a handsome volume of touts' advertising, and the tipsters' ads in turn drew circulation, as the home front was well supplied with venture capital.

The war bore seeds of disaster for the *Enquirer*, but their gravity was not then apparent.

"The wartime shortage of cigarettes and chewing gum gave rise to our gravest postwar problem," William Scott Griffin, who succeeded his father as publisher, told me a couple of years ago.

"The small neighborhood candy-and-newspaper stores, which were a vital outlet for us, took to closing on Sundays because they could sell all their smokes and sweets during the week. It wasn't worth their while to stay open just to sell *Enquirers*. The proprietors learned they could make a living by working only six eighteen-hour days a week, and now most of them still take Sunday off."

Young Mr. Griffin added that he was working on a scheme to put the *Enquirer* on sale in delicatessen stores, which do stay open on Sundays.

Thus the *Enquirer* depended more heavily than ever on headlines designed to make the paper "jump off the stands," as they say in the trade, in such outlets as it had.

THREE GIRLS RAPE
QUEENS BACHELOR

an eight-column front-page streamer in type three inches high was one such headline that minimized the number of returns from dealers, Mr. Griffin said. The follow-up the next week:

NEW YORK SEX LAWS FAIL TO PROTECT MEN

UNSUSPECTING
MALES WIDE
OPEN TO ATTACK

was almost as successful.

Last spring, the *Enquirer* was purchased by Generoso Pope, Jr., son of the late publisher of *Il Progresso Italo-Americano*. It thus embodied two family journalistic traditions. The new management of the *Enquirer*, incidentally, has eliminated from its pages the Colonel Stingo line cut with the starting gate and the soubrette, possibly in an effort to make the paper look more like the New York *Times*. In partial compensation, it has awarded the Colonel an extra "Verily." The standing head on the column now reads "Yea Verily Verily."

The old *Enquirer* combined its headline style with a reverently sentimental approach to organized religion and the Democratic Party machine in the five boroughs. In national affairs, however, its heroes were General MacArthur and Pat McCarran, and its editorial outlook would not have displeased Colonel Robert Rutherford McCormick. This has been somewhat modified under young Mr. Pope, who endorsed Governor Stevenson's candidacy in the last election.

Colonel Stingo, incidentally, never shared the Griffin political orientation. His policy was simply, "Let Paris be gay!"

Back in 1943, as I continued to read his columns, the range of the Colonel's acquaintance, like that of his specialized knowledge, amazed me every Sunday, as when he began:

"Watching finish, $25,000 Empire City Handicap, 3-year-old special, 1 $\frac{3}{16}$ miles, here this matins is Old Man 'Jim' Kirk. Saddled great colt, Dobbins, for Richard Croker just 50 years ago to dot. Though turning 82, 'Jim' still can rig nice fat boob with anybody. . . . Well-liked 'Jack' Levine, celebrated 'Jewish Cowboy,' makes sturdy Hit with Numbers this past Friday. Little over $2,800 drawdown. . . . 'Johnny' Gillieu dealing for O'Brien Bros. oldtime Bank Game outside Troy, N.Y. . . . Popular 'Big Jim' McMahoney now The Eye at Hotel McAlpin. . . . That tobacco-spitting gnat, Spindle Jack, making Midnight Handbook, Night Trots, Buffalo, N.Y., on Batavia, N.Y., nocturnal harness heats. And scoring good. . . . Duke of Windsor back on Park Ave. on hustle, incog, past Tuesday. Gurnee Munn his standbye with limitations."

This cast of characters included only two, the Duke and Mr. Munn, of whom I had ever heard before, unless you want to consider Dobbins and Croker among the dramatis personae. But they seemed more interesting than the celebrities who turned up in columns like Leonard Lyons's and Louella Parsons's. And the Nestor who could still rig a boob at eighty-two was a comfortable subject of reflection for a reader getting on to forty. As for Spindle Jack, a character who recurred in the Colonel's notes, usually reporting on aleatory conditions in the hinterland, I wondered about him until, as a friend of the Colonel, I was in a position to inquire.

"He is a gambler who acquired that sobriquet during years of peregrination with carnivals," the Colonel said. "He conducted a wheel of fortune, one of those large vertical wheels with numbers divided by brass pins," the Colonel particularized. "The wheel is set in motion by the operator and slowed down by the pins hitting against a leather spindle attached to a stationary frame. When it comes to a stop the number at the top of the wheel wins the prize. The more nearly rigid the spindle, the more deliberate the last few turns of the wheel. The operator thus has a better chance to stop the wheel just where he wants it, inducing it just barely to kiss off a number on which some yokel has wagered, and stop on a number which has not been played at all or is being played by a house shill. He effects the stoppage itself by a slight pressure on a device known as the gaffpit, imperceptible except to the initiate. Jack's fingering on the gaffpit was lighter than the pianissimo of a De Pachmann—you wouldn't think he had touched the wheel. And his spindles could make the thing stop as fast as a quarter horse trying three furlongs. In the days of hippomobile carnivalry he was known as the Canfield of the Crossroads. He graduated into dealing games like chuck-a-luck and shemmy, but the name Spindle Jack adhered."

This of course puts me out in advance of my story. I soon knew from "Yea Verily" that Colonel Stingo was a reading man. "Description by correspondents of drab London life makes you think of Charles Dickens' narrated impressions of New York in 1855," he wrote one 1943 Sunday. Market conditions of all sorts engaged his attention:

"Two mighty shipments of topgrade Scotch whiskey, July 21 and August 1 into New York and Philly reported," he wrote on another Sabbath. "Cargoes evaluated at $16,000,000. And not a case of it reaches thirst frenzied public market. Being cached under reserve for Christmas trade when John Begg, instance may retail on hustle at $11.20 a fifth."[4]

I also learned to recognize his portentous manner, one of his best, as in these paragraphs:

"Through many of these clearing houses [for bookmakers] is washed an ocean of money wagered in hundreds of Cities and Towns over the land on Base Ball, Football, and Hockey. Scores of stockbrokers in Wall Street district, today, gross more 'commission' on 'the games' than they do 'clearing' dull and slow moving Stocks and Securities in the Market, believe me. Today the players in the handbooks, off trackside, or the Punter pasting away at Pari Mutuel slots, on trackside, want daily lines from Professional Turf Information purveyors. . . .

"Truly, under legalized Pari Mutuel betting today, Coast to Coast, our Turf speculation becomes a mighty financial and social factor in the Nation itself. Ordinary laymen scarcely visualize its immensity. Futility and fallacy of attempting to 'prohibit' betting on Racing and Sporting Events is, more and more, becoming apparent to students of public order and wel-

---

[4] The Colonel's loyalty to John Begg, described in the Garden State column as "liquorial ecstacy," was not unconnected with an advertisement that ran regularly on the sports page of the *Enquirer*, extolling that brand of scotch. He collected a commission on the ad, which had been placed through him. Thus, in a column reviving the glories of P.T. Barnum's Jumbo, he included several gallons of John Begg in the historic behemoth's daily ration.

fare. It can be regulated, licensed and taxed but never stifled. If legal within a racetrack enclosure, why not outside that Race Track? Experience of the 'noble experiment' rises in memory like a spectral gnome at this time.

"Tonight, there is all sort of talk in Hotel Mayflower bar about this and that concerning impending tustle. One thing certain, revived Turf Committee of America is to have campaign Bank Roll which will tremendously overshadow Half Million swagged around at Albany, N.Y., in 1908 to offset Governor Charles Evans Hughes' onslaught on Racing and its Book makers, for, never in over 100 years of sport have Race Track Stockholders ever stood so deep in Dividends, thanks to crimson sister of one Arm Slot Machine, viz., sacred Pari Mutuel Slotways. They say, tonight, an Ohio henchman, big Lawyer and Senator, will Boss this fight on Racing's behalf. Liason man up in New York, and, here in Washington, would be Herbert Bayard Swope, most able Talleyrand. Our ancient Turf owes much to his talent and devotion.

"During 180 racing days, 1943 New York season, just $266,435,000 was betted through Pari Mutuel Slotways. . . . Approximately, sour faced Taxman in Albany, N.Y., will take off $17,715,500 as his share. . . . Game almost doubled in all departments in one year.

"Jockey Fred M. Smith, now retired these many years [here a couple of paragraphs on Jockey Smith's sterling career] looks little different from sturdy appearance of two decades ago. For many recent years 'Freddie' has been engaged in purveying inside Information to widespread betting clientele. Always, he is a familiar figure on Gallop Grounds of a nippy morning. His large plant and offices are at 131 W. 42nd St., Manhattan, where, periodically, many a lovely long priced winning overlay adds joy and emolument to the scores and scores of his speculative followers and admirers."

The abrupt switch in subject matter in this column was, I suspected, explained by a large advertisement which appeared in the lower left-hand corner of the page:

Jockey Fred M. Smith,
Bootin 'em In Over Quarter Century.
I Have Worked For America's Foremost Owners
—N-O-W I Am Ready To Work for Y-O-U!!
—Dealing Exclusively in "Exceptional" Moves.
I release on days when conditions are right.

Plans are made in advance,
and every "Move" bears my personal Okay. . . .
Three ($3.00) Dollars brings you all three
"Exceptional Moves."
This is merely an introductory offer.
The idea is to get acquainted and get the best.
Make all remittances payable to Jockey Fred M. Smith.

15/"Moby Dickiebird"

I FINALLY had to forsake the Colonel for my trip and when I returned to the United States in the last week of 1944, I found his mood funereal. Unduly alarmed by a slight temporary success of the Germans in the Ardennes, Mobilization Director James F. Byrnes, subsequently Governor of South Carolina, had shut down the race tracks. This was perhaps because they caused absenteeism from the war plants that had been prematurely reconverted to the manufacture of peacetime goods.

When I renewed acquaintance with "Yea Verily" I found that Colonel Stingo was down in Washington, judging from his dateline, trying to discover what there was left to us worth fighting for. I did not then understand his elastic use of the dateline; he holds that a writer is entitled to use in perpetuity the dateline of any place he has ever been once. Thus in the summertime he will sometimes begin a despatch: "Clubhouse, Belmont Park," when he has in fact spent the afternoon on the Hudson River, on the deck of the Bear Mountain steamer. "I have been to Belmont," he says. "I know what it is like."

The Colonel's datelines are subjective, like those of a correspondent I knew in North Africa whose colleagues called him Magic Carpet Mac. The Carpet would lunch aboard a submarine tied to a pier in Algiers and date his despatch: "Aboard an American submarine in the Mediterranean." On the next day he might take the *aperitif* with an officer of the Camel Corps at a bar in the center of the city and dateline that piece: "With the French Sahara Camel Corps."

In similar fashion the Colonel, before we began to share professional secrets, used to amaze me by sometimes dating one week's *Enquirer* piece from Yellowknife, Ontario, the scene of what he terms the last great gold rush, which is within the Arctic Circle, and the next from the Oriental Park racecourse at Havana. Considering the modest appearance of the *Enquirer*, it seemed to furnish him a lot of traveling Tease.

"One notes the sharp repercussion here today, resultant from the Kiss of Death administered the American Turf by Mobilization Director Jimmy

Byrnes when he 'requested' the closedown of racing throughout the nation," the Colonel wrote. ". . . After a week's sobering reflection, the question remains in the minds of Turf Leaders, viz., 'Why was Racing, of all professional and commercialized sports, singled out for the Crusher?'" The Colonel seemed to feel that it was because the racing people, like Dr. Sykes and the Rev. Dr. Orlando Edgar Miller, had overweened themselves. "No question the Pari Mutuel lobby is one of the most powerful 'educational' camaratti here in Washington today, and, for many years, going back to the nefarious Standard Oil, Southern Pacific, and Anti Saloon League protectory movements of 60 years ago. . . . It is said the Pari Mutuel Lobby has suffered at times from over aggressive and flambuoyant Bellwethermen, especially Col. Herbert Bayard Swope, a sincere and able devotee and Defender of the Faith of the Turf, lo these many years." ("Flambuoyant," so spelled, seemed to me so fine a description of Mr. Swope that I almost forgot my country's troubles in my aesthetic wonderment.) "Many wisenheimers around here tonight opine it would have been the simple act of elementary common Horsesense (which, after all, they of all people should have had) for the Turf leaders to have accepted the new 1945 Tax proposed for the Pari Mutuels without a Squawk, and, with ready alacrity. But no, even the smartest Lobbyist gets bullheaded."

I learned, further along in "Yea Verily," that the Turfites were preparing for a Dunkerque, rather than a Pétain armistice. They were going to sail off to Havana and continue the war there, at Oriental Park.

A "Yea Verily" in mid-January considered the sad case of the horse players who had not been able to make Havana.

"What are they going to do for 'action'?" it began. "Meaning the Gambler who had been always with us, and the Speculator who is irradicably a part and parcel of our organic economic life. Through intensive study and experted practice they hold an edge upon the haphazard Player, and, thereby, earn a luxurious living upon the Racetrack, the Stock Market, and across the Gaming Board throughout the land. Where there is one professionalized Gambler there are a multitude of Schukels [Boobs] serving as ready material for the exercise of craftsmanship. Director 'Jimmy' Byrnes picked Christmas to launch his Squelcher closing down the Racetracks, and great had been the panic of readjustment of Life for hundreds of thousands of persons, directly and indirectly effected, since then."

A month or so later the Colonel reported in "Yea Verily" that the boys had found something. This one was dated from Lakewood, New Jersey, where, I learned subsequently, the Colonel was during this period engaged in dealing a faro bank.

"Lakewood, N.J., Mar. 3rd (Special):—We've engaged in, or observed, the Tango Marathon, the Bunion Derby, the Stork Derby, the Flagpole Sitter Contest, Commodore Dutch's Annual Ball, the Pie Eater Handicap, the Frog Jumping Championship, the Irish Royal Hospital Sweep, and the Roller Skating Gold Cup, but, the White Robin Authenticity setup takes the confectionery.

"About middle of last month, 'Bonehead' Barry, the Original, surprised the weary eyed company at the All Night Drug Store, over in New York, after the shutters had clattered down at Armando's, Duffy Tavern, Golden Pheasant, Stork Club, Paddy The Pig's, El Morocco, and Hogan's Irish House, with the astounding assertion that the White Robin had come back to Lakewood. He had been seen by that distinguished Ornithologist, affable 'Abe' Potal, Commander 'Sam' Moorehouse, and 'Mike' Todd. Sure sign of early spring and a favorable Training Season for the New York Giants[1] explained 'Bonehead' Barry. Fitting in nicely with the pattern of things planned by the devious 'Bonehead,' grave doubt and challenging apprehension of Mr. Barry's assertion immediately arose. What, a White Robin? Never heard of such a thing. There's no mention of it in Frank C. Menke's Encyclopedia of Sports. Impossible, 'Bonehead,' you're sure daffy.

"Then old 'Sad Sam' Jackson, the Booking Agent and All Night Sitter Up of substantial repute, offered to lay 3–1 that no one could prove there is such a thing as a White Robin. Quick as lightning for the Overlays, 'Jack' Bart, the Pharmacist, demanded 16–5, and, on acceptance, loaded 'Sad Sam' with a hundred. That started it. The nice fat Schnuckles[2] cut in hefty, too. Night after night, the Mob had been betting off its collective head on the White Robin proposition. Over the All Night Drug Store's steaming Java many a wager, one way or another, had passed on the gentleman's word.

WHITE ROBIN CINCH

"Appears, this 'Buddy' Prior, across at the Golden Pheasant steam beer Peelau, side-kicker of Wingie of Philly, consistently laid against the White Robin proposition, still posting 12–5 right up to 5:00 O'Clock, yesterday (Friday) morning. Other good Players booked against the White Robin too. Strange how iron faced Sophisticates will take Gamble Action on anything these days,—and nights,— with the Horses on motatorium? With plenty a money around the Mob will go for anything. And, so, the White Robin was made to order.

"And now 'Bonehead' Barry was going to prove his case,—that there is a White Robin, and, that he is back in Lakewood again

---

[1] During World War II, when there was a limitation on unessential travel, the major-league teams forewent their training camps in Florida and other southern states. The Giants trained at Lakewood.

[2] "Schnuckles," or "Schnuckels," is correct. The Colonel's unorthodox spelling, "Shukels," in an earlier column, had drawn a blizzard of protesting letters, I subsequently learned. "Shukel" must have sounded to him like a word more closely akin to "shekel," an old word for a kind of Tease.

this Spring as pouty and chesty as ever. This past Wednesday Night the 'Bonehead' declared he had a friend, Lawyer Frank A. Murchison, whose country home on Forest Drive, beyant the Rockefeller Estate, is surrounded by the Red Berried bushes[3] of the Paunsa Tree.

PAYOFF

"This sends 'em. Schnuckles go for White Robin hook, line & sinker. Soft touch.

"The hardy Long Island Thrush, the early Spring visitor, the long tailed Bluebird, and the Robins thrive lustily on these Red Berries as well as the wild Pidgeons, fast becoming extinct, the Jersey Ravens, and the shiny owl like Toebills. 'For the past ten days,' says 'Bonehead,' 'the Birds have been appearing in the bushes, opposite the large bay window of the Murchison home, which commands a full view of the red berried feeding grounds.

" 'Several red breasted Robins have been noted, and, for the first time in many Springs the very rare specia, the White Robin. He, or she, is the same in size and contour of brother Red Breast. Has the same song, hop, and trot of Mr. Redbreast, and, is quite as chesty too. Feeding time is around 7:15 O'clock every morning, soon as the light of Dawn is tolerably clear.' Continuing, 'Bonehead' said, 'It is my Idea to have you Betting Men appoint two Representatives and let Pricemaker Prior nominate the third one. You'll all ride out to the Murchison country manor house in my car leaving Paddy the Pig's ice free Barge Landing at 3:30 A.M.' Agreed. 'I'm taking along Photographer "Ben" Cohen, post graduate pupil of I. Kaplan, and we'll see what we can do as to proving that there is such a thing as a White Robin.' Readily agreed.

PAYOFF ON PICTURE

"Quickly the Anti-White Robin Mob selected as representatives Oldboy 'Bitzy' Ascher, ancient Bookkeeper for roly poly 'Sam' Boston and 'Jack' Durnell, the Parker & May, Bar Harbor, Me., credit man. The trip was made, the Birds fed as per schedule, and Picturetaker Cohen caught a corking flash of rare White Robin through the Murchison large bay window. The illustration, poised herewith, tells eloquently that there is a White Robin, and, the Payoff of quite some money was made last night on the Committee's Report and this visual confirmation of the fact.

"And now the denouement, the finale, the Grand Sendoff, if you don't mind. This ostensibly Silly Johnnie, the red headed 'Bonehead'

---

[3] I am not familiar with this deciduous conifer.

Barry, may be knave or fool? I'm just after learning from Tillie the Toiler, in effect, Mr. Barry is a Brother of 'Ringer' Barry[4] who did a little Remembrandting on the good racehorse Ahmaudon,[5] $5,000 Claimer, at Havre de Gras, Maryland, ten years ago.

"Made this Ahmaudon look like a certain $1500 Claimer entered in a race that same afternoon. The conspirators got the Price and they reaped the harvest. Without customary Easel or Pastel, somebody could have done a neat job on White Robin. I'm only Saying, that's all. Ever, and always, the Honest Rainmaker, as related in Job, the 2d Verse, is among those with the Prattle of a Babe and the soul of Jimmy Hope, the Bank Robber. Some of the Lads haven't cooled out as yet. Anyway, I lay 'em down, and you guess 'em. Yea, Verily."

This was the piece that sealed my determination to meet the Colonel.

Besides the narrative merits of the story, I was impressed by a historical oddity few other readers may have noticed. Ben Cohen, the photographer privileged to photograph the white robin, is described by Colonel Stingo as a pupil of I. Kaplan, who was the first observer to report on the naked duck, another creature previously little known to ornithologists.

Mr. Kaplan, who must now to my sorrow be referred to as the late, was a photographer employed by the *Daily Mirror* in its sport department, and was not a man of the type to build a blind near the nest of a tawny pipit and then patiently wait. But, as any correspondent of the *Field* knows, opportunities a convinced bird watcher would give his best field glass for frequently fall by luck to a Philistine.

Mr. Kaplan, who told me the story in an automobile chartered by the Twentieth Century Sporting Club, on the way back from Max Schmeling's training camp for the first Joe Louis fight, related that he had accompanied the New York Yankees baseball team to their training camp in Macon, Georgia, in the early spring of 1916 or 1917, he forgot which, and that the roster had included the usual large complement of left-handed pitchers.

One evening Mr. Kaplan had wandered out to sample the native corn whiskey,—there was already a state prohibition law in Georgia,—and two of the left-handed pitchers had attended a carnival being held for the

[4]Skillful horse-ringers do not usually resort to the paintbrush. "That paint look streaky when the horse sweat," a learned clocker of my acquaintance explained to me. "What they do is get two horses that look the same to anybody but maybe me, only one of them is something and the other one ain't nothing. Then they enter the nothing in a race and they run the something." That is what Barry the Ringer did when he ran a four-year-old named Akhnaton instead of a three-year-old named Shem at a Maryland track in the late thirties. But the traditional notion that ringers do use paint is essential to this fable of the kalsomined robin, which is equally evocative of La Fontaine and Damon Runyon.

[5] "Ahmaudon" is Third Avenue Irish for a graceless fellow, a schlemiel, and is a friendlier name for a horse than Akhnaton anyway.

benefit of the Knights of Pythias. There was an artful dodger concession, with a colored man who stuck his head through a hole in a backdrop for the customers to throw at. "Five baseballs for twenty-five cents; hit the dodger in the head and win a fat white duck!" The baseballs were large and soft, which cut down on their velocity, making them easier to dodge, and also obviated any lethal result in case of a hit. The pitchers, both canebrake southerners, had brought on their persons a supply of league baseballs, which they switched with the concession's own. In consequence they scored six hits out of ten, winning half a dozen ducks and disabling half a dozen colored men, all for fifty cents.

Then they returned to their hotel, where all the sports writers were staying as well as the club, and knowing Mr. Kaplan to be out on the town, they entered his room with a passkey, filled the bathtub with water, threw the ducks into it, and left, closing the bathroom door as well as that of the bedroom.

When Mr. Kaplan came home, barely conscious, he sat down on his bed, undressed a hundred per cent, and then went to the bathroom to brush his teeth before retiring. He opened the bathroom door and was almost knocked over by a flight of naked ducks, as pink and wrinkled as newborn babies. He swore they flew, although I don't see how they could without wing feathers. They must have looked like the pterodactyls in the illustrations to Conan Doyle's *Lost World*.

The pitchers, in their haste to leave the Kaplan premises before he returned, had not noticed they were running hot water in the tub, and as often happens in hotels, the hot had been near the boiling point. It had taken all the feathers off the ducks, and when Izzy unwittingly released them, they fluttered and tumbled all over the bedroom, squawking like burning witches with head colds.

Mr. Kaplan, thinking he was going mad, flung wide the door that opened from the bedroom to the hall and ran out as nude as a scalded duck, falling in a faint at the feet of a group of baseball players who had assembled outside his door to enjoy the joke.

"Ven dey saw da naked dogs," Mr. Kaplan said (he pronounced "duck" in this unique canine fashion), "dey damn near fainted too, I betcha."

He thought it was one of the funniest things that ever happened to him.

Remembering Mr. Kaplan's story, I was reminded of the experience of a Frenchman I know who on his first visit to New York was staying at a super-palace-hotel with his wife. The wife had retired, and he, in a state of undress like Mr. Kaplan's, opened a door which he thought led to the bathroom, on a hook within which he had left his pajamas. The door he mistakenly opened was that which led to the hall, and as he gazed dismayed about him, he heard a loud bang which told him that the door had swung shut in his rear and that he was locked out. He turned, rang the bell, pounded the door, but discreetly, since he did not wish to arouse the sleepers in other rooms, who might come to their doors to see what was happening. The discreet pounding was not enough to awaken his wife, who had fallen instantly into a deep sleep. The Frenchman sold wine, and they had been out until night-club closing hours, drinking his firm's brand of champagne with proprietors. He himself had been in a moderately thick fog, which accounted for his mistake about the doors, but his situation, he told me, sobered him instantly. The best thing he could do, he thought, would be to make his way to the row of elevators, ring the bell and then flatten himself face to the wall until a lift man arrived, when he could explain his predicament and send him for a passkey. Since it was between four and five in the morning, he would probably not be seen waiting. He rang and pressed himself against the wall for what seemed an interminable time. At last he heard the hum of the approaching elevator. He was on the forty-second floor. It came nearer and nearer. His appeal had been heard. It stopped at his floor. The elevator door slid open, and my friend sidled toward it, but he heard voices within. The lift had passengers. He froze, and after a pause the door shut again and the elevator continued. As soon as it departed he worked his way to the bell and rang again. The elevator stopped again, on the way down,—and out walked four men and four women, all in evening dress. They were guests at the hotel, who had been attending a party in some other guest's suite. My friend was at the right of the row of elevators, frozen to the wall, trying to make himself *mince, mince.*

"It was as during the Resistance one time, when I knew the Gestapo was looking for me," he said. "I could hear their footsteps, their voices. . . ."

The men and women, absorbed in one another's conversation, turned left and went off in the other direction, without having seen the Frenchman. The elevator paused again, for 42 flashed on the operator's board. The lift man looked out. But the Frenchman did not dare attract his attention because the men and women, although moving toward the other end of the hall, were still in sight. The puzzled flunkey waited a few seconds and then continued downward.

"I had fear that if I rang again he would think somebody was playing him a joke and would not respond," my friend said. It seemed to him that he had been out there for hours when the ultimate horror arrived. The door of one of the suites swung open and a woman in a *robe-de-chambre* appeared in the doorway. She stood peering about, as if for the source of some noise that had disturbed her. My friend was on the point of losing consciousness, he thinks, when he heard her say, "Oh, there you are." It was his wife.

The whole incident, he said, had lasted five minutes.

This has turned into what may seem another labyrinthian digression, but I mean it to show that Colonel Stingo's writing, like that of all major authors, has the quality that Stendhal attributed to great music. It starts you thinking along parallel and then tangential lines, and reflecting on the inwardness of the meaning of experience, your friends' and your own. The Colonel's nature story is just like *Moby Dick* in that respect, except that it is about a robin instead of a whale.

16 / The Navasota Murder

MY FIRST ENCOUNTER with Colonel Stingo, like Boswell's with Dr. Johnson, was not the result of accident but sought out. I began my active quest for the Colonel at Madison Square Garden, on the night of January 6, 1946. A long, lanky colored heavyweight named Al Hoosman was fighting an untalented but experienced fellow named Lee Savold, and the attendance was so sparse, even including a couple of thousand paratroopers who had been admitted free, that opportunity for seeing friends and visiting with them was unlimited.

I asked Harry Markson, then the Garden press agent, if he knew who Stingo was, and he said he didn't but would find out from the *Enquirer's* boxing writer, a fellow named Billy Stevens. Markson went off and came back to my seat in a couple of minutes with a slip of paper that said on it, "Jimmy Macdonald, Hotel Dixie."

I called the Dixie on the morrow and on several succeeding days, but the operator said his room never answered. I left my name and telephone number on each occasion, and on the fifth or sixth day I got a telephone call, at my desk in *The New Yorker* office, from the author of "The White Robin."

His voice was mild, fresh and courteous, untinged with regional accent. A certain measured orotundity of phrasing reminded me of his prose style, but his tone bespoke amusement with his own rhetoric. I told him I wished to meet him because of his writing. His voice reflected a modest incredulity, but he made a rendezvous in a joint on Fourteenth Street near Irving Place. "I would suggest," he said, "that you ask for me at the bar." I acted upon his suggestion, and the bartender pointed out to me the protagonist of this chronicle.

I have already furnished, in places scattered from the beginning of this work to here, bits of description of the Colonel. It is difficult to remember, when you have known a man a considerable time, what there was about him that particularly impressed you at first sight. In the case of the Colonel, I think it was his boyishness. He seemed rather a very old youth than a youthful old man. He was as astonished at the maturity of my appearance as I at the juvenile quality of his.

"From your voice," he said, "I judged you to be a young neophyte. But

I see before me a man with the outward aspect of a Russian heavyweight wrestler."

Nothing flatters a fat man more than the suggestion that he is in fact a mass of muscle.

The Colonel, had he presented stock-subscription blanks and a fountain pen, could have signed me up right there for ten units in the American Hog Syndicate or one hundred shares of the Stray Dog Manhattan Mining Company, both promotions of which I was in time to learn from his own lips. But he contented himself with accepting a peg of John Begg.

Contemplating Colonel Stingo as he sipped his drink, I noticed he wore a bow tie, a white carnation in his lapel and a dashing suit of the period of the Great Gatsby. His neatness and dash made me wonder whether he had ever been a military man, and I was impelled to ask.

"I deny the impeachment, but I come of a military family," he replied. "One of my ancestors, a giant of a man, led the last despairing charge of the Clan Macdonald at Culloden. It is possible the genes have marked my physique." The Colonel had, I now noticed, a wide mouth, which, when he smiled, presented a full crescent of square teeth, several of them braced with wires, and his nose, wide at the base, was uptilted at the end. His confiding eyes were of the color of a washed-out blue shirt. The full face was disarming, the profile less so. The bridge of the nose was high, and so were the cheekbones. The lids hung heavy over the eyes when he wasn't looking straight at me. From the side, the head reminded me of a not particularly benign tortoise.

I asked him what papers he had worked on before the *Enquirer*, since his column offered internal evidence that he had been active long before the foundation of that organ in 1926. This is a good way to get an old newspaperman started talking, sometimes, and it worked with the Colonel. (It is never hard to get him started, I have learned since, but, like Scheherazade, he takes his own way home.)

"I began in my native city of New Orleans," he began, not at the time entering into any details on his debut, "and by the time I was twenty I had achieved the position of handicapper on the *Item*. My selections appeared on the first page of the early edition during the winter racing season. At that time New Orleans offered the most important winter racing in America. There was a track at Jacksonville, but it didn't amount to much, and neither did Florida.

"Stopping in at the *Item* office one day on my way to the Fair Grounds track I found a note asking me to call on a Mr. Charles Phillips Cooper at the St. Charles Hotel. The name meant nothing to me, but I went. Mr. Cooper introduced himself as the managing editor of the New York *Evening Sun*. He said he was in town with his wife and daughter for a holiday, and the women had played my selections in the *Item* and won thirty-four hundred dollars.

" 'That proves to me, my boy,' he said, 'that you are the best racing writer in the business, and I offer you the post of turf editor of the *Evening Sun*, at a stipend of fifty dollars a week.' I accepted his offer, but delayed my departure after he had left. When he wrote that he wouldn't hold the job any longer unless I took the next train, I finally made up my mind and quit the City of Mardi Gras, where I had been raised under the tender care of my grandmother's household slaves."

"But surely you don't go back before the Civil War," I said, astonished.

"I was born in 1874," the Colonel said. "People in New Orleans held slaves long after the end of Mr. Lincoln's war. It was like bootlegging.

"When I was a little tad my grandmother and her mother, my great-grandmother, would send two of their male slaves and a white-haired black-faced mammy over to Newtown, beyond Canal Street, to the 'big house' where I was born, to get me and return me in regal splendor in a Creole-type open barouche behind a big jack mule who could roar like a lion. He liked me, that I remember, for I always maintained an adequate supply of sweet yams for his delectability.

"On one of those cavalcades I saw General Beauregard. The mammy called him to my attention.

"It had been twenty years since Beauregard had smelled powder at Chickamauga but nevertheless he was still the Napoleon of the Promenade at Old Spanish Fort on Sunday afternoons for all the fashionable Deep South world to pop an eye and heave a sigh at the wondrous sight of the little man in large wavy black hat, encrusted with a gold ribbon and bonbon tassel, and sporting a goat whisker trimmed down to a pin point. He was the President of the Louisiana Lottery then. His shiny black Prince Albert coat caught my eye, and I wondered did he wear that black coat, almost to his knee cap, into battle.

"My great-grandmother, whose maiden name was Angelica O'Reilly, lived to be ninety-four, and my grandmother, whose maiden name was Elizabeth O'Regan, to be ninety," the Colonel said. "Since Great-grandmother had been only sixteen when she gave birth to Grandmother, the two at the age when I recall them seemed to me like sisters. They would call each other by their first names.

"My great-grandmother spoke but little English, but she was fluent in Spanish and very handy with the Gaelic tongue. She looked like the monument you see of the pioneer mother. She was rough but kindly, I recall. All the slaves adored her.

"My wonderful grandmother sang and played most acceptably on the first Steinway piano ever brought into residential Vieux Carré. She had once acted upon the stage of the French opera and could handle a Springfield rifle like a soldier at Shiloh. Well I recall seeing my grandmother, many times, smoking a big black plantation cigar while knocking off with fine appreciation Brahms or Liszt in G Minor at the Steinway. Her expectoration had remarkable capacity as to distance and accuracy, her objective being right through the open window to the green lawn in the garden across the pedestrian walk. If ever the flapping window curtains interfered with her trajectory, vent would be accorded her annoyance by an indulgence in choice profanity."

The Colonel ordered us another brace of drinks.

"It is not yet the hour of the Great Transition," he said, introducing me to that now familiar term. "I drink hard liquor only before breakfast. But I got up at five o'clock this afternoon and have not had my breakfast yet. After breakfast, on principle, I drink only the Gambrinian amber."

When the barman set down the drinks, the Colonel went on, flicking a tear off his right eyelash:

"It is the wonderful dining hall at Sarsfield House, our ancestral demesne, that sticks uppermost in my childish memory with its two immense and positively beautiful old antebellum crystal chandeliers, the soft and generous old-time Irish linen at table overspread with silver 'right from Tiffany's up there in that hateful place New York,' as my grandmother would explain. Out of forty-odd slaves who manned Sarsfield House not one accepted freedom at the close of the war, though invited to do so. Grandmother directed them with regal authority, but she was also kindly and considerate. The old-time darkies just loved her. She would get up in the middle of the night and go out into the pelting storm to help one of them in an hour of anguish or emergent necessity.

"My father was Macdonald, a descendant of the Highlanders who came to Louisiana while it was still Spanish," the Colonel said. "He was a highly successful attorney. But by and by hard times came knocking at the door, and the result was my precipitation, at an early age, into the branch of letters which first suggests itself to the non-holding, namely, journalism."

"Well, what happened after you got the job on the *Sun*?" I asked, ashamed of my intrusion upon these deeper recesses of Mr. Macdonald's early private life. I could see that every time he thought of those antebellum crystal chandeliers he felt terrible.

"I was highly successful," the Colonel said, "and by adhering to bad habits I scored one of the greatest beats in the history of the newspaper business. It happened in the summer of 1902. My work had already attracted the attention of Arthur Brisbane, who had been appointed managing editor of the *Evening Journal*, and he had sent for me. 'What are you getting over at the *Sun*?' he asked. I had the presence of mind to answer seventy-five dollars. I was getting sixty by that time. 'We'll give you a hundred to come over here,' he said. I said I would have to have time to think it over.

"I meant it, because I felt safe over at the *Sun*, and I didn't know what would happen once I entered that Hearst volcano.

"I was a perspicacious observer around the racecourses, although I never bet my own money, and one day I got a hot one and passed it on to a fellow who bet heavy Tease. It was a two-year-old filly named Navasota that hadn't been out since the Fair Grounds meeting, and she came down at ten to one. The fellow made a big score, and he slipped me five hundred.

"She ran on a Saturday, at Morris Park. It was the same day Compute won the Withers Stakes. There was no evening paper next day, so Saturday was my night of revel Babylonian. Another fellow and I took a couple of girls from a Weber and Fields show to the Woodmansten Inn, a roadhouse over by the backstretch.

"It was nothing but bubbling Irroy *brut* and *toujours l'amour* until far into the night, and we stayed right there, but the room with private bath was not so ubiquitous as it has since become. Shortly before dawn I had to go to the second floor and I was aghast to find the hall outside my room filled with the muffled bustle of clandestine activity. There were two employees of the inn carrying a blanketed form on a stretcher, and escorted by the night clerk and the owner. As I came out of my room the latter placed his finger to his lips, giving me the office to keep quiet.

"Realizing the boss would not offer physical hindrance, since he wished to avoid a row, I stepped over to the stretcher and lifted the blanket from the recumbent's face.

"It was one of the richest and most powerful men in America, a pillar of the turf, a big politician and a great thief, and he was barely breathing. I couldn't be mistaken about who it was because he was a man I talked to almost every racing day. I had seen him out at the track that afternoon. I pulled down the blanket to see what had happened to him. The nightgown over his bulging belly, an onion-shaped kiosk, was slotted with dark blood, around which fluid more freshly pumped from the interior formed a burgundy border, ever spreading. He had evidently been shacked up with a woman and opened to the wrong knock, perhaps an outraged husband or a cadet to whom she had refused an agent's commission. I gave no sign of recognition and went about my errand. When I returned to my room the hall was empty.

"The Sunday-morning papers, which I read over my coffee at the old Imperial Hotel, Thirty-second Street and Broadway, carried no account of the sensational event, so I knew I had a scoop. It was by that time midafternoon, and I proceeded to Park Row by the Elevated Railroad and went up to the city room of the *Evening Sun* which was then on Frankfort Street, just off the Row. I typed out my story, left it on the managing editor's desk and departed, feeling I had performed above and beyond the call of duty. The party of the second part in the shooting was one of the most famous men in the country. I got a first edition of the *Evening Sun* with my breakfast next morning. Evening papers then went to press at 7 A.M. with their first editions. The story was spread right across the front page. I dressed and breakfasted, feeling good, and made my way downtown again to stop by the office and receive congratulations before starting out for the track. On the way I bought another copy of the

Sun, a later edition. There was no trace of my story in it. I was perturbed.

"On entering the city room I was met by the managing editor, who asked me if I knew that the assassinee's brother-in-law owned the money behind the paper. The family had had the story jerked, and had managed to keep it out of every other paper in the city. I told him that I could not possibly be mistaken,—I knew Mr. —— well. He said he was sure I was right, but I could not remain on the *Sun.* But he invited me to continue as racing writer until the paper could find a successor. I thanked him warmly and went right over to Mr. Brisbane's office at the *Journal,* which was then published in the old *Tribune* Building. Luckily the *Sun* gave no by-lines on local stories in those days, a circumstance which I had deplored when I thought it would deprive me of public credit for my scoop, but of which I was now glad.

" 'Mr. Brisbane,' I told that old fraud, when I had penetrated to his presence. 'I have been thinking over your offer and have decided to accept.' He was delighted. I worked out my two weeks at the *Sun* and then went over to the Hearst empire."

We had another round, and the Colonel said:

"The experience shook my faith in the integrity of the press."

17 / Honesty Is Not

THE COLONEL had told his story complete with names, and I was disappointed, when I looked the victim up in newspaper files, to learn that he had died in a hospital a couple of years after Compute's Withers, of what were described as natural causes.

Colonel Stingo, however, insists to this day that he saw the man after the shooting, and that the family hushed it up. "He may have been patched up and lived a while afterward," he says, "but he was never healthy again and that is what he died of."

This is the kind of difficulty that comes up frequently in editing the Colonel's reminiscences, but his reply, when consulted, is to say that reminiscences are not meant to be edited, but enjoyed. "Memory grows furtive, Joe," he will sometimes say when faced with a fact right out of the Columbia One-Volume Encyclopedia, the New York telephone book or Philadelphia Jack O'Brien's legacy to me, a copy of Tom Andrews' Boxing Record Book for 1913.

But with equal frequency he will maintain that his version of the past is right, and that conventional history is wrong. He believes assassination a far more common cause of decease than commonly supposed, and it is no worse than even money that any prominent figure of the past you happen to discuss with him will turn out to have been a victim of a very thin blade or of slow poison. In the Colonel's opinion, a man who avoids getting murdered is likely to live to a ripe old age.

In speaking of the heroes and demigods he has known in the past, he denotes their success by the appellations, "a rich man, a powerful man." He signifies his own approbation by adding, "a great thief," "a great old thief," or "a *pisseur*." He reserves the three-point accolade for a group including Elbert Hubbard, William Randolph Hearst, George Graham Rice and Boss Croker. He will never refer to a man he dislikes as a thief. Brisbane, for example, he considers a petty figure. "His show of erudition was a phony," he says. "He always played it close to the chest." "For instance," he said once, "while demanding of me during my tenure as racing editor a succession of sensational stories on the turf, which he deemed salutary for circulation, he would enforce the publication on the sports page periodically of the admonitory slogan: 'Race-track betting is the downfall of millions. . . . Don't be one of them.' And while we ran more boxing news than any other paper, including much citation of the fluctuations of odds, we published often at his behest, the injunction: 'Don't bet on fights.' He was a facing-both-ways, like Double Deck Tobin, the two-headed baseball pitcher, who was able to visualize simultaneously both first and third bases while working in the pitcher's box. It is a fact that Tobin existed," the Colonel said, retracting his heavy eyelids and looking me full in the chin. "He pitched for Hanlon's Brooklyn Superbas, but only briefly, because there arose Dr. Henry Ward Beecher to protest against parading him in public, an ungodly offense, according to the great lover and pious old humbug. He could have gone with Barnum but he disdained to earn his living as a freak. So a fellow named Jim Ryan gave him a job in a loan brokerage shop, or hypothecary, as chief overseer, where he did all right, all right.

"This old Buzfuz Brisbane had me write a Sunday story in the summer of 1907,—it was a full page magnificently illustrated by Hype Igoe, then a young cartoonist,—entitled: ' "You Can't Beat the Races—and Why," by J.S.A. Macdonald, Racing Expert of the *Evening Journal*.' In it I related the sad case of a one-legged man who hovered storklike about the betting ring in the grandstand at Sheepshead Bay because he had hocked his artificial limb to play a three to five losing favorite. 'Everyone is surprised at the meteoric rise of the sport,' I concluded, as if disturbed by the shadow of a bird of ill omen, 'and no one dares to think where it will end.' We were furnishing the sinister Hughes with ammunition for our own destruction."

But Mr. Hearst ranks only just behind Al Jennings the train robber, Rice and maybe Bet-a-Million Gates and Aneurin Bevan in the Colonel's all-time list of standouts. "Although," he once said affectionately, discussing his old boss, "I must admit the man was mad as Nero, and eschewed self-criticism."

Aneurin Bevan,—the Colonel pronounces it BeVAN,—is his choice in the future book among the world's statesmen. "The Red Napoleon," the Colonel calls him. This, I have learned from him, was the title of a peering-into-the-future book by the late Floyd Gibbons, in which Gibbons predicted a Communist world dictator would be English. The Colonel clips newspaper stories on BeVAN and saves them. He is probably the champion long-distance reader of the New York *Times*, which is perhaps the nearest thing the Colonel has at this moment to a wife. When he has been riding the magic carpet too hard, hovering like a helicopter over the Gambrinian waves, he shuts himself into his Hotel Dixie retreat and reads back numbers for days at a time.

"It is both soothing and educational," he says. The only drawback to this habit, from my point of view, is that he sometimes tells me Arthur Krock's column without assigning credits.

Of all the Colonel's idols, a man named George Graham Rice (born Jacob Simon Herzig) is the one he most frequently invokes.

On the first evening of my acquaintance with Colonel Stingo we walked, as we best could, from the bar in which I encountered him to the restaurant Barney Gallant ran on University Place near Eleventh Street. As we emerged from the bar, Colonel Stingo looked up at the vast Consolidated Gas Building across Irving Place. There were lights in hundreds of windows scattered along its sides.

"When George Graham Rice would see windows lit up like that," said the Colonel, "he used to say, 'Jimmy, behind every one of those lights there is a man staying up thinking how to get the better of the fellow across the way.'"

The Colonel first met Rice, he told me, when both were reporters in their twenties in New Orleans. Rice had come down there from New York, where, previous to embarking on a career of letters, he had had what he called "a very youthful past" consisting of nineteen months in the Elmira Reformatory for grand larceny and another couple of years in Sing Sing for forging his own father's name to a check. Rice, who developed into something of an author, later lumped the two episodes as, "One incident in his youth that left a blot on his escutcheon and placed in the hands of unfair opponents an envenomed weapon ready for use." He often wrote of himself in the third person.

He not unnaturally refrained from placing the envenomed weapon in the hands of his newspaper colleagues.

"George Graham Rice entered upon many and diversified fields of endeavor," the Colonel said to me as we walked toward Barney's, "but in a general sense his flaunting banner will be best remembered always on the turf and in the stock market, both reservoirs of romance, money and adventure. No baccalaureate wreathed his brow, but he soon acquired in the practical world of men and affairs a grasp of matters no formal education might afford. Down in New Orleans he was known to the rest of us as Ricecakes, a thin, wiry, young fellow with an extraordinary bump, or protuberance, on the pointed end of his cranium. He wore his top hair very long so he could comb it back over this bump. He was always fashionably attired.

"Even then Rice had foreseen the golden horizon of newspaper advertising looming in the early morning of his career, a perception that did not fade from his vision the rest of his days; it may be said truly of him that he became a master of the science. But for yet a space his genius was confined within the limits of the non-profitable, or editorial, department.

"His chance came suddenly, at a period shortly after I had left New Orleans for the *Evening Sun*. He was assigned to the hotel beat, and one night, late, he was over at the St. Charles, a block away from the publisher's office, in Camp Street. He knew the rudiments of telegraphy, and he heard a call for help come in over the Western Union wire running into the Hyams & Co. brokerage office in the lobby, from Galveston, Texas; a giant tidal wave had engulfed the entire city, thousands dead, an outbreak of fire, and all communications fast going out. 'Greatest disaster of the century,' clicked the operator, which, if you held that 1900 was the first year of the twentieth century, it certainly was.

"Over to Camp Street in a hop, skip and jump went Ricecakes and got from the drowsy business office cashier a requisition for five hundred dollars and transportation over the Texas, Pacific & Western to Houston. From Houston he got into Galveston just before communications went out altogether and got out by rowboat and mule a few days later with the material for a nationwide scoop.

"Ricecakes, when he arrived at a telegraph office, didn't see why he should turn over such a bonanza to a hick newspaper that was paying him, tops, thirty dollars a week, so he queried the editor of James Gordon Bennett's *Herald* in New York, sold them an exclusive story, with a follow-up series, and cleaned up. He was a genius. He said afterward that he sent a duplicate story to the *Times-Democrat*, but that didn't make them happy. They took the narrow view that just because he was their reporter and had gone to Galveston on their money, national rights belonged to them.

"So Ricecakes, when he finished his series, came on up to New York, bypassing New Orleans en route. He had got five grand from the *Herald* for his series, and it looked like a fortune.

"Our paths crossed again, possibly at the bar of the Knickerbocker Hotel, or the old Waldorf-Astoria. He was thirty and I twenty-six. We were fortunate to be at our prime in the much discussed golden era, which embraced the halcyon period in Wall Street, upon the race tracks and in the fashionable seasons at Saratoga, and in Europe upon the Riviera,—from 1896 to 1906. To have lived it is an experience unforgettable and priceless. It exemplified the method of fine gracious living without the raucous perplexities of frenzied taxation, sordid politics, and displacement of solid social status resultant from the parlous conditions of war, past and to be.

"Ricecakes had been infected by the contagion of turf fever while in New Orleans. In New York he bought a declining racing weekly called the *Spirit of the Times*, but a printers' strike caused him to miss several issues. By the time he came out again, the circulation had evaporated and so had his five grand. His reportorial services were in weak demand on Park Row, even though he had demonstrated his prowess, because the Galveston sequel had made his reliability appear dubious. It was then, with his fortunes at a low ebb, that he made his first ten-strike.

"Ricecakes recounts its genesis in his book, *My Adventures with Your Money*. Published in 1913. It is one of my head-of-the-bed favorites. I read a chapter every other night, alternating it with episodes from *Get-Rich-Quick Wallingford*, by George Randolph Chester. But Ricecakes is not completely accurate, tending always to over-dramatism. He says that he was down to a cash capital of $7.30 when he met Dave Campbell, an acquaintance of the turf world who was flat broke. It was in March, 1901. Campbell had a letter from Frank Mead, another friend, who was at the races in New Orleans. In the letter Mead tipped a horse named Silver Coin to win next time out. He said it would be as good as ten to one. Silver Coin was entered to run next day.

"Campbell wanted Rice to bet the horse, but Rice suddenly got a better idea. He would publish an ad giving the tip free, and including an office address. If it won, he would have more suckers than he could handle coming to his door with bundles of lettuce to spend for further information. In one cogent paragraph he disposed of the dry adage frequently proffered by the platitudinist: 'If the tipster thinks the horse will win, why doesn't he back it himself?'

" 'If the seven dollars was used to bet on the horse,' he propounded, 'the most we could win would be $70. By investing seven dollars in the advertisement, it was possible for me to win much more money from the public by obtaining their patronage for the projected tipping bureau. I was taking the same losing risk as the bettor—seven dollars—with a much greater chance for gain.'

"He took all the space in the *Morning Telegraph* that seven dollars would buy,—four inches of a single column, according to his account,—and the ad ran, 'Bet Your Last Dollar on Silver Coin Today at New Orleans. He Will Win at 10 to 1. Maxim & Gay, 1410 Broadway.' In agate type at the bottom of the ad it stated usual terms for information would be five dollars a day and twenty-five a week, and that this would be the first and last free horse. They then rented an office and stalled the agent for the rent, promising to pay after the first week.

"Well, in came Silver Coin, paying ten to one at New Orleans, but the betting on the horse was so heavy in the New York poolrooms that at post time six to one was the best you could get in New York, according to the book version.

"Next day when Rice and Campbell went down to the office they found a line of men stretching all the way around the block and clear up the stairs to their door, each with five dollars to pay for the next sure thing. Mead had telegraphed another horse that morning, and they gave it to 551 customers at five dollars, taking in $2755. The horse was forty, twenty, and ten, and finished second. They had given it to win, but at a price like that, a lot of the bettors had played it across and they cleaned up. They established the firm.

"It's a good story that way, but I think Maxim & Gay had a less impetuous inception. Ricecakes during his short flyer with the *Spirit of the Times* had gained insight into how much money could be made by the exploitation of avarice. He saw how crude the tipster's ads were in the racing papers of the day, and knew that with big display and his genius of persuasion, he could draw the boobs in swarms. But he planned the enterprise with deliberation, not, as he recounts, on the spur of the moment.

"Then inscrutable Fate steps in upon the scene. Always an inveterate horse player, Ricecakes had formed the acquaintance of a hefty bettor at Sheepshead Bay through a mutual friend, Belle Corwin, afterwards to gain renown as the inamorata of John Jacob Astor. The name was Amby Small, a great theatre magnate of the age, with headquarters in Toronto. This Dave Campbell mentioned by Rice was Small's executive assistant, and knew the equine realm in all its manifestations. At Campbell's solicitation Small advanced three thousand dollars as a pump primer to start the tipping business, and the boys made careful preparations. They wanted a real good thing to advertise as their initial free tip, a premeditated stratagem.

"Both, and I, had a sterling friend at New Orleans, Frank Mead, named but not described by the master in *My Adventures with Your Money*. Mead was a sheet writer for a bookmaking firm supreme known as The Big Store. The sheet writer records the bets and does the arithmetic. This firm was so ramificated it employed two money takers and two sheet writers. No one man could grab the cash fast enough, neither any other one man keep track of it. At night Mead was a croupier in an emporium of chance, and he also wrote racing news and did a daily handicap for the New Orleans *States* under the pen name of Foxy Grandpa. He was a jim-dandy and always well occupied, conversant with the flow of money, the gossip of the in-the-knows, and the welter of commentation that always surrounds the world of turf.

"The new firm wired Mead to send them 'an advance horse that might win at ten to one.' In due course, he complied. Silver Coin, a three-year-old maiden, was the horse, entered in a modest selling stake. The good jockey, Winnie O'Connor, after the Hughes stab in the back a favorite of the European turf, but then still in dawn flush, was to ride.

"Far from being broke, they still had $825 left of the $3,000, which, considering their proclivities, was a remarkably large fractional residue,

for they liked to play the wheel available then in innumerable and dignified establishments. This was ample for a full-page ad in the *Morning
Telegraph*. The advertising text was in the dignified verbiage, with an
artcraft spread, that only a master like Ricecakes could devise and articu-
late; as you read along, the vibration of a piece of copy from the house of
Morgan, announcing the flotation of a new issue of United States Steel,
seemed to be confronting the reader.

"It invited the turf-speculative populace of New York to visit the office,
the unpretentious demeanor of which was not stressed, and receive, without charge, the name of a horse, its rider, and the stake in which it was
engaged to run in two days. It would, without peradventure, win at ten to
one or better.

"For two days long lines of seekers of the golden info led from the
Maxim & Gay Company's office door down the street and around the
corner. Each received an envelope with a slip inside containing the name
of Silver Coin. Names and addresses, with telephone numbers, then not
so common, were duly taken and registered in the mailing list department, keystone of Ricecakes' subsequent success in promotorial capacities.
So far as history records, it was the first sucker list he ever compiled, and I
would venture that on the successive peaks of his crenelated career, over
a span of forty years, he continued to hold the confidence of some of the
investors upon whom he created this first favorable impression.

"The day of the race comes to hand bright and early, with all the
forebodings that such a situation might well hold. Repair by Messrs. Rice,
Campbell and Peter Grant was made to Gallagher & Collins poolroom in
Sands Street, Brooklyn, to learn what Fate might have in store—triumph
or disaster?"

The Colonel paused, for dramatic effect.

During his narrative we had walked clear down to Barney's, been
seated by Dominick, the headwaiter, and been served with two bourbon
old-fashioneds without sugar or any fruit except lemon, which I had
ordered in a whisper without interrupting the Colonel's outflow. Gallant's
is gone now; I am sad when I think of the generations of good restaurants
the Colonel and I have survived.

It was the first chance I had had to ask a question since the Colonel
broke on top.

"Why didn't Rice and Campbell use their own names?" I asked.

"Because they wanted to be able to try again if the first horse missed,"
the Colonel said. I could see from the change in his expression that he
was putting a couple of bugs next to my name in his roster of acquaintances. (Two bugs, or asterisks, next to a jockey's name in a program indicate that he is an apprentice, one of small experience, a
neophyte.)

"It was while dining at Browne's Chop House, on Broadway next to the
Empire Theatre, one evening, that the ingenious Ricecakes picked up

Colonel Mann's scandal sheet, *Town Topics*, noting a story about 'gay times at Maxim's, Paris.' Hence Maxim & Gay."

This is not the way Rice accounted for the name in his published version, but it seems more plausible. Rice says he looked at the entries for the next day's race, and took the name of a sire, St. Maxim, adding Gay "for euphony." I was to find in all my experiences with Colonel Stingo that where he diverges from recorded history, he improves on it.

"But the horse won, as he said?" I asked, wondering for a moment if Rice had known anything at all about his own venture.

"Everything came in off the call wire just as advertised," the Colonel said, "the horse, the jockey, and the price on the opening line. Why prolong the agony? The dandy Silver Coin thing got off in front and just winged all the way. Every quarter call was so much music to the sinners' sore-distressed souls, conveying visions of limitless lamb chops in the future.

"That launched the firm. On the next day they handed out Annie Lauretta, the forty-to-one shot, and then they played it safe, giving out a couple of odds-on favorites, which did not let them down, but provoked some sensation of anti-climax among the boobs,—why pay five dollars for a tip on a one-to-five shot?

"It was then Mead furnished them with the name of a mare named Brief, owned by a man named Mose Goldblatt, handy with a needle and syringe. Racing at winter tracks then was not so sanctimoniously supervised as under the aegis of the august Jockey Club in New York. Visiting a race track in Puerto Rico only a couple of years ago, I was informed by one of the stewards: 'We do not discourage the use of helpful medicines.' That, in 1901, was the practice on the mainland.

"The favorite was Echodale, strictly a hophorse, trained and owned by the notorious Bill Phizer. Echodale closed that afternoon at sixteen to five and Brief went only mildly supported at six to one, with eight to one available in spots. Both went to post frothing and preening like unto De Quincey's opium addict you read about. It was a competition in stimulative medication. Brief, a stretch runner best ridden by Jockey Redfern, just did get up to beat Echodale on the post by a head. At the precise moment of passing under the imaginary winning wire, Brief toppled over dead.

"The success of Brief, under circumstances that denoted Maxim and Gay knew the very stride a horse would drop dead on, appeared symbolic. The high-riding Maxim & Gay people were now in the lap of the gods running before the wind with all sails bellowing. The heavy play on Brief put out of action two Herald Square books, while all the newspapers carried stories on 'Broadway Cleanup of the Bookies.' Next day the boys took in ten thousand dollars, their highest gross yet.

"Mr. Ricecakes boarded a streetcar, rode down to the Stewart Building at Broadway and Chambers Street, No. 280, and rented a suite of offices of a sober magnificence commensurate with Anaconda Copper. He wired Mead, empowering him to get the very best information that money could buy, setting up a staff of clockers, figurators, and toxicologists. Mead would wire one horse a day, which the full-page ads would advertise daily as 'The One Best Bet.' It was the first time the term had been used.

"The country was race-mad and bet-mad. There were some weeks when the business netted over twenty Gs. In one Saratoga meeting of three weeks they took fifty grand. He averred to have paid a thousand dollars a week for information, and in advertising he spent an unparalleled amount, which I remember as usually twenty-two thousand dollars a month. The great Chicago firm of Lord & Thomas handled the account, and ads appeared in Chicago, Toronto, Dallas, Detroit, New Orleans, San Francisco and Los Angeles newspapers, as well as the *Morning Telegraph* and a similar sheet in New York called the *Daily America,* not to be confused with Hearst's *American,* as yet unborn but soon to be.

"His methods of advertising were unique. He used full pages wherever possible, and proclaimed to his subordinates that small type was never intended for commercial uses. He claimed to have coined the word 'clocker,' as well as 'one best bet.' If so he permanently enriched the language.

"He enlarged the variety of his services,—from sending out one horse a day, he progressed to putting out complete ratings, a Three-Horse Wire, an Occasional Wire Special at fifty dollars and a Maxim & Gay Special Release, in return for which the recipient promised to bet a hundred dollars for Maxim & Gay's account."

The prosemaster paused for purposes of imbibition, and I had an opportunity to order two shell steaks, of a variety known to Barney that sliced down the side like bricks of chilled pâté de fois gras and cost at *sotto voce* 1946 prices less than you now pay for a slab of pink gristle in a store.

Getting his empty glass on the table quickly,—he is considerate of waiters and does not like them to make extra trips for his drink orders,— Colonel Stingo continued: "I was in New Orleans myself when Silver Coin and Brief scored, covering the meeting for the *Sun.* After that I went on to Bennings, the track near Washington which filled the gap between the close of winter racing and the New York opening, which in those days occurred at Aqueduct. By the time I returned, Ricecakes was in full stride, lashed on by the divine inflatus. I remember it as a time of literary production like that of Shakespeare. Some of Ricecakes' ads were so good I still remember them." And closing his eyes reverently, the Colonel intoned:

" 'The Whole Question is one of Money, Plus Brains. We know we have one; we think we have both.

" 'We invite you to join us. You never struck a better investment proposition in any field of speculation than our Three-Horse Wire since you joined the Human Race.' "

"It's beautiful," I said.

The Colonel opened his eyes and looked me full in the nose.

"Thank you," he said. "I wrote that one myself.

"Besides this species of ad, which I may call the exhortatory," the Colonel continued, "he employed another of his own devising, the confidential, or cards-on-the-table. He had a remarkable run of luck through that summer, and he would frankly review on Sunday in the *Morning Telegraph* the results of all his selections for each week, with commentation, such as:

"Our selection for the Metropolitan, second, was beaten by a fair horse, but not the kind any sane man would pick to win such a race in a hundred years.

" 'Our selection in the Juvenile was practically left at the post and then beaten by an added starter of unquestionable class.

" "A flat bet of a hundred dollars a horse on our Three-Horse Wire for five days is only a five-hundred-and-forty-dollar winner,—a distinct disappointment. The element of racing luck will creep in occasionally, but when it does it is the exception that proves our rule of many winners. The Three Best Bets given by us daily, famous to the racing world as Maxim & Gay's Three-Horse Wire, and backed by almost every plunger of note in the country for thousands daily, is worth your serious consideration, whether a big or a small bettor.'

"The 'disappointment' about winning only $540 was the convincer. Readers could see Maxim & Gay were on the level. The money flowed in like the waters of the Columbia River over the awesome Grand Coulee Dam, spreading beneficence in all directions. The fallacy undermining Ricecakes, like so many great men standing unwittingly upon the brink of disaster,—Hitler and John L. Sullivan are examples—was that he overweened himself. He began to think he really had something.

"Like the sheik in the story, he bet on those horses. And so when his intelligence department turned up a succession of stiffs, his reserves diminished rapidly.

"On March 15, 1902, he was enabled truthfully to advise the public: 'We sold our information to sixty-four thousand individuals during the twelve months just ended. What was in it for them must be in it for you.' A few days later Maxim & Gay promulgated:

" 'This is getaway week at New Orleans. Our experts burned the wires yesterday with startling inside information, which, added to knowledge already in our possession, points to the fact that this will be the banner week in the history of the Maxim & Gay Company. We are conservative in our promises. Each word is weighed well, and when we say there will be sensational doing during the next six days the statement is a positive one. Opportunity is knocking at your door. It is the time for action! Any two days of this week should show better results than the backing of our wire during the entire fortnight just ended. We know what we are talking about!' "

It was like hearing Carl Sandburg recite his own verse.

"The results of that week compelled Maxim & Gay to assume an apologetic tone," the Colonel said sadly.

" 'New Orleans is the hardest track in America to beat on any system of selecting probable winners that is based on workouts,' the faithful readers were instructed at the end of the meeting. 'The reason for this is that the horses which race here have little or no class and cannot be depended upon to repeat their morning workouts in their afternoon races. Again, the jockeys—most of them—are a lot of pinheads who are as unreliable as the horses. In the East it is different. The horses are classy, reliable, and their morning workouts are a safe indication of their evening performances. Entire eastern season, four hundred dollars in advance.'

"The reputation of Maxim & Gay was so firmly established in a year that even after the bad week at New Orleans, a number of boobs sent in the four hundred dollars," the Colonel said. "But the Bennings meeting was barely a standoff for Ricecakes' tips.

" 'Our performance at Bennings was fair,' the next series of ads began. 'At Aqueduct it will prove to be brilliant. This week, beginning with the first race Monday, we will give the pencilers the worst dose they have had in 1902 to date. Get aboard!'

"Aqueduct was grim for Ricecakes," the Colonel said. "His policy of frankness proved a boomerang when the hypothetical flat-bet-of-a-hundred-dollar customer, mainspring of his advertising, showed a loss for several successive weeks. When he dropped this type of advertising the boobs demanded the reason for the abandonment. By midsummer his enterprise was on the verge of collapse.

"It impressed upon me indelibly the lesson that in advertising honesty is not the best policy."

18 / Farewell to Ricecakes

WHEN THE Colonel referred to Mr. Rice it was with the tone of Joyce's Mr. Casey talking about Charles Stewart Parnell: "My dead king."

I could see that the two experiences the Colonel had just narrated, both coming in the fateful summer of 1902, might well have engendered the cynicism he professed.

I also had a memory of Rice, more recent than the Colonel's. I had interviewed the great old thief in January, 1934, when I was a reporter on an evening newspaper and he had just come out of the Federal Penitentiary in Atlanta, where he had done the fourth, and last, prison stretch of a long and accidented life. (He had successfully defended himself against at least as many indictments, including one for evading $1,700,000 in income taxes from 1925 to 1929.)

He was a pot-bellied, round-faced man of sixty-four, with spectacles and fine white hair,—I did not remember noticing the bump,—and his asseverations of continuously misunderstood good faith had seemed to me almost comic. I remembered he had told me he had "a phosphorescent mind," and that he was "the only honest financial writer in America," for which reason the big interests had always persecuted him.

It would be unkind to tell this to Colonel Stingo, I knew, since he remembered Mr. Rice at the top of his form. That is how fans who saw the second Tendler fight remember Benny Leonard. They do not like to be reminded of how Leonard looked in his attempted comeback nine years later. Long Riders, like prize fighters, should be remembered off their best.

So I merely asked Colonel Stingo if the 1902 run of losers had meant the end of Maxim & Gay.

"No," he said, "the mind Napoleonic will never concede defeat. In Ricecakes' book he records that it was the wont of the firm's track salesmen, dressed in khaki paramilitary uniforms, to appear at the office at noon every day and receive a bundle of envelopes containing the tips. They would then go on to the track and sell them at the gates for five dollars each. The stupendous gall of the procedure becomes apparent if you reflect what five dollars was worth in 1902.

"One day, while Ricecakes was out sick," says he, "a man in his office put slips of blank paper in the envelopes. The salesmen were forced to refund money to the handful of faithful boobs who still patronized Maxim & Gay. A horse named May J. came in at two hundred to one. The next day's papers carried full-page ads of Maxim & Gay claiming they had tipped May J. Nobody could prove they hadn't.

"And such is the power of suggestion that in the afternoon a boob, not a plant, came into the office and laid down five dollars on the counter, averring that he had played May J. on Maxim & Gay's tip, and wanted more like her. They got him to make an affidavit to that effect and published it in another series of full-page ads. Business picked up immediately.

"When the clerk who performed this stunt was asked for more information as to how he came to secure such an affidavit," the Colonel said, "and I quote Ricecakes: 'He gave absolute assurance that he did not offer the customer the slightest bribe to make it, and that nothing but an innate desire to call himself "on top" had influenced the man to perjure himself.' The duplicitous employe was promptly discharged, Ricecakes says, although he does not go so far as to state that Maxim & Gay ever repudiated the May J. ads. He fails at any point in his narrative to identify the clerical scalawag, and I think his disclaimer of origination is due to modesty.

"To me the May J. coup is reminiscent of Jack Dempsey's triumph over Luis Angel Firpo, when, knocked out of the ring and groggy, he climbed back and felled that huge black-browed man, the incarnation of misfortune. Maxim & Gay gave a string of winners, and within a month net earnings again reached twenty thousand dollars a week. Shortly after May J., the president of Maxim & Gay found a bankroll man, or source of new capital if needed. He was Sol Lichtenstein, one of the mightiest bookmakers of the day.

"There grew up at about this time in the tremendous business of Maxim & Gay, engineered by this truly astounding old Ricecakes, a problem. Their nationwide advertising and resounding success had created a vast public of small-town investors who knew no bookmakers but wanted to get in on the rich profits envisioned in such copy as:

"'This will be a bonanza week! Our Three Best Bets Wire every day this week beginning Monday should prove a bonanza! We know what we are talking about! It will sizzle with good things this week, beginning with the first race Monday. You are invited to get aboard.'"

From the Colonel's expression I could divine who had written that one.

"Rice moved his entire office staff to New Orleans at the beginning of that winter racing season. He took twenty thousand dollars' worth of display advertising to run in thirty newspapers in the United States on the same day, announcing that Maxim & Gay would function as a commission house, accepting money orders for any amount and *betting the money for clients* on Maxim & Gay information. Maxim & Gay charged ten dollars a week for the information and retained five per cent of the winnings. It was a sure method of preventing holdouts, since they knew exactly what was coming to them. They made seven thousand dollars a day for the one hundred days of the meeting.

"As offices they rented in New Orleans the entire floor above Parson Davies' Crescent Billiard Academy on Canal Street, the lurking place, Bourse and Lloyd's Clearing House of the sporting gentry. The volume of mail addressed to Maxim & Gay was so great that Ricecakes had to hire a couple of trucks to haul it from the post office.

"Nothing like it was ever seen. But Ricecakes kept betting his profits back on the losers. He became crazed with the megalomania of octopus-like expansion. Not content with selling information, wagering his clients' money, clipping them five per cent of their winnings, shaving the odds and occasionally slipping them a wrongo, he decided to become a newspaper publisher, run his own ads and make a profit off himself.

"He may have had visions of becoming a second William Randolph Hearst. In pursuit of his ambition he bought a New York racing paper called the *Daily America* and announced he was pulling the Maxim & Gay business from the *Telegraph* and giving it all to his own sheet. He might have put the *Morning Telegraph* out of business, but William Collins Whitney, one of the richest, most powerful men in America at that time, bought a controlling interest in the *Telegraph*.

"It was made known to the upstart that unless he sold the *Daily America* to Mr. Whitney there would be a Federal investigation of the affairs of Maxim & Gay. It was also conveyed to him that the Jockey Club considered the methods of Maxim & Gay injurious to racing, since there was implicit in them a suggestion that racing was primarily a form of gambling. This is a heresy denounced to this day by the owners of the patents on the pari-mutuel machines. Therefore, even if he sold the *Daily America* on Whitney's terms—a squalid pittance—the *Morning Telegraph* would refuse his ads.

"The words in which Ricecakes has recorded his defeat are ever present in my memory. They are of a sombre chastity divergent from his florescent vein:

"'Having lost the *Daily America* and having "blown" the Maxim & Gay Company, I was again broke.'

"It is said that Stendhal, the French gambler, used to read the Code Napoleon to learn stylistic restraint," the Colonel said, just as the waiter began to cut up our steak. "It is also said there was another distinguished Frenchman, whose name I do not at the moment recall, who used every year to reread Stendhal's masterpiece about roulette, *The Red and the Black*,[1] for the same reason. Personally I read George Graham Rice."

We fell to upon the steak, which offered small test of the Colonel's mandibular powers but a brilliant field for the demonstration of his appetite. "I am a good doer," he said, and proved it.

As frequently happens when food is voraciously ingested after several rounds of drink, we became torpid and conversation lagged.

In this first meeting I had heard more about George Graham Rice than about the Colonel himself, but I felt we had established a rapport.

19 / The Honest Hog Caller

SHORTLY AFTER our first rencontre, I paid my first visit to Colonel Stingo at his eremite retreat in the Dixie. Having forgotten his room number, I confused the desk clerk by asking for Mr. Macdonald. He looked through

---

[1] Much later, when we had become habitual associates, I remarked to the Colonel that *The Red and the Black* was not about roulette. "Memory grows furtive, Joe," he said. "I meant *The Gambler*, by Volodyovski." Volodyovski, a horse leased for the occasion, won the Epsom Derby for William Collins Whitney in 1901.

the list of guests, found what room Mr. Macdonald had, and then said, "Oh, you mean Colonel Stingo."

The Dixie is a seven-hundred-room hotel with entrances on both Forty-second and Forty-third streets, between Seventh and Eighth avenues. From the Colonel's single-with-bath, on a corner of the seventh floor on the Forty-second Street side, he can look out over a block of shooting galleries, cafeterias and third-run movie houses—a block that he knew in more glorious days, when the New Amsterdam Theatre housed the *Ziegfeld Follies* instead of Tarzan pictures, and Murray's Roman Gardens Restaurant occupied the building presently tenanted by the flea circus. The ramps of a bus terminal plunge beneath part of the Forty-third Street side of the hotel, and the buses bring many of the Dixie's guests—earnest young honeymooners from the South, and servicemen with their wives. The crowd in the small plywood-and-aquamarine lobby at the core of the building is younger than the crowds in most hotels, and this, the Colonel says, is good for his mental tone. "It makes the sap rise just to look at them," I have heard him declare.

The Colonel's room is simple and functional. It contains a single bed, covered with a rough gruelly cloth, a writing desk, a typewriter table, a dresser and two chairs. It is about the size of the chief steward's cabin on a small ship, and the Colonel's gear is stowed as neatly as a seaman's. His greatest periodic dread, next to rent day, is the approach of the time when it will be necessary to change the ribbon in his portable typewriter. Usually he delays this operation until he himself is unable to read what he has just thumped out. "Have a new ribbon for Mr. Underwood," he wrote to me once. "Put it on myself, single-handed and unassisted. As great an engineering feat as a triple play in the clutch." There are a few framed photographs on the walls, the most noteworthy of which is a picture clipped from the New York *Press*, a sporting sheet. A headline over the print reads: "Grand Old Hickory Jims of the Turf Writers," and the caption underneath identifies it as a reproduction of a picture of "the organization meeting of the American Turf Writers Association, January, 1902, in the popular Old Hickory Restaurant, Jackson Square, New Orleans." There are fifteen men, nine standing and six at a table, and there are fifteen stiff collars and five handle-bar moustaches in the group. Fourth from the left among those erect is J.S.A. Macdonald, New York *Evening Journal*. The Colonel, considerably more solemn of aspect at twenty-eight than he is at seventy-eight, is wearing a white scarf and watch chain with a dark suit. His hair, quite long, sweeps low on the right side of his forehead, his cheeks are leaner than today, but otherwise he is much the same. He has his right hand on the shoulder of the racing correspondent of the Buffalo *Express*, who looks like Herbert Hoover, and stands directly behind an old deep-south gentleman denominated Captain Williams of the New Orleans *Times-Democrat*. In Captain Williams I recognized the true original of the Colonel Stingo cut, complete with

white moustache, goatee, long hair, and frock coat. They were an imposing lot, the turf writers of 1902, like some weighty committee of the
American Federal Bar. Colonel Stingo and a man named Harry Brievogel
of the Chicago *American* seemed to be the youngsters of the band.

The Colonel first bivouacked at the Dixie in 1940, at a time when
Broadway hotels welcomed residential guests at a weekly rent lower than
the transient rate. When World War II brought a great rise in demand for
rooms at any price, the Colonel and many another Broadway solitary sat
tight, protected by the emergency rent laws, and he still pays a rent he
describes as "inexorbitant."

When I first visited him I congratulated him on his *bonne mine*. He
was then, by his own count, seventy-two. "I have three rules for keeping
in condition," he said. "I will not let guileful women move in on me, I
decline all responsibility, and above all, I avoid all heckling work. Also, I
shun exactious luxuries, lest I become their slave."

He was at that time prosperous, if not precisely holding,—his relation
to liquid assets, at best, is that of a conduit, not a cistern. He was making
and therefore spending a couple of hundred dollars a week,[1] all in
commissions on ads in the *Enquirer*, and when I called on him insisted on
taking me to dinner at Dinty Moore's, a place where an order of celery
costs as much as the blue-plate luncheon at the Dixie. Within Moore's
mirrored walls I tried to get him to resume the train of his autobiography
where he had abandoned it in favor of the great George Graham Rice's.

"Was it on the *Journal* that you began to use the Colonel Stingo by-
line?" I asked him.

"No," he said. "It was not until I came back to San Francisco after my
betrayal by Tommy Burns, who wouldn't fight Ketchel for me, that I
adopted the sobriquet. Colonel Stingo was a character in Bret Harte's
Luck of Roaring Camp. He was a wise old fellow, held in universal
reverence, who would settle all disputes among the desperadoes. And he
would conclude all sessions with the solemn words, 'Yea, Verily.'[2] I was
conducting a legitimate advertising agency under my own name, and I
used Colonel John R. Stingo as a nom de plume in a little weekly newspaper I owned called the *Referee*."

"And what does the middle initial *R* stand for?"

The Colonel reflected.

"Randolph," he decided. "A great southern surname.

"San Francisco, in the years immediately subsequent to the Fire," he
said, "was a magnificent city. Everybody had money and nobody went

[1] The Colonel told me at our first meeting that he had purchased an annuity to
mature when he was ninety. When, during the plug-in-the-door flap of 1951, I asked
the Colonel what had happened to the annuity, he said, "It has been hypothecated
to the ultimate degree,—extinction."
[2] I have never been able to find this Colonel Stingo in Bret Harte. But when my
Colonel Stingo told me about him I hadn't tried. There is an old guy in *Luck* called
Colonel *Starbottle*. But I don't think the Colonel meant him, either. It seems to be a
case of the Colonel's creating a character that Harte had forgotten to [create].

to bed. The insurance companies had paid off so many claims in cash that the town was a maelstrom of liquid capital. It was wonderful and remained so until the reform element got in its deadly work.

"It was a life gracious and delightful," he said, "and not at all sordid. I remember the weekly embarkation of Tessie Wall and her bejeweled girls for the races at Emeryville, across the Bay. It was like a painting by Watteau, or a story by De Mossopont. Tessie had been for years the reigning madame of the city, the arbitrix elegantrium or, as the troubadours would say, the queen of love. She wore so many diamonds she was attractive, in spite of her grenadierian mustachio and not inconsiderable seniority. But the girls were pips.

"Emeryville was across the Bay, and to get there you took the ferry to a jetty called the Mole. There you boarded streetcars to ride out to the track. Drinks were served on the ferry, going and coming, and if you didn't have a place at the long table with Tessie and her girls it meant you were an outsider, a rustic. Nobody ever ventured to order anything but champagne, which in the parlance of those days was just called 'wine.' For other sorts you said claret, hock, or any other specification.

"After the return from the track the girls and their favored escorts embarked in Stanley Steamers, Wintons and the like and proceeded to Tessie's, a noble mansion with an anteroom like the rotunda of the American Museum of Natural History at Seventy-seventh Street and Central Park West. In this anteroom the gallants would remain while the girls changed to their work clothes."

This is something that often happens with the Colonel. He contemns precise chronological sequence. You try to hold him to New York in 1904 and he ducks under your arm and turns up in San Francisco in 1910 or '11 or '13. In his handling of years he holds to an axiom of his managerial days: "It is ever the part of sagacity, in making a match, to give or take two pounds."

"I bought the *Referee* for thirteen hundred dollars," he said, "and put it over big, selling it at all the fight clubs, with enclosed in each copy a printed slip listing the boxers and their weights. San Francisco was the pugilistic capital of the nation then, the sport being obstructed by hampering laws in New York. The sporting pages of New York papers were filled with stories of California pugilistic activity, and the state contributed a disproportionate share of the fistic talent. Corbett, Jeffries, Tom Sharkey, Choynski had come out of there, and among the lighter men there were stars like Abe Attell and Willie Ritchie. Not only the boxers but the best fight writers came from the Bay region,—Bob Edgren, Tad, and Hype Igoe, all great names already in New York. The patronage of the fights largely corresponded with that of the select resorts which advertised in the *Referee*. But when the reformers, urged on by Fremont Older, an editor skillfully avid of circulation, succeeded in jailing the mayor, a man named Schmidt, who led the orchestra at the Tivoli Opera House, and also Abe Ruef, the political boss of the town, I had a premonition of woe. I sold the *Referee* for fifteen hundred dollars, glad to find a sucker in the person of a journalist recently arrived from the East.

"But I had been prematurely discouraged. Abe and the mayor continued to run the city from San Quentin. Life went on as merrily as before, the henchmen being but put to the trouble of going out to the can daily to receive their instructions, a trajectory they accomplished in an Overland automobile driven by a young friend of mine who is now a mighty advertising executive here in New York.

"So I bought for twenty-six hundred dollars another paper, denominated the *Wasp*. It followed much the same pattern. I have always found there is nothing like having a medium of personal articulation. The *Wasp* had a yellow front page, in allusion to the yellow jacket, and when we mentioned anyone we would send him or her a penny post card with the message: 'You are stung on page 8, column 3,'—or whatever it was,—'the *Wasp*.' I took care to mention about a thousand people an issue, and for a small paper it developed a mighty circulation,—fifteen thousand."

" 'Colonel John R. Stingo' was a great by-line for the *Wasp*," I ventured, but the Colonel stuck to the Bret Harte etymology.

"Disasters never run singly, but always as an entry," he said, an aphorism I was to hear many times from his lips. "The monarch of the California turf was a man named Tom Williams. He controlled the racing at Ingleside, Tanforan and Emeryville. There was no good racing in Southern California then. Tom put up fifty thousand dollars bail for Mayor Schmidt, merely as evidence of his sympathy for a musician. The incensed reformers took out after Tom too, and the result was the Walker-Otis Law, repeating in California the Hughes crime in New York. It spelled the death of the sport of kings in California, not to be revived for twenty years. It flourishes there now, but, as always happens, the vulgar parimutuels, while contributing mightily to dollar prosperity, have at the same time wrought a depletion of the sporting festival's charm of artistry and selective quality.

"Next they assailed the boxing ring, limiting bouts to four rounds and rendering it the most innocuous fight town in America. San Francisco hasn't sent out a good fighter since. And as the international Panama-Pacific exposition approached, the black-visaged band of ascetics assailed the robust pleasures of the Barbary Coast, the dance halls like the Thalia, the Hippodrome, the London Music Hall and the Midway, all good advertising accounts of mine. The Hearst paper, the *Examiner*, imitative of Older, supported the inroad. Coblentz, the editor, hired Pinkertons to take the names of respectable citizens entering the purlieus. Then he published them. Sex became a hole-in-corner affair, politics without savor. I sold the *Wasp* for a paltry sum and devoted full time to the boresome pursuit of legitimate profit."

The Colonel polished off an order of large oysters, drank a bottle of ale and continued.

"I dislike humdrum occupation; it lacks solidity," he said.

"Avoid merchandise, it's ethereal, whether it be coffee, sugar or butter. The only solid value is a concept. There was a woman named Cassie Chadwick, for example, who convinced a couple of hick bankers from Ohio that she was an illegitimate daughter of Andrew Carnegie and had a bank vault full of securities. She took them up to Carnegie's house in Pittsburgh in an open barouche and got out and went in right in the door. She spent half an hour inside on some premeditated pretext, and when she came out the butler carried a package to the carriage for her. Maybe she had slipped him a sawbuck. They loaned her two million dollars on the securities she said she had. If she had had a tangible house and asked them for a mortgage they would have demanded eight per cent and her right eye.

"In the early fall of a year that I recall as 1914, because it coincided with the beginning of the war in Europe, I was in the wonderful bar of the Palace Hotel in quiet contemplation while gazing rapturously upon Maxfield Parrish's vibrating canvas,—'The Pied Piper of Hamelin.' It was a spot to which I repaired when in need of spiritual replenishment. I was still in quest of a concept.

"Suddenly, the shadow of a quietly approaching man in a long black coat, homburg hat and carrying a heavy stick, falls upon me, reflection in the back-bar mirrors affording me a moment in which to effect recognition and identity of the sidling figure before he could make introduction himself. Yes, sure enough, it would be none other than Harry Brolaski, true soldier of fortune, whom I had not seen for many the year.

"This Harry Brolaski," he said cheerfully, "was a freebooting Barbary corsair of horrendous background, but a good fellow withal, although not to be lightly trusted unless you were armed to the teeth. He was bereft of the full use of his left leg, and I shall cite the manner in which he suffered this mishap as an illuminating commentary on this Long Rider. In his very early days he worked week ends for his father, owner and personal operator of a piratical craft on the Mississippi River, plying between Natchez and New Orleans. The ship never was known to have freighted more than two bales of cotton on any one voyage. The craft's chief item of revenue arose from that grand old institution of postbellum days, faro bank and stud poker.

"The Brolaskis were insatiable,—they began ascending the river as far as St. Louis. There was engendered a matter of disputation there, for a St. Louis mob suspected the character of the seemingly innocent craft. They learned of the gaff roulette game below decks, to which landlubbers were admitted while the vessel lay at dockside. It was a muscle-in job. No moving the Brolaskis, father and son, to a sense of reason. 'This is our racket, and we're a-going to keep it that way. No one is going to cut in here except over our recumbent cadavers.'

"So, one moonlit night, as the *Sea King* drew hawser and moved into the stream from the Temple Street docks, St. Louis, with the games going big guns, wheels turning and cards falling, a hefty pineapple exploded aft in the captain's cabin when the stud-poker game roared along.

"It is interesting and pertinent to note that on the casuality list, his leg fractured in three places, was young Brolaski. Tenaciously, he refused surgical suggestion of immediate amputation, but he limped for the rest of his mortal span.

"In a later period of his life he bank-rolled the Palmetto Club, a book-making plant in the Fair Grounds race track, New Orleans, and at Montgomery Park, Memphis, Tennessee. He was singularly prosperous at both spots, but one day he was discovered to be laying heavy odds against horses with whose jockeys he had prearranged their stoppage, while betting considerably on others for whose jockeys he had made friendly wagers. This led to his requested departure, but he little wreaked. We find him a year later as the builder, owner and operator of the sumptuous Arkansas Jockey Club, Little Rock, Arkansas, where he was both judge and jury at all times.

"He was a rare good fellow, and as expatriates from the southland we were mighty glad to see each other. His plethoric pocketbook did not increase the size of his head, and he was always full of schemes.

"After the customary salutation and the setup of new drinks by the impeccably white-appareled man behind the stick, the fat is in the fire with Mr. Brolaski dilating, with great and convincing fervor, upon the opportunity which now presented itself, whereby we two could now make a whole ton of money, without hurting anybody, says he, particularly ourselves. So we talked and talked, with many a relation of an experience shared interlarded in the intercourse to leaven the sales approach my old friend is waging unremittingly at thirty-four strokes to the minute.

"After the third Ramos gin fizz, a drink chosen as appropriate to a southland reunion, Mr. Brolaski divulged to me that he was the inceptor of a potential mint called the Great American Hog Syndicate. The beginning of the war, he pointed out, had jumped pork prices sky-high, Europe had to buy here to feed its armies, and if we went in, which he thought, with perspicuity, likely, we would have to feed an army of millions as well as civilian war workers, with plenty Tease to exchange for nourishment. 'Pork is the big chance, the main chance right now,' he said, and adduced in evidence the evening newspaper which showed that prime bacon was bringing seventy-six cents a pound as compared with twenty-four the year before. Please remember that I quote these prices from memory, so do not vouch for their exactitude, but that was the general idea.

"I said that might be all right for people without any imagination, like the Swifts and Armours, but how did it concern us? Harry looked at me reproachfully, and I am lucky that he did not konk me with the cane, which concealed within its ebon sheath a keen Toledo blade.

"His idea was fraught with that divine simplicity that denotes genius," the Colonel said, after an interim marked by the partial demolition of a portion of chicken in the pot with broth and noodles.

"At the fourth round we deem it better to sit down at a table in order better to comprehend the inviting opportunity offered by the incubating enterprise to make money in large gobs without too much exertion and no risk whatsoever.

"But before beginning operations, Mr. Brolaski divulges, he needs a farm of at least six hundred acres within an hour's motor ride of San Francisco. He must have two offices in a prestigious building and we must have ten grand for newspaper advertising. If I can supply these requisites, he says, I'm in for fifty-fifty. Generosity was never the quality for which this old Brolaski was most noted."

The Colonel tore elegantly at a drumstick and then said:

"Peculiarly enough I was in a position to comply with these demands."

"How?" I asked naturally enough.

"A Long Rider's most precious resource is a well-catalogued mental file of acquaintances," the Colonel replied. "A good friend should not be lightly used, but put away in a drawer like a good pair of pajamas, for use on a special occasion. But I shall not denoue the identity at this moment. De Mossopont once wrote that more than half the value of a story was dependent upon the maintenance of suspense, and I concur.

"It is enough at this point to say that within two days we had a suite of three offices on the ninth floor of the Crocker Building,—conveniently across the street from the Palace with its mighty bar,—and on the cuff. In a week more we're installed, with 'Great American Hog Syndicate' lettered with chaste flamboyancy across all the doors and front windows, and a staff of six handy people hired on. Behind us we have a one-year lease on a farm of twelve hundred acres at Millbrae, California, just twice the size stipulated by the wily gambling man. I also have a bank roll not of ten grand but of twenty-five hundred dollars, promoted from the same beneficent source and origin.

"We decide to invest twelve hundred of it in newspaper advertising the following Sunday."

By now the Colonel had me, and I crudely asked, "What was the scheme?"

"The first effort in preparing a sale," the Colonel said, "should be to stimulate curiosity. But I shall be clement." He ordered two coffees and, by excepiton to his rule of the Great Transition, a couple of brandies, and then said:

"I threw together the advertising display copy and it had a pull like a horny-handed backwoods dentist. I knew just how to talk to my public, having been successfully advertising 'sun-drenched apartments' for years in San Francisco, city of mists, where the sun never shines. It is what people haven't got enough of that they want to read about in advertisements. The sunshine is an example. One thing they never have in sufficient quantity anywhere is easy money. The Monday after the Sunday on which our copy ran in both *Examiner* and *Chronicle*, the corridor in front of our office was packed-jammed with boobs holding money in their hands. They couldn't wait lest they be short-circuited, excluded from this heaven-sent opportunity.

"It was a unique proposition, entirely fair and on the face of it sure to pan out good."

"All right," I said. "Put me down for one hundred shares and tell me what the scheme was."

The Colonel held up a reproving palm.

"No shares," he said. "Units. There was an important legal difference. The screaming advertisements, in effective position next to vitalized reading matter, bore the modest suggestion that Pork is King, and His Majesty has it in mind to make the reader rich and happy through a moderate investment in what might turn out to be a modern Golconda;—turning the poor into the rich, the depressed into the elated and all is to be as merry as a wedding bell.

"In my early copy-writing esquisays," Colonel Stingo said, after knocking back his brandy, "I modeled my style upon that of a man named Dr. James W. Kidd, a savant of Fort Wayne, Indiana, but a national advertiser.

"'After years of patient study and delving into the dusty records of the past, as well as following modern experiments in the realm of medical science, Dr. James W. Kidd, Fort Wayne, Indiana, makes the startling announcement that he has surely discovered the elixir of life. State what you want to be cured of, and the sure remedy for it will be sent you free by return mail.'"

"Listen," I said, but was put off by the reproving palm again.

"Be no longer impatient," said the Colonel. "Here it is. The proposition, so adroitly, and with utmost native caution, worked out by the illustrious Mr. Brolaski, invited the reader to undertake an investment of two hundred dollars in the purchase of a unit partnership in the Great American Hog Syndicate. This, it elaborated, was a movement in furtherance of the laudable purpose of supporting the food creation campaign so necessary to our national survival in a time of crisis. Once a unit partner, the subscriber became a half owner of a high-blooded sow which the incorporated Syndicate agrees to maintain in reginal splendor at its farm in the Santa Clara Valley.

"It is important to note that the subscriber would not acquire a share in the Syndicate itself,—just in the hog.

"In addition to this commitment the subscribing unit partner would be entitled to the ownership of one half the litter of the aforesaid sow during her fecund lifetime,—generally two years. On its part the Syndicate pledged itself to acquire and maintain in stud ten of the best boars from the sales and catalogue of the National Hog Breeders Association, Kansas City, Missouri. They were to be of the finest bloodlines extant, viz.,— Berkshire, Cochin China, and Hertfordshire, with a dash of St. Simon and an outcross to the line of Commando.

"Our pulsating Syndicate did business with Long Brothers & Pidgeon, Kansas City, Missouri, in buying these ten porcine monarchs.

"On the first day of business we took in just thirty-two subscriptions to unit partnership, sixty-four hundred dollars, encouraging. But on the next day we took but one, and that by dint of concerted persuasion reinforced by a gratuitous libation at the Palace bar when the boob seemed on the point of withdrawal. It was obvious that the Hog Syndicate was the sort of promotion that must have continuously plenty of newspaper space. In such circumstances it was the wont of the great Ricecakes to use the incoming money with which to buy more display pages, a dangerous practice if carried to extremes, like continual reliance upon strong stimulants. Because of my longer and more congenial association with the newspaper racket, I improved upon this device.

"Within a week of our establishment, the Oakland, California, *Daily Post-Enquirer* thought the enterprise so unique and praiseworthy that it deserved news treatment, resulting in a two-column spread with a double-decker head and drop sublines enlivened by a startling picture of Red Alexis II, the Gold Cup winner at the New York State Fair in Syracuse in the Berkshire class. He was the Best Hog in Show, too, and had earned during the year in prize money thirty-two hundred dollars including a small purse in a trotting race and fifty dollars for fighting a pit bull terrier.

"WILL THE GREAT RED ALEXIS II COME TO CALIFORNIA?"

the headline demanded. The story, written by an enthusiastic dairy farmer named John R. Stingo, went on to say that our Great American Hog Syndicate had made an offer of six thousand dollars for Red Alexis II but without avail.

"It was the highest price ever quoted on a blue-blooded prize-winning boar in this country, and, of course, other newspapers followed with stories and layouts on the matter, all most beneficial in stimulating the sales campaign of the Great American Hog Syndicate. The newspaper stories were embellished by accounts of the reporters' visits to our on-the-level indubitably tangible farm, where Mr. Brolaski had installed a never-failing supply of bourbon whiskey under the governance of an agriculturist known on eastern race tracks as the Millionaire Kid. The Kid was glib with the figures on hog prolification. He had dutched many a book in his time, taking thirteen to five in thousands and laying it back at eleven to five, thus insuring against loss while retaining the chance of a handsome profit. He was therefore well qualified to bedazzle even the mathematically expert, especially after plying them with nectar, and the stories reflected the roseate impression the Millionaire Kid managed to slip the pressmen.

"We reinforced this free publicity, which is the best kind, with a regular salvo of paid space on Sundays, and we mowed them down. Mr. Brolaski, betraying an unbecoming lack of confidence in me, moved to bring the Millionaire Kid into the office as money taker. He himself was not qualified to occupy the spotlight, since he had a record as long as Bob Fitzsimmons' arm, and public confidence might waver if he were identified on the premises of our public-spirited venture.

"After six weeks of drum-thumping we finally offered Long Brothers & Pidgeon the spot-cash sum of eight thousand dollars,—our final bid,—for prodigious Alexis. He weighed 464 pounds, or perhaps 1,464,—memory grows furtive, and I don't think I've seen a live pig since my one porcicultural experience. He was quite young, coming up to his two-year-old season with engagements in all stakes, as I remember. In his first time at bat he had fathered seven litters of eighty-four little pigs, which is perfect, like a score of three hundred at bowling, for the mother pig is equipped with but twelve outlets for nutritional contact with the young, and a thirteenth piglet would starve to death. The residuum of information from my avatars is variegated. All this statistical data caused Mr. Brolaski to smack his thin cruel lips in contemplation of what the leviathanic Alexis would do when given a chance at the beauty chorus of piquant young sows we were assembling.

"To our surprise and delight an acceptance came through from Kansas City by wire."

20 / Enter, the Duchess

MY CURIOSITY now at fever heat, I demanded of the Colonel, "But who was your backer? Abe Ruef?"

He smiled cryptically, and then, with quasi-parental indulgence, said, "Since the purpose of my narration is not to beguile but instruct, I shall sacrifice at this point the veiling concealment which is the pointer-upper of the storyteller's art. With a bow to De Mossopont, whose precept I am violating, I will allow you in."

He ordered a replenishment of the aquavital supply, and said:

"It was a beautiful woman. She was a Nouvelle-Orléanaise, a true Creole, of an admixture of Spanish, Irish and Italian blood, known to me in my cub days on the *Item* as a glorious ornament of my native city.

"In her late twenties then, she was tall, dark and winsome. Willowy as a reed in the Babylonian Gardens, she was sophisticated and daring. Her true name, Frances Miro Valin, her father had amassed a fine competency in cotton and passed on as chairman of the board of a mighty steamship company. Miss Valin, our the Duchess, among her members of family and circle of friends was addressed with appreciation and affection as Frankie but in no time became known upon two continents as the Duchess. She had lost no time in precipitating a career, for she had married into the proud and brave blood of the celebrated Torlonia family of Rome and Naples, one of the foremost industrial components in the economic fibre of Italy. In the fourth year of her married life, coming to New Orleans with her noble Italian husband and her young son for a brief visit, she lost her husband, who succumbed to yellow fever. She had then migrated to California. There she had been again married, again widowed, and when our paths crossed once more there she was in her mid-forties but still enchanting,—a solitary, haunting figure."

The Colonel took a pensive slug, sighed, and continued.

"Her second husband had been one of the California Midasei, a man of coruscant wealth," he said. "Name of William Sutro Tevis, heir to a monumental concentration of Tease. At their residence of true ducal aspect, Hillsborough House, Santa Clara Valley, the Duchess held lonely court.

"We had many old touches to cut up together and we got to be great pals. The world of the Long Riders enchanted her, although she had no incentive to participate, being incurably holding. She just wanted the fun and distraction that a rich lonely woman sometimes craves. A wealthy woman, she was a power in her own right, and one of the most remarkable characters who ever lived." Colonel Stingo sighed again, and ground the end of his lighted cigarette into the ash tray, as if extinguishing the embers of an ambition he had never dared acknowledge at the moment of possibly fruitful temerity. Later I learned that during his San Francisco days he led a commendably uxorious married life.

"One characteristic thing about her, I recall," he said, "she appeared always to be lonely, searching for somebody she never seemed to find.

"When Mr. Brolaski popped his proposition, I thought of the Duchess instantly. So down to Santa Clara station I scamper next morning after duly informing the Duchess of my coming. She laughed and laughed and willingly proffered the necessary help, on condition she be allowed participation in the inner councils of the enterprise, for she liked to be on the inside of everything. All financial assistance, however, was to be in the shape of loans. Her position did not allow direct involvement in the enterprise. It was she who arranged for the farm, the offices and the initial wad. Her native caution, as intense in its way as Mr. Brolaski's, had caused her to limit the amount to twenty-five hundred dollars, lest Harry lam with the scratch.

"The journalistic furor about Red Alexis, however, and the resulting gusher of boobish Tease, hinting at the vast reservoirs still untapped, indicated to her that we had good cards to draw to, and she willingly shoved over another stack of chips. She advanced another ten thousand for purchase of Red Alexis II, but insisted we give a note to the small local bank for that amount, bearing six per cent interest. When Brolaski heard that he bellowed like a harpooned behemoth. He said he had thought of the Duchess as a sister, and now she was demanding his signature on a legal document.

"But these preliminary bellowings were nothing compared to those the great man emitted when it dawned upon him in due course that he had failed to pin upon Long Brothers & Pidgeon the onus of safe delivery and competent attendance for Red Alexis during his long trip from the Mississippi Valley. Finally, a Dr. Shepherd, a California veterinarian of repute, was engaged at a five-hundred-dollar fee and expenses to escort Big Alex to his new home at Millbrae.

"Meanwhile I had indulged in a staccato of cogitation, and come up with an idea worthy of a P. T. Barnum, of Cecil de Mille. A civic and state reception for the monster swine came to mind as a natural. The concept impressed both the Duchess and Mr. Brolaski. We agreed that there should be a representative committee of reception, and the Duchess's feminine flair for the aesthetic really developed an angle in conjunction therewith; it was that the members of the committee should all wear long red-and-gold badges and bright shiny opera hats.

"At this juncture, although protected in every case by the statute of limitations, I shall not explain the why and wherefore, but the Great American Hog Syndicate, Inc., did enjoy, even in moments that might otherwise have proved distressing,—a kind, friendly and generous press. This is a most essential circumstance in all undertakings in which the Long Riders engage.

"After five days' travel in a palace horse car, all to himself, Dr. Shepherd and an attendant, the royal Red Alexis II came home to California in all the regal glory of an ancient Caesar returning from the Carthaginian wars a mighty conqueror to receive his people's homage in spontaneous outburst of love, admiration and affection.

"This Big Alex had to be bathed twice a day, a fresh bed of imported Argentine grass laid down nightly and to satisfy his temperament not be left alone.

"The day of days had come to hand. At the snug little station of the Southern Pacific Railroad at Santa Clara, near San Jose, there had gathered the reception committee, headed by the sixty-piece band of the University of Leland Stanford, Jr., and Senator James D. Phelan, Lieutenant Governor Frank J. Moffat, representing our dear friend, Governor 'Jim' Rolph, solid citizens, crums, bums and sharpshooters in large number, buttressed by all the cameramen that Mr. Hearst's ponderous San Francisco *Examiner* could level on the momentous event, plus an army of reporters and special writers. In fact, Annie Laurie, the famous sob sister, long identified with the Hearstian press, was there as the guest of the Duchess, together with other of her friends, including Mrs. William H. Crocker, Mrs. Charles Stuart Howard, Ethel Barrymore, Helen Wills, little Poker Face, and Kathleen Winsor, youthfully innocent then, with no indication at hand of the guileful sophistication of *Forever Amber* to come some years later.

"A passer-by enquired audibly,—'What's the occasion? Who is coming home today?'

"Someone answered,—'Mr. Herbert Hoover.'

"Apparently satisfied, the interrogator went on his unlearned and elfin way, gratified at the gladsome scene.

"Mr. Washington Dodge, Jr., the cashier at the bank where we negotiated the ten thousand dollars through the gracious help of the Duchess, acted as chairman of the reception committee and made a nice speech but spoke more about Mr. Rolph's bright chances for re-election as Governor than an espousal and character study of Red Alexis II.

"Of course Mr. Brolaski, approaching the speaker's stand, where he would be in full view of friend or enemy, came forward mincingly, for who knew, there might lurk there an ancient foe from Arkansas who perchance might accord him leaden recognition, which would not be viewed as a buoyant circumstance in the upward climb of the Great American Hog Syndicate, Inc.

"Luckily there ensued no fusillade, indicating he had not been recognized, nor were any visiting prison wardens or sheriffs among the invited guests to call attention to his heroic past, so the occasion was unmarred.

" 'I am just a simple hog farmer,' Harry told the assembled multitude, 'unaccustomed to address such distinguished gatherings. But I am here to tell you that the Great American Hog Syndicate is going to bring home the bacon.' It is impossible to be too corny on such occasions, and the rustic Santa Clarans applauded as if for David Warfield. Senator Phelan said to me, sitting beside him on the platform, 'Who is that man? He would have a great future in politics.' "

At this point I made a tactical mistake which I have since learned not to duplicate when I wish the Colonel to maintain the tenor of a narration.

"I saw Helen Wills play at Forest Hills in 1922 when she was still in pigtails," I said. "She was supposed to be fourteen years old and looked it. That would make her six at the time of the reception. And Kathleen Winsor must be even younger."

"I can see," the Colonel answered, "that you are essentially interested in the unessential, a spoilsport. You will remind me next that Caesar did not partake in the Carthaginian wars. If you know better than I do who was at the reception, why don't you tell me about it? I have made my submission. I await your rebuttal."

The Colonel, as I was to learn from reading his column as well as listening to him, shares with the painters of the *quattrocento* and *cinque-*

cento the practice of placing favorite contemporaries in his historical canvases. It amuses him.

It does not detract from the verity of a martyrdom by Mantegna or his great contemporary, Calamaretti di Posilipo, that the face of the officiating centurion is that of the artist's greengrocer, whom he liked, while the holy man getting the works displays the distorted but recognizable countenance of the landlord who had him dispossessed for throwing empty wine jugs out of the window at the watch.

Nor, to cite an example from "Yea Verily," does it take away from the Colonel's word picture of the great race between Man o' War and John P. Grier that in his enumeration of those watching the finish that day in 1920 he placed me between Samuel D. Riddle, Man o' War's owner, and Kentucky Babe, a light lady from Louisville who had been associated with the Australian prize fighter, Young Griffo, in 1895. I didn't even see the race. What made the piece great reporting, though, was the Colonel's description of the sleek millionaire, a ringer for Samuel Seabury in white-haired, rubicund dignity, seeing John P. Grier gain for a few strides on his immortal champion. "The hair on the back of Mr. Riddle's neck stood straight up," the Colonel wrote, "like the bristles on the back of an enraged Deer Creek porcupine."

This is a labyrinthian digression.

On this particular evening at Moore's, though, I was sobered, or nearly sobered, by the impasse into which my brashness had got me. In calling attention to what I had misinterpreted as unwitting anachronism, I had jeopardized my chance of ever finding out what happened to the Great American Hog Syndicate.

"Please by-pass the interjection," I said. "I have a compulsive habit of blabbing out the irrelevant."

The Colonel was mollified but still hurt, like a boxer whose opponent offers to shake hands at the end of the round after sticking a thumb in his eye. He said, "Let's get out of this dump. It's getting on my nerves."

When we emerged and headed for an institution known as the Formerly Club, the Colonel looked about him appreciatively at the double alignment of marquees, stage doors, saloons and restaurants that forms Moore's block on Forty-sixth Street. "What a mighty and wonderful city," he said. "I'd die on the vine anyplace else."

As we took our way down Eighth Avenue to the Formerly, he continued in the same strain. "Some Friday nights I sit up in my room at the Dixie," he said. "Working away on my column. I finish, and it is perhaps one o'clock. If I were sagacious, I would put on my hat and go to bed. I always keep an old felt hat by my bedside," he said, "because I like to sleep with my windows wide open, and bedclothes make no provision for the protection of the thinly veiled cranium. The brain, like Rhenish wine, should be chilled, not iced, to be at its best. Women, however, are best at room temperature.

"Up there in my retreat I feel the city calling to me," he said. "It winks at me with its myriad eyes, and I go out and get stiff as a board. I seek out companionship, and if I do not find friends I make them. A wonderful grand old Babylon."

The story of the Great American Hog Syndicate apparently was finished for that night, but scarcely had we arrived at the bar and ordered drinks,—the Colonel reverting to his Gambrinian conservatism,—when there occurred a manifestation corroborating one area of my friend's reminiscences.

For as long as I could remember,—and I had been almost a founding member of the Formerly,—one of the peripheral personages there had been an old ex-bookmaker named Benny. Suffering from some wasting malady that closed in on him slowly from year to year, he became with each lustre more spectral, his nose longer in proportion to the rest of his face, the veins on his wrists more prominent. The doctors had got all his money. It is the only way they can beat the books, being notoriously incompetent horse players. Benny would earn an occasional skin by placing a bet for one of the patrons of the Formerly. If the bettor won he might slip Benny a buck, and if he lost Benny might get a commission from the bookmaker. It wasn't much of a living, since the Formerly is chiefly patronized by newspapermen, who are two-dollar bettors. But Benny might have had a couple of other places of call.

The Colonel and I had just bellied up to the bar, like Mr. Mori and his friends in "Yea Verily," when Benny entered, returning from some mysterious mission of small import. Waves of recognition passed between the two old men and they grabbed each other by the shoulders, as if they had been dressed in funny clothes and attending their fortieth reunion at Old Nassau.

"I haven't seen you since 1906, when we were both running for that train out of New Orleans," Benny said.

"I made it," said the Colonel.

"You were always an all-around athlete," Benny said admiringly. "I missed it, but I got out on a banana boat."

"This fellow used to win bets on how fast he could run around the block," he told me. "He'd race you around the block for a round of drinks."

The Colonel smiled at this evocation of his agility.

"The circumstances suggested the advisability of a hurried departure," he said. "We had touted Dynamite Jack Thornby onto a horse that had failed to justify our confidence. It had been well meant, but dear old Dynamite was irascible, and we thought it best to let him cool out."

Benny had been rapidly taking stock of the Colonel's appearance, which was debonair, and the Colonel had been casing Benny, too. It was obvious their fortunes were at this point disparate, but the Colonel fortunately remembered something to his old friend's advantage.

"I had completely forgotten that sawbuck you let me have on getaway day at Bennings the previous spring," he said. "Here it is and God bless you," and he shoved a crumpled bill into Benny's hand.

"I never thought twice about it," Benny said.

I am pretty sure he had never thought once.

This was the incident that first made me suspect the sincerity of the Colonel's representations.

It reminded me of the time I took a distinguished Armenian-American author of my acquaintance to call on an astute Armenian-British friend in London. The author opened, in English, with several of those naïve, sunny sentences that light his prose with a happy, childlike glow. My friend parried with banal observations indicative of a dull, heavy mind. Suddenly they broke into Armenian and for about twenty minutes fired volley for volley in the tongue of Tigranes the Great. Disengaging, they returned to discoursing English amenities open to the rest of the company, and when the author left the room for a moment, I asked my friend what he thought of him.

"He is what we call a false fool," the host answered. "He is really very intelligent."

Walking back across the green park in the blackout, I asked the author what he thought of my friend.

"He's a nice guy," the author said, "but who does he think he's kidding? He's not dumb."

I had an intimation that the Colonel might be a false Long Rider.

The intimation was confirmed years later when I met a man who had known the Colonel in his San Francisco days. "Jimmy Macdonald has been playing cops and robbers all his life," the man said. "He likes to think of himself as a Robin Hood, but he is really a Santa Claus.

"I hit San Francisco in 1911, as a young man of twenty-one, and went into the outdoor advertising business with a chum my own age. We had to buck what amounted to a national monopoly, the two big firms that controlled billboard space all over the United States. Any national advertiser who rented our boards would find himself denied billboard space in all the territories where we didn't operate. So we got only local accounts, and we were paid in whatever the advertiser peddled,—whiskey, automobile tires, hotel rooms or ready-made clothing. Then we in turn had to sell our takings. Jimmy was a man about town then, noted for his patent-leather shoes and his New York air, and he used to go out of his way to introduce us to saloonkeepers who would buy our whiskey. He even gave us a job selling advertising on the *Wasp*, so that we could pick up a bit of cash on the side.

"I'll never forget one day when the three of us, none well heeled, despite Jimmy's imposing exterior, were walking over from our office in the Crocker Building to the Palace Hotel bar for a drink, and the most awful human wreck I've ever seen came along, without even enough energy to panhandle. Mac walked up to him politely, handed him a ten-dollar bill and said, 'Pardon me, I think you dropped this.' Then we went into the bar and rolled dice with the bartender for the drinks. Luckily we won."

When I repeated this to the Colonel, he sulked and hinted he had once helped Al Jennings rob a train.

21 / Da Sissantina

I MET WITH the Colonel several times more before I could get him to resume the story of the Great American Hog Syndicate, about which I had by now developed a curiosity of my own. I could not see what there was about the scheme which would redound to the disadvantage of the customers, and I would have suspected the Colonel of conducting a legitimate enterprise, if I had not known that in that case he would never have mentioned it.

On occasions I expressed my misgivings to him, but he maintained a mien inscrutable, having returned, he said, to the axiom of De Mossopont that the element of surprise must be reserved for the last round in order to make a showing and catch the eyes of the referee and judges just before they render a decision. "The referee and judges in the case of a narration, either spoken or written, being the auditors or readers, as the case may be," the Colonel said, "and especially those readers who come under the classification of potential investors.

"I will concede," he said, "that the enterprise had a reassuring aspect of benevolence, since it was based on a well-known phenomenon,—the tendency of animals to proliferate, which was traditionally exploited by the patriarchs of Biblical days,—sheepherders all of them. This has imbued animal husbandry with such a respectable air that people who would shy off from gilt-edged copper stock will sink their all in a chicken farm, a vastly more speculative form of investment. The American Hog Syndicate had this quirk running for it.

"I myself, in an anterior period of my life, had devoted time, if not money, to the promotion of an enterprise known as the Mid-Continental Chinchilla Rabbitry, under the aegis of a figurator named Kelly Mason, who had become entranced by the multipular possibilities of those rodents. In Kelly's mind it presented the aspect of a progressive bet, or endless winning parlay. He had read in some newspaper, doubtless discarded by somebody else on the seat adjoining Kelly's in a race train, for he himself never purchased anything but the racing form, that the air and track conditions in Kansas were so favorable to rabbits that the state was spending thousands of dollars in the form of bounties for their extirpation. 'That,' he said to himself, 'is of a surety the place to breed rabbits.' He had seen two of these animals in a pet-shop window, marked at fifty cents apiece. Further inquiry instructed him that rabbit pelts were used in the manufacture of hatter's felts and a fur called royal seal,—there was a market for them as illimitable as for four to one against Roseben.

"He leased a farm of twenty-two acres near Wichita, Kansas, after asking the yokel who leased it to him specifically whether it was good rabbit ground. He installed hatches, a kind of coop covered with earth to make the rabbits feel at home. They are so denominated, I suppose, because the rabbits hatch their young therein. The rabbits needed little encouragement; they spawned monstrously. Kelly made contracts with furriers in Kansas City, Missouri, and with hatmakers in Danbury, Connecticut, to take all his output, but as the production increased, like a mighty gusher of oil it proves impossible to cap, he had to sell farther afield, his operations reaching the Brunswick-Balke-Collender Company, manufacturers of billiard tables, which are of course felt-covered, and also Luchow's Restaurant, the Blue Ribbon, Hans Jaeger's and the Hofbrau, New York; the Golden Ox, Chicago; and the Techau Tavern, San Francisco, all manufacturers of *hasenpfeffer*.

"Things began to look so good that Kelly sent for me to undertake a campaign of national promotion, but on the very day of my arrival we were visited by a representative of a newspaper who demanded Kelly buy a full-page ad, reading simply, 'Compliments of a Friend.' I remonstrated that this did not seem to me the type of pulling copy we needed. It said nothing about our wares. 'It better not,' the small-town newspaperman said, 'since there is a state law that makes it a misdemeanor to raise rabbits in the state of Kansas, imposing a fine of five dollars, or three days in jail for each rabbit so produced. You probably owe about sixty thousand dollars now, if anyone wanted to get tough about it.' We took the ad, and business went on as usual for a couple of weeks when another dumb rural newsman appeared from the sheet published in the seat of the adjoining county. He said they were getting out their annual centennial edition. Every year is the centennial of something, he said. He wanted two pages of complimentary advertising. So we gave him that.

"After awhile the sheriff came over for a contribution to his campaign fund, and then the fellow who was running against him, and a committee of ladies from a Congregational Church, who said it was so nice having us in the area, they knew we would be glad to donate five hundred dollars to build new pews. Then eventuated delegations from the Campbellites, and the River Brethren and the Methodists and the Greek Orthodox. They were all on the shake. Even the WCTU got us for a grand." The Colonel looked glum. "Even a stick-up man will let you keep coffee-money," he said, "but not a woman engaged in God's work.

"The reason for the ban, we learned, was that rabbits are prone to escape,—they become stir-crazy, although not, like the poor souls at Alcatraz, sexually deprivated. It is a wonder to me," the Colonel said, "that they had any energy left. Having escaped, they would proliferate extramurally, thus nullifying the efforts of the state to exterminate them. They were a menace to the great universal granary, the Kansas wheat fields. They cost more than Professor Hatfield with his Gatling gun.

"Our rabbits kept right on breeding," he said, "unaware that their activities were without legal sanction, and Kelly continued to market the pelts, because he had a bite to meet every time a strange Ford honked at the gate. He figurated by now if anybody sang he was in for a million and a half dollars in fines, nine hundred thousand days in durance laborious. 'I haven't the heart to think of it in years,' he said, 'but it's a long rap.'

"Eventually the rube who was renting him the place came around and told him he had broken the lease by conducting illegal activities, but it would be all right if Kelly and I cut him in for fifty per cent.

"That was the day before the night Kelly got drunk with the husband of the president of the WCTU and they turned all the rabbits loose.

" 'I don't want any incriminating evidence left on the place when the law comes,' Kelly told this good old countryman, so after they had run a tractor through the wire fence that surrounded the Mid-Continental Chinchilla Rabbitry they loosed a pack of beagles on the property. Next morning there wasn't a chinchilla on the farm.

" 'Here is something for your wife,' Kelly said to the benevolent rustic as we climbed into our Winton racer to depart, and he handed him a sawed-off shotgun loaded with deer slugs. The old fellow looked as pleased as a ballplayer accepting a free automobile. He promised to give it an early trial. Within the next year the state of Kansas had to pay out $723,000 additional bounty in that county alone."

The Colonel paused.

"The moral of Mr. Mason's adventure," he said, "if any, may be expressed: 'Never enter a race without reading the condition book carefully.' "

"I should have thought that experience would have made you leery of participation in the Great American Hog Syndicate," I said.

"The circumstances were radically different," the Colonel said. "We had the deal, an inestimable advantage."

The Colonel is a great coffee drinker, being particularly devoted to that black Italian brew, with lemon peel on the side, that is erroneously supposed to be conducive to insomnia. He sleeps like a lungfish.

On the evening when the Mid-Continental Chinchilla Rabbitry came to his mind, we were sitting in the Red Devil on West Forty-eighth Street, a deservedly crowded place at dinner hours, but tranquil as you could wish once the theatre crowd has gone.

The Colonel ordered a third cup of coffee and looked so soulful that I divined he was thinking of the Duchess. I thought this was a favorable moment to animadvert to the Great American Hog Syndicate, and it proved so.

"You were just beginning to tell me about the reception for Red Alexis II at Millbrae," I said, "the last time we talked about your venture with Mr. Harry Brolaski."

"Ah, yes," the Colonel said, softly. "An occasion unforgettable. To be observed all through the activities at the Southern Pacific Railroad station and the rest of the eventual day of days is a naughty twinkle in the eye of the Duchess. This is her day, and resolved she is to enjoy it to the full. The furor at the station is but hors d'oeuvre. Scarce returned to the New House in the foothills of the Coast Range, filigreed in a forested park of redwoods, fifteen hundred acres in extent, our Duchess, the perfect chatelaine, is beaming in exaltation at the thought that here now is to come the crescendo of the home-coming-of-Red Alexis festivities.

"The great manor house, a sixty-two-room job, with a ballroom as large as the Crystal Room, Hotel Ritz Carlton, New York, had undergone a special furbishment for the occasion. The splash, I afterward learned, cost her sixty-two hundred dollars, which constitutes but a trivial item when set, back to back, against an annual income from vast inherited holdings.

"So here we are at the great table, a huge oaken plank affair, 18 feet by 5, purchased by the late Frederick Charles Crocker, builder of New House, for thirty-five thousand dollars translated into pounds, from Christie's, London, many years gone by. It was originally in Tower Hall, the residence of Henry VIII at Bath, even today a favorite watering place in succoring the gout-afflicted, for centuries the national malady in well-stuffed Blighty."

The Colonel maintained a most serious demeanor. I had already informed him I am subject to attacks of gout, a circumstance which he finds inexhaustibly amusing.

"For luncheon this fine and historically redolent item, the table, is battened with cottoned mats and then overspread with Irish linen tablecloths, inherited by the Duchess from the Torlonia family years prior, and now to be activated in service to his lordship, the prolific American pig. Members of that proudly defiant Savoyan family would flop over in sepulchred rest did they but know the situation of the moment.

"So, in files for luncheon the thirty-three guests led by Mr. Dodge, the banker, and the six other members of the reception committee of the Red Alexis II welcome celebration; all in high silk hats with long red-and-gold badges displayed upon their Prince Albert-coated breasts, an impressive spectacle to be sure; there they be, the State of California sent the lieutenant governor, Mr. Will Crocker, Mr. Dudley Field Malone, Mr. Seabiscuite Howard, and Herb Fleishhacker, mighty men of politics, finance, the law and insurance. As a representative gathering it would serve to background a more consequential event, but the gentlemen were all friends of the Duchess, and it is pertinent to bear in mind their banks, brokerage offices and professional services had been requisitioned by the Duchess to their monetary advantage through the years. Such is life west or east of the Sierra Nevada, a puppetry with the strings pulled by the acquisitive instinct.

"Of course at table head appeared the urbane Mr. Brolaski, wise as a serpent, with all the top cards reposing in his capacious mitt. Dazzling in her happiness, and impatient for the business to begin, sat in queenly poise our the Duchess."

The wall lights at the Red Devil are screened by parchment tambourines, on each of which is recorded some Neapolitan saying the proprietor, Don Ciccio, considers amusing. The Colonel's glance rose to one of these as he sought Ernesto, the waiter, in order to command another cup of coffee. It read: *"Da Vinta a trenta giovane valente."*

"Are you conversant with the Mediterranean idiom, Joe?" he asked, "and if so, pray what does that mean?"

"From twenty to thirty, a potent young man," I ventured.

"And the next?" asked the Colonel.

"Da trenta a quaranta valente ma nu tanto,—from thirty to forty good, but not that good," I approximated.

"Next?" said the Colonel.

"Da quaranta a cinguanta, nu o crerere si s'avanta,—from forty to fifty don't believe him if he boasts," I said miserably. This is the line I take most to heart.

"And then?"

"Da cinguanta a sissanta uno ogni tanto,—from fifty to sixty just one in a while."

"And the finale?" he demanded, pointing to the last of the row of tambourines on that wall.

"Da sissantina a sittantina lass' e femmene e piglio o vino,—from the sixtieth to the seventieth year, abandon women and stick to wine."

The Colonel ruminated a while and then said:

"Who wrote that, Dante? It is one of the saddest passages in all literature."

He ordered the coffee and then said, "Besides, it is prematurely pessimistic. A man of seventy is a mere boy."

22 / The Apotheosis of Alexis

WHEN THE waiter had brought the coffee the Colonel resumed his narration.

"Directly across the table from the Duchess is Mr. Dodge and the other members of the committee ranged and intermingled with the guests round about and on both sides of the huge board, which in its day had heard the flagoon and trencher platter of good King Hal impinge upon its solid fibre," he said.

"The huntsman's trusty sharp-beaked Falcon had fetched the meaty bird and vinters their tumbler of red Kent wine full to brim for ho my lads they lived high in those thumping days of old.[1]

"The ancient oaken planks of the treasured table must have felt *en rapport* as the chattering merriment of present company voculated into their creaky recesses, bringing suggestion that perhaps there yet lived the spirit and the guile of Robin Hood and of Moll of Flanders.[2] After the dishes had been cleared, and the period of pleasantries before guest dispersal had drawn to close, Mr. Brolaski and the Duchess decided much important business affecting the Syndicate would be discharged forthwith.

"And now we're in the smoking room with its high-paneled Tudor oak wainscot and marginal eaves around its expansive walls in the late afternoon of a California summer with its dry but chilly fogs which drift in from Half Moon Bay with the trade winds from the far-stretching Pacific Ocean. Suddenly, as we're seated round about, the butler announces a call at telephone for Mr. Brolaski, now in the midst of the delightful incineration of a genuine Principe de la Porta, from out the recesses of the Duchess' cherished humidor continental. 'No stinker, a real two-dollar torch,' he had boasted to me *sotto voce*.

"Returning to the company's midst this marvelous knight of opportunity brought gleesome news, in effect: 'The Millionaire Kid is on the way down with plenty dirt to spill.'

"So we awaited in expectancy but in no wise allowed this significant development to interrupt the forward trend of business at hand.

"I could see the Duchess was just bursting with some tremendous suggestion which, to her feminine mind, spelled drama and money. After Mr. Brolaski had explained to Mr. Dodge, the genial old codger who initials the credit slips for the teller at the San Mateo National Bank, that a Principe de la Porta has a more aromatic pungency on a 'relight than before,' we cuddled closer and finally came to grips. Looking back over the years it's so consoling to see Mr. Brolaski work in mind's eye. What a man!

"So it came to be the Duchess exploded all of a sudden. Breathlessly, her idea was that a swine evaluated at eight thousand dollars should have a spot in Burke's Peerage with a chronological background befitting a monarch of Berkshirian blood and ancestral distingué.

"He had already proved his capacity as a family man, a very good point in the favor of Red Alexis II.

[1] The Colonel, I fear, is not much of a medievalist. Falcons do not fetch their quarry to the table but stay with it until the falconer arrives with transportation. And Henry VIII drank French wine.
[2] George Borrow's apple woman on London Bridge called her Blessed Mary Flanders.

"He had been received in his new California kingdom with a pomp and circumstance befitting a regal liege.

" 'He ought to hit .336 in this California climate,' chimed in Mr. Dodge. 'And he is going to have nothing but chic young sows,' emphasized the Duchess, now about to retire at any moment to reappear outfitted in blue jeans and shoulder braces befitting any up-to-date manager of an American-type breeding-farm swinery.

"We had received so far bounteous publicity and the fullest co-operation from the newspapers, and Mr. Brolaski remained perfectly aware of the necessity of a continuance of that generous attitude on the part of the gazettes. On three long draws off the Principe de la Porta the cogitating president came to surface with this one; he said, with glee in his eye and competency in his voice, 'I'll tell what it is. We name this Big Red after William Randolph Hearst.'

"So it came to be that Red Alexis II, as he appears registered in the American National Swine Breeders' Association Stud Book, fell heir to a new and glorious nomenclature,—William Randolph Hearst. The Hearsts and the Stingos are only collaterally related, I may say, the two middle-name Randolphs having been mere acquaintances on their respective mothers' sides.

"Now then the butler announces Danny Haggerty, the Millionaire Kid. His affluence having come to a terminancy with the collapse of racing in New York, the Kid had come to California in that great diaspora of talent which followed the cruel Hughes holocaust, like the dispersion of the Huguenots following the revocation of the Edict of Nantes. New York, like the France of Louis XIV, lost many of its keenest minds after this triumph of intolerance."

The Colonel looked glum for a moment.

"The city has never entirely recovered," he said. "Only last week I was having a light collation of lentil-and-pasta soup and beef *braciola* at the Antica Trattoria Roman, near the Criminal Courts building, and encountered Francesco Salerno, an old friend of mine engaged in the bail-bond business.

" 'You must be in a flourishing condition, Frank,' I vouchsafed to him. 'The papers record a multitude of arrests, and high bail is set in almost every case.' 'It don't do me any good,' he replied. 'I would not write a bond for the cheap-class crooks they got nowadays. They skip.'

"It all started with Charles Evans Hughes," the Colonel said. "In American history he will rank with the chestnut blight.

"Well, to return to the main thread of dissertation, the Millionaire Kid is just chuck full of news respecting the day's operations in the offices of the Great American Hog Syndicate up in San Francisco. The headline publicity about the preparations for the arrival of big Alex has served as a hypodermic for sales, we hope.

"Mr. Brolaski, so eager to hear about it he rests the Principe de la Porta in its dying and fragant stages upon one of the Duchess's heavy Venetian gold-encrusted ash trays, arises with both hands in his money pockets. 'Is the news good, Kid, and how much, tell me quick, Kid,' Mr. Brolaski kept volleying as he approached the lone traveler.

"As the Millionaire Kid drew from his black pocket case a roll of bills a cheetah couldn't jump over, I thought Mr. Brolaski would revert to cannibalism and devour the Kid alive—boots, hat and all.

"He kept pushing and jabbing his forefinger into the Kid's mid-section, forcing him half around the table while we all looked on in amazement. Finally, the Kid sidles into a chair belching the latest advice from the battlefield's front lines in bated and hurried respiration. Mr. Brolaski, meanwhile, in menacing attitude, looking down upon his victim much after the manner of a Siamese cat surveying a captured mouse.

"Proclaimed the Kid in triumphant tone: 'We did sixteen subscriptions, and the take was thirty-two hundred today, with two hours to go. I have eleven hundred dollars in cash here and the checks I leave up in the office safe. Thought you might be wanting some of the ready, and here it is. I've got to have a cut of it myself before leaving you all.'

"Drawing himself up to a commanding poise the pleased master promoter,—how he relished that designation,—replied, 'Well, Kid, I see you took all necessary steps to assure yourself that the money would be available. You leave me without an alibi. Now I'm slipping you five hundred.'

"The Millionaire Kid thanked Mr. Brolaski, briefly but pointedly: 'That's so good of you, Mr. Brolaski,' he said. 'Three hundred would have been O.K.'

"I'll never forget the reaction on the master promoter's well-weathered face, the storms of the centuries behind it, as the realization of the Kid's remark arose within his comprehension. Fleecy clouds lacing the blue summer skies suddenly displaced by a black intruder from nowhere with the depressive forewarning of rain and bluster. But nothing happened.

"With the Millionaire Kid gone and on his way, we all reverted to the matters of moment concerning the destiny of the Great American Hog Syndicate.

"We long ago had figured that an average of ten subscriptions a day, a take of two thousand dollars, would be tops. Now it looked as if we might exceed this. To supply the necessary number of little piggies to offset this phenomenally rapid growth of the business would require more than one William Randolph Hearst at royal court.

"This wonderful Mr. Brolaski, with all the brains and nerve in the world, had overlooked nothing. At the very moment of our social amenities at New House as the guests of the Duchess, the master has working under lights until far into the night at the offices of the Great American Hog Syndicate two young actuaries from the Equitable Life Assurance Society, poring over an overwhelming number of figures cryptic to the layman, but to them reassuring right down to the last decimal point on blue- and red-lined paper marked out in quadrilaterals to keep them from going blind. They were being checked by Kid Bloggs, the same figure man I had employed in behalf of the rainmakers.

"We the board of directors and strategy of the Great American Hog Syndicate would soon know how many little piggies we must produce, how many boars in the stud, the cost and source of feed, overhead and other esatorica. Already the experts had informed us that when we would reach a thousand unit partnerships we must have twenty-five high-class, well-bred, boars of top prolificigacy, the best that money would buy, to keep the production line moving, and four thousand acres with expert trainers, grooms and exercise boys, or their taxonomic equivalents in the idiom of the hog business.

"It appears the actuaries had it down so fine they told us that after 255 days' operation we could count on at least a net profit of 37.01 per cent with pork on the hoof ruling in the market at Chicago, Kansas City and San Francisco at sixteen cents the pound or better. It was now twenty-eight cents a pound with continual uprise; to what heights nobody could predict beneath heaven's vault. A year later it did reach fifty-seven cents, and two years after that drovers were willing to pay as much as ninety-six cents a pound at the sty with a bonus of a free baseball bat and glove to the seller if a member of the 4-H Club, a nationwide organization of juvenile agriculturists."

Here, as in the episode of the rainmakers, I must trust the Colonel's figures, having no way of checking up on them. The newsprint on which papers of the period were printed is so friable that it crumbles at the touch, or I would look through the commodity price tables for the period of the First World War. I have been unable to get in touch with Kid Bloggs, now said to be an inmate of a blind men's home, where he is running a pea-and-thimble game. What I got out of the Colonel's recitation was, in a general way, that the Great American Hog Syndicate was sucking up a lot of Tease.

"As an office manager," Colonel Stingo said, "the Millionaire Kid was even better than at conning reporters. It was no time until we find him daily lunching with boobs of moment. He was a guest of honor at the weekly luncheon and gabfeist of the Rotary Club, for example, addressing the august assemblage upon the subject of 'Pork is King.' Ostensibly espousing the cause of increased food production in support of war preparedness, he did not fail to emphasize the chance to turn a clever buck in the units of the Great American Hog Syndicate selling at a sacrificial two hundred dollars a throw. All the Mr. Babbitts from Main Street perked an eye and bent an ear at the alluring prospect delineated by the Millionaire Kid.

"They showed an eagerness to try one shot anyway equaled only in enthusiasm by the rainbow trout in springtime as he contemplates the juicy angleworm covering up for the shiny hook in the sunny waters of Valley Junction Creek. The trout has the excuse of hunger resulting from the difficult foraging conditions of the winter," he commented, "but the more replete the boob is with currency the more rapaciously he reaches for another helping.

"Then there was the day when the school children of South San Francisco and their teachers, at the invitation of the Millionaire Kid, visited the farm to see the much vaunted and sensationally advertised and publicized World's Heavyweight Champion Boar, William Randolph Hearst. The cameras snapped and the Duchess, in blue jeans and heavy long boots, surrounded by her society friends from Burlingame and Hillsborough, performed beautifully as the lady of the manor. She even wanted to sing, finally moderating her enthusiasm by directing her secretary, Miss Mary Muffins, to present the leader of the school's twenty-piece brass band with a five-hundred-dollar check.

"Then came that day when Mr. Hearst, moated at San Simeon, 180 miles down the Coast Highway, must be apprised of the honor bestowed upon him by the acceptance of his nationally acclaimed monicker as the name of a very tremendous porker of expensive progenitory capacity.

"Someone had to carry the Message to Garcia and the honor devolved upon the Millionaire Kid, since, we reason, Mr. Hearst, who read his own newspapers and had an elephantine memory, might well recall Mr. Brolaski's oft-implicated name or physiognomy, frequently in the past photographed over such captions as: 'Missing from his usual haunts.' As for that distinguished agriculturist, John R. Stingo, Mr. Hearst would have known him immediately as a horse fellow, and so have doubted the solid gravity of the whole operation. So the Kid tooled down the wonderful new Pacific Coast Highway, around mountain peaks, into green valleys, and then close to the ceaseless hiss of the combing surf, in the special Jaguar job from the garage at New House, as directed by the Duchess. By prearrangement he was waved on by the postilioned castle watch in the medieval arched block house at the foot of the precipitous hill upon which crested the turreted ménage of the mighty dragon of American journalism. The Duchess's writ ran everywhere.

"Once in the presence of the august Caesar Imperator and Heliogabalus combined, the Kid duked him with aplomb. Brevitating his pitch, for the American emperor, always a busy man, had allotted him but one three-minute round, the Kid asked Mr. Hearst whether he objected to the use of his name for the furtherance of the food-production racket,—effort, rather,—he said, retrieving his verbal burble. Mr. Hearst, amused, queried, 'Why hit upon me for the honor? Why not Mr. William Jennings Bryan?'

"The Kid, returning from his mission, reported that he sensed beneath the good humor a modicum of annoyance, and the Kid was highly sensitized to such emotional nuances. His flair had enabled him on a couple of occasions to drop under a table or otherwise escape a second before opponents opened fire.

"I therefore suggested we change the big hog's name to Governor Rolph, as I could not afford to turn the Hearst papers hostile.

"A politician, I knew, would welcome publicity in any form."

23 / The Iron Was Hot

"As I view retrospectively the progress of the Great American Hog Syndicate," Colonel Stingo said, "it seems to me that the reception for Red Alexis II marked it indubitably with the stigmata of success. From that point on it proceeded on carefully stimulated impetus. We had broken on top, but like a skillful jockey equipped with a stinger we took nothing for granted, applying the whip of high-voltage advertising whenever our enterprise showed signs of going limber.

"A stage soon arrived when, left to my own devices, I would have refused further subscriptions. I trembled in thought of how we were finally going to get out with sails bulging and craft unscuttled. But Mr. Brolaski was insatiable, and the enterprise, moreover, had developed a sordid commercial aspect of tangibility. Within a year of our establishment, we were selling pork on the hoof, tons of it, and sending out dividend checks to the owners of the units that had produced the progeny sold down the river. Had not Mr. Brolaski advised me in advance of a denouement delectable to anticipate, I would have suspected him of embarking me in a simple exercise of entrepreneurage.

"With the rise in the pork market the prices of eligible debutante sows and bachelor boars of old stock naturally increased, but Mr. Brolaski refused to raise the price of unit subscriptions. 'We will breed our own stock,' he said, 'and sell it to ourselves at Kansas City on-the-hoof prices, thus saving the cost of transportation thither and consequent loss of weight, also insurance and commissions.' He was mad with greed, like an ordinary businessman.

"For the enhancement of prestige, however, and in order to harvest more publicity, we sent the vet, Dr. Shepherd, east to recruit nine more glamour hogs like Alexis. His mission was followed by the California press with the same interest that attended the signing of players for the San Francisco Seals or the recruitment of gigantic high school all-state football beehemotheye for the University of California Golden Bears. He soon apprised us, to our dismay, that prices for boars of even the allowance class had risen to an average of four thousand dollars. Sows of scrub type, not recognized by the Jockey Club, were available at their comestible or stockyards price, and Mr. Brolaski decided, while authorizing the purchase of the new lot of porcine aristocrats, to encourage *mésalliance* between them and the girls from the wrong side of the track.

" 'Half the aristocracy of Virginia,' he said, 'is descended from marriages between Cavaliers and indentured women.'

"A less recondite argument that might have influenced his decision was embodied in the contract of unit partnership. In the writ and scroll it was provided that the Syndicate owned one half of each sow and one half of each crop of sibling swinelets. At all times the Syndicate retained full ownership of the blue-blooded boars of ancestral distinction,—we were whole-hog on them.

"We therefore wired Dr. Shepherd, our scout, to close the deal,—we must have more names to exploit, like Hollywood, or we would lose our grip on the public, and the Frankenstein monster we had reared would engulf us all.

"I urged caution upon Mr. Brolaski," the Colonel said. "But he replied, 'Always step inside a punch, not away from it. It's safer.' He therefore despatched the thirty-six thousand dollars, still hot from the Millionaire Kid's hands, through which they had passed with such speed that none had had a chance to adhere on their journey from new subscribers' pockets.

"The personalization of Red Alexis II had yielded such generous dividends of free space and public interest that we immediately decided the new rookies of the year should be baptismically monickered after the best-known good fellows in California. They were accordingly denominated Doug Fairbanks, Charlie Chaplin, Ty Cobb, Jim Jeffries, Gunboat Smith, Sunny Jim Coffroth, Clark Gable, Daddy Browning and Legs Diamond."

I noted that the Colonel had here repeated the cinquecento device of historical displacement, as in the case of Helen Wills and Miss Winsor. Neither Mr. Gable, Mr. Browning, nor Mr. Diamond, I was sure, had been public characters as early as the First World War. But I had learned my lesson and said nothing, lest I never hear the end of the adventure of the Great American Hog Syndicate.

"Remember," the Colonel said modestly, "I was in charge of the general advertising and publicity activities of the Great American Hog Syndicate. And it was the style and pull of the appeal in the copy of the Great American Hog Syndicate's advertising campaign which sensationalized the whole career of the fabulously successful enterprise.

"To describe it: we used 280 agate lines by 2 columns wide, which made an area of 2 columns by 20 inches. An artcraft border, heavy and challenging, with ornamentation in the way of a drover herding a wriggling mass of little piggies out of the lush meadows into the stock pens, was used with a minimum of lettered type face.

"The appeal to self-interest was promulgated chiefly through tables in box form setting forth the rising market for pork, on the hoof, in dressed form, canned, or bottled, at the emporia of trade throughout the land. Chitterlings, I remember, had risen in value five and three quarters times in a space which had produced an increase of only 113 per cent in a selected group of twenty-four industrial and twelve public-utility common stocks. Coupled with this evidence was a mild intimation that price per unit might soon rise.

" 'Pork is King,' read the punch line, relieved with a picture of our Jim Rolph, formerly Red Alexis II and William Randolph Hearst, with a royal crown mounting his swinish brow.

"But the feature which made of each ad a conversation piece, sought after with the same eagerness as the daily standing of teams in the Pacific Coast League or the race charts, was a heavy-bordered box showing the standing of the ten prize boars in number of pigs credited to their prowess during the week terminating with the Sunday on which the advertisement appeared. We also showed monthly and lifetime product. Heavy betting developed on this feature, and also numbers games paid off on the three last digits of weekly accouchements. We published a regular price line, twelve to five against Clark Gable, seven to two Hiram Johnson, or whatever it might be. It varied according to the fluctuations in their recently recorded potency. It was surprising how some hogs would do better in warm, others in rainy weather. They seemed to fall like horses into a classification of fast-track or mud runners, also sprinters and routers. Lagging behind the others in weekly output, Governor Rolph would occasionally put on a bonanza burst, coming through when the price was right with a production like Bethlehem Steel.

"But over the route Clark Gable reigned supreme. In three years of competition, he and thirty sons produced over sixty thousand dollars' worth of pork in varied finished form and nailed Doug Fairbanks by a nose on the post. Each weekly summary was accompanied by a footnote in chartmaker's style, penned by the old master, Jimmy Macdonald, as: 'Charlie Chaplin, a prominent contender from the start with three litters totaling thirty-five attributed to him on Monday, continued in good style through Friday, but hung in the stretch. Gunboat Smith came with a rush and got all the money with a week-end four-bagger!'

"My purpose in initiating this feature was orthodox. As any county-fair promoter knows you've got to give the public a show to get them into the place. After they have been attracted they buy. I would pull them in with my race chart. Then I would sell them with my pork-production tables. But as interest in the weekly chart increased astonishingly, it became apparent that in it we had the key to another Montezuman treasure chamber of Tease. We installed in our offices a couple of bookmakers, discreetly dissembled as order takers, and the handle soon attained as much as ten thousand dollars a day. We contented ourselves with a modest 110 per cent book, not having before us as yet the national example of unsyndicated hoggishness, the pari mutuel with its bite of sixteen per cent. The ten per cent profit insured us a steady thousand dollars a day, sufficient to meet the office nut and keep Brolaski in two-dollar cigars and old Farmer Stingo in good spirits.

"It almost lost us the services of the Millionaire Kid, who said he would forego all the commissions accruing on his sales of units if we would just let him have the bookmaking privileges in the town's four leading saloons. Then the Duchess called up from the breeding farm, now extending over four thousand acres by the leasing of juxtaposed acreage and its addition to our original twelve hundred.

"She said she had caught her most trusted stable foreman out in the boar barn with a syringe, just on the point of slipping Daddy Browning a hypo which would diminish his ardor. 'He said he expected a big play on Daddy Browning this week, and he was going to lay him two points over the house price,' she said in cultured trepidation. 'Jimmy Macdonald, I think you have demoralized our employes.' "

The Colonel looked about him dolefully, and said:

"Gambling spreadeth pollution in its wake, Joe. It is like one of those ships that go up the Hudson and pump out their old bilges at night, imparting to the shad a gasolinic taste, so that after despatching a portion priced $3.50 you are afraid to light a cigarette.

"Scarcely had I put down the receiver, when I saw Mr. Brolaski, with a lowering air of conspiracy upon his trust-repelling features, standing in the door of his private office and beckoning me to enter. There, secreted from the public, he watched through a number of armored judases the operations of his subordinates, particularly the three cashiers, or money takers, constantly employed.

"When I joined him and he had snap locked the door, he said, 'Jim, I've got a great idea. We lay five to one against Gable and slip him a line of bashful sows.' 'There are none,' I said at a venture, wishing to discourage this train of thought. 'And moreover, what are we running here? A handbook or a mighty corporation? Next thing you know the cops will be in for ice. Do not let us imperil this stupendous operation for the sake of any extracurricular larceny.'

"I could see on his lowering façade an expression of agonized indecision; my suggestion that he pass up any form of booty outraged his natal instincts. But he said, 'Jim, I agree with you. We will can that lousy foreman and let it be understood around the farm that every one of them hogs is well meant.' It was a decision that demanded a great deal of moral courage."

The Colonel, having reflected on the advisability of ordering more coffee, decided against it, and suggested a bottle of Canadian ale. "It is not in the tradition of the Mediterranean cuisine, I know," he said, "but my tastes are eclectic."

Encouraged by the ale, the Colonel continued:

"In full bloom, the operation, under precise and punctilious direction, as already explained, proceeded untrammeled into pleasing fruition both for sponsor and investor. The situation arose where our earliest boobs had by now accumulated in semiannual dividends a total of $907.10 for each unit of $200, a result little typical of the average opportunity marketed by Mr. Brolaski. Others had reaped lesser profits; still more were in the clear, or nearly. Pork on the hoof ruled at a high of eighty-three cents a pound; here and there stray lots brought up to a dollar.

"Three years had passed. With the United States in full-fledged belligerency the price of hogs hit a new zenith at close of each day's market.

"It was the hour when the Syndicate's full board found the iron at furnace heat,—the fateful moment for the great move in the carefully contrived stratagem. One learns from history that whatever soars must some day recede to a rational basis. The market might at any moment break adversely. That great patriot, Mr. Brolaski, had a statesmanlike intuition of the collapse of the Hohenzollern empire, although it was apparently in ruggedly ebullient bellicosity.

" 'Suppose them bums quit?' he said. 'We are buried in lard.'

"We therefore decided to wind up the business with assured profits of gladsome proportions in the offing. The multitude of subscribers, or partners in units, as legally and speculatively set up, were duly informed to claim and remove from the four farms, which the rapid growth of the business had made necessary, the half sows and half litters pertaining to them within a week, as our lease was up. They retained the option of buying our half of the sow at current Kansas City rates, but, we informed them with regret, we would not buy their half of the sow because we had no premises suitable for porcine harborage. The countryside literally swarmed with little piggies, for the Big Ten had done a noble job in the department of genetics, and the young home-bred boars had followed their noble example.

"Consternation reigned wherever the United States mails were delivered, for our subscribers were all over the United States, and most of them were urban, unequipped to receive hogs into their domestic premises. Checks on the Syndicate treasury for all the various earned and accumulated accretions went out, together with notices to hurry, hurry, hurry, pick up those pigs. One little lady, a schoolteacher, on confrontation with the necessity of taking possession of a half sow and five pigs, wrote from New York on stationery of the Martha Washington Hotel, 'I never heard of anything so awful.'

"After a week another batch of letters went out, imploring recalcitrant subscribers to come and get their pigs, since we were being dispossessed and the animals would become a public charge and cause of destruction, rendering their proprietors of record liable for any damage they inflicted on the watermelon crop.

"If this proved impracticable, we said, we would consent to take them off our partners' hands at a nominal price, although we did not know what we could do with them. Meanwhile Mr. Brolaski was considering competitive tonnage bids from representatives of Swift & Company, Armour, Wilson, Morris, Cudahy, Timothy Shine of Shine's Restaurant, Barney Greengrass, and the Maryland Market, Amsterdam Avenue, New York.

"In the end 95.42 of the subscribers ceded their porkifers to us at a price 79.2 below prevailing market price. Yet they did not lose money in all cases; some of them broke even, a happy result which is not subject to income tax.

"Mr. Brolaski received a certified check for $512,011.30 from the successful bidder, Cudahy or Wilson, I forget which. The Duchess was happy for our sakes and offered to sell Mr. Brolaski an ancestral chateau of the Torlonia family in a romantically malarial part of Italy. 'It offers the best pheasant-shooting in the Old World,' she informed him."

The Colonel finished his bottle of ale and called over to the waiter, "Ask the man at the cigar counter if he has a Principe de la Porta two-dollar straight."

"And what was your share of the proceeds?" I asked him.

"Fifty per cent of the net," he answered without elation.

The waiter returned to say the cigar man had never heard of a Principe de la Porta, and the Colonel took a pack of Kools instead.

"There was only one drawback," he said. "Mr. Brolaski left town with the check. His object was honorable, he explained several years afterward when we met in a shop at Saratoga, where he put the bite on me for five cents to buy a glass of vichy. 'I just wanted to make another spot of Tease for both of us,' he said, 'so we would have something to show for our trouble when we cut it up.'

"So he bet the money on a horse that was going at Havre de Grace at a price of three to five," the Colonel said, "and it ran eighth in a field of nine. The last horse broke a leg."

24 / An Exercise in History

COLONEL STINGO does not conceive of history as a photogenic cake, with successive layers placed precisely on one another and all held firmly together by a mortar of Toynbee or chocolate goo to give it cohesion, like a picture magazine's history of Western man. He sees it rather as a slow stream, often doubling back, and while he will concede that nothing is as dead as yesterday's newspaper, he believes the day before yesterday's is already slightly less so.

"That old fraud Brisbane once told me that any first-class news story, if revived and recounted years after it happened, is fifty per cent as potent as it was in the first place," he said to me in one of our first disquisitory interchanges, "and for once he was right." It is a principle the Colonel had exploited in the redaction of "Yea Verily," in which he periodically reconstructs such mighty episodia as the burning of the steamboat General Slocum in 1904, the great Rubel Coal and Ice Company holdup of 1934 and the Battle of Gettysburg. Other events he from time to time commemorates are the unexplained disappearance of Amby Small, a Toronto theatre owner, in 1913, the defeat of Terry McGovern by Young Corbett at Hartford, Connecticut, in 1901, and the charge of the Irish Brigade at Fontenoy.

The Irish Brigade got him out of a tight spot last Christmas, as it had the Maréchal de Saxe in 1745. Lacking Tease wherewith to buy Christmas presents for his friends, he told me at the year's turn, he had sat in his room at the Hotel Dixie too dispirited to hunt up a fresh story for his next "Yea Verily." As he had not done the Fontenoyset- piece for a couple of years, he painted in a couple of new rhetorical touches and sent it in. The day after it ran he was sitting in his room again, equally dispirited, when the telephone rang and the desk informed him that there was a man below with a package to deliver.

"I instructed them to forward him," the Colonel said, "and presently there appeared a large Irishman, red of neck and countenance, carrying a cardboard carton of the size that contains a dozen fifths. 'Merry Christmas from Mr. Ignatius McGonigle,' he said, naming a member of a large firm of booze wholesalers. 'Mr. McGonigle says he always enjoys the part of that piece where they mow the redcoats down in swathes, and will you please mow down an extra swathe for him the next time you write it.' He departed, leaving behind him the remembrance, which consisted of tastefully bottled grain neutral spirits flavored with whiskey. It solved my gift problem instantaneously. I bought some seasonal wrapping paper and appropriately packaged the twelve individual bottles for distribution."

As tangible evidence of the truth of his story, the Colonel offered two bottles of the blend, which I am sure he would never have bought of his own volition.

"The incident illustrates the pulling power of an old story," he said, and then added, a trifle ungratefully, I thought, "Next season I'll *exterminate* the English. Then maybe he'll send me some whiskey worth not giving away."

Gettysburg, to which he returns in fancy at least once a year, is a flexible anniversary,—he can run it either on the date of the battle itself, in July, or of the Gettysburg Address that followed it in November. Each time he writes it he develops a news lead. Once it was an interview with Eddie Plank, the old Athletics pitcher, who lives near the battlefield, and again the fact that a boy from Gettysburg town was playing fullback on the University of Pennsylvania varsity. Last year it was the news that General Dwight D. Eisenhower had bought a farm near by. In all the years he has been writing the piece, however, he had never succeeded in getting it into the *Enquirer* intact, a failure which causes him artistic distress.

"The current Newsprint shortage raising hob," he wrote back in 1946, soon after our acquaintance began. "After our Mr. Make-up, the Great Deleter, had done with his emasculation of last week's Stingo, there remained absent several pickets from the wooden fence."

Not only Gettysburg has suffered from this species of mutilation, to which the Colonel is peculiarly susceptible. "In last week's compendium of the famous renewal of the Dwyer Stakes in 1920, wherein the heroic John P. Grier ran Man o' War, the winner, to a neck finish," he was once compelled to write, "the Kite lost its Tail through constriction due to a tight paper."

I have no copy of his 1946 Gettysburg story, but one excerpt haunts my memory: "As the sweet River Shannon began to flow softly and copiously, although I like Trommer's White Label a deal better than the local Conestoga brew. But this Mennonite cheese is surpassing."

"Gettysburg is the kind of subject I like, Joe," he once said to me. "I can really wind up and throw. The description of lesser events is like a half-mile race track, on which a horse with a long stride is at a disadvantage. The fear of hyperbole restrains. But with a theme like Gettysburg or J. P. Morgan it can be disregarded."

One November—he had chosen the anniversary of the address this time—he sent me an advance manuscript of his Gettysburg so I could catch it uncut. The unabated paper shortage precludes my reproducing it that way, but I can quote some.

"I had been here before, many times for many reasons," the Colonel says, setting the mood, "but one finds the quiet old Dutch countryside changed but little, while the sleepy old town remains just the same as ever." Then, after working through the Eisenhowers' purchase of a farm "composed of rolling land of hill and valley while the historic Cherry Creek comes in off the Battlefield nearby to scintillate the vistas," the Colonel gets into his battle. "From the long verandah of the Manor House of the General's lovely new home to be, you gain a sweeping concept of the expansive Battlefield and figurate for yourself how the awful conflict was won and lost.

"The catastrophic Third Day of the titanic struggle remains the crescendo of the momentous almost man-to-man grapple in utter death on the outskirts of the Little Dutch Town. Recently a summarization was given you of the first and second days' operations. Now let us hop to the line in respect to this vital and crucial Third Day, one of the great military episodes of all history."

Instead of hopping immediately, however, the Colonel wheels for another run, like a horse-show rider bringing his mount up to a high obstacle.

"But a final word of Devil's Den itself, centre of the Second Day's fighting. Within this gigantic Rockery are the celebrated Five Rocks. They are not of volcanic upheaval but came into the cosmic in the Paleozoic Prima Period,—some 200,000 years ago according to Darwinian Theory. . . .

"It is said that 3,700 odd youngsters, both sides, lost their lives within Devil's Den at Gettysburg, within a space no larger than the Baseball Diamond today at Yankee Stadium, New York, as explained recently.

"Night falls again. The tumult dies. There is a full moon over Gettysburg. The living and the dead are in tumbled heaps. Men breathe their last amid the overwhelming fragrance of the Sweet Clover, in Hayfields and Wheatfields ripe for Harvest. Lights burn late in the opposing Headquarters while the tired thousands of the unwounded of both armies drop where they stand and sleep. . . .

"Then comes the Third Day at Gettysburg . . . Sparked and emblazoned by the Charge of Pickett's Brigade, its result is to affect all men and history in its trend for a thousand years. . . .

"It is sublime and pitiable. . . ."

The Colonel would have made one of the great war correspondents of all time, if he had had the luck to find himself in a war.

Personally I prefer the kind of historical writing he does about his own era. For example:

"Clubhouse, Aqueduct, L.I., June 10 [1944]—Squeezed in like Monterey sardines in a tin packet case a great, and motley, throng of rabid Pari Mutuel fanatics strained at girth here this afternoon for the annual renewal of oldtime Carter Handicap, 3 y.o. & u., 7 furlongs, $10,000 added, in this tight little racetrack known as Aqueduct.

" 'How long can it last?'—It's the cry on every side. Deep students of the economic problem involved in Pari Mutuel operation now foresee the restrictive value of Bookmaking as opposed to rampant mechanized Pari Mutuel legalized gambling.

"Mayfair was well represented on Balcony and out in Box Row. . . .

"It's no secret to New York *Enquirer* that David Windsor appreciatively evaluated the parties given for him and his American Duchess by 'Her Grace' last summer which brought out the most interesting of the Belgravia. . . ."

But the kind of history in which the Colonel is at zenith, I think, is in the mid-ground between Gettysburg and the present. It is represented by his narration, last summer, of a great betting coup and its sequelae.

"Saratoga, N.Y., Aug. 11—This here United States Hotel Stakes is not so rich in endowment, but it is redolent in warm tradition as one of the most important juvenile fixtures in the entire Saratoga Book of Events. . . . In 1902, if recollection serves rightly, it was Blonde Plunger Charlie Ellison from Norwood, Ohio, who sensationalized the Ring and Club House by scoring a smart coup with his colt, Skillful, son of John E. Madden's top ace stallion, Mirthful.

"Late Kansas Price and Mose Fontilieu placed the Ellison Commission in the betting ring, Cad Daggett in the Club House and elephantine Hughie Quinn in the populous Field where quite some 80 summerily attired bookmakers operated. Joe Ullman and Kid Weller, operating the celebrated Big Store for John W. Gates and John A. Drake, the notorious prodigals in the Main Ring, stubbornly decided to lay Skillful with an opening price of 10–1. Coyly, the chalk showed 12–1 over at the mart of Sol Lichtenstein and Lucien Appleby. At crowded club house imperturbable Johnny Walters offered 12–1 as a feeler while English Bill Jackman and Humming Bird Tyler in the Field were reported to be overboard with as good as 15–1."

The Colonel's historical characters, like those of the reign of Robert the Pious,[1] have sobriquets that stimulate the curiosity. I have learned that it is unwise to interrupt the flow of spoken narrative to ask him how they were acquired, for the explanation, while beguiling, is so long that it prevents the completion of the anecdote in which they figure. But in the case of stories already committed to paper by him, I have no such inhibition. So the first time I met him after the appearance of the specimen of his art now under consideration, I asked him about Humming Bird Tyler.

"Humming Bird was a fellow who would have a horse marked up at four to one on his slate," the Colonel said, "and then some fellow who looked as if he were betting for somebody else would walk up and bet him a substantial sum, perhaps a thousand. Old George would start humming, 'On the Banks of the Wabash,' or something like that, as if he hadn't heard him, and he'd turn around in an absent-minded manner and mark that horse down to five to two before he casually turned to the stranger again. Humming Bird was a cautious type, like Circular Joe Vendig, so denominated because he would act as his own outside man and circulate among the other books, to see what they were doing."

But I must return to Saratoga in 1902:

"Afterwards, it was learned Skillful had been highly tried and the great jockey Otto Wonderly, then at the very zenith of his riding flair, was in the saddle. Blonde Charlie, then a rich man and heavy bettor himself, really represented a syndicate and Mid-Western high-money operators as well. . . .

"Well, sir, suddenly, a farmer-looking fellow, dug up by Kansas Price, modestly approached the Big Store where Kid Weller, on the block, was invited to take on $500 at 12–1. Accepted. Then a tender of another $500. 'You're on,' replied Weller. Then a proffer of a $1000. Accepted. Two minutes later the yokel came back beseeching $5,000 more at the prevailing 12–1. Hadn't Mr. Drake instructed Weller & Ullman to 'take anything offered and don't rub until you hear from me'? But now the cat's out of the bag and where is Mr. Drake? By the time that rough toss Outside

[1] For instance, Hugues Eveille-Chien, or Wake-Dog, the Count of Maine, and Olaf Krakaben, or Break-a-Bone (or possibly Break-a-Leg), the King of Norway, known after his conversion as Saint Olaf.

Man Red Sam Friedlander had knocked down [here a long catalogue of people who might have been standing around] and caught up with Drake and 'Ort' Welles cooling themselves beneath a wide spreading elm tree in the Paddock, fully some $162,000 had been eased upon the bookmakers and Club House commissioners.

"Then came the break in George Wheelock's market, followed by hurried chalk rubbing.

"To make a long ancient story abbreviate, it will suffice to say that the Syndicate got down to the last penny. Skillful closed at three, even and out.

"Next day, in New York *Herald*, the erudite Judge Joe Burke approximated the Ellison syndicate had won upwards of $470,000. It is a bye-thought today, in the speculative world of American racing, that Blonde Charlie Ellison, who afterwards won a Kentucky Derby in 1903 with Judge Himes, took down on Skillful's win a figure which surpasses all the known single top takes by either Pittsburgh Phil or Riley Grannan in their halcyon heights. Of course William Collins Whitney once won close to $2,000,000, though his Commissioners collected but $1,400,000, on George W. Jenkins, a steeplechase horse. Them were the days when men were men and women used no talcum powder."

A member of the Hearst politburo once informed me that the three only elements of news were blood, money, and sex in four letters. This particular commissar has since edited an anthology of great American reporting. By his criteria, the Colonel's story has everything. Right up to the talcum powder, it dealt only with money, but the other essentials were coming right up.

"But there is a climax to this reminiscence. The day after Skillful's win all hands are at Hotel Fort William Henry, Lake George, where Blonde Charlie had gone to escape the Bee and ubiquitous reporters, and the wrath of the Jockey Club's emissaries, who decried 'loud and vulgar betting' even as today. It was a gaudy dinner that night with Edna Mc-Cauley and Lil Russell honored guests and Diamond Jim Brady and Joe Seagram, foremost Canadian distiller and breeder and racing man, vying, one with the other, in sustaining a running river of choicest vintage, all the way, Mumm's Sec to fragrant light Paul Masson and White Seal, the champagne of the dilettante and gourmet. . . .

"Pleasing and natural event was the presentation to Jockey Otto Wonderly by Blonde Charlie of a cheque for $25,000, apart from his regular riding fee and winning stake bonus. Joe Seagram (who had won $144,000) chipped in with one for $15,000, and Abe Frank, representing another winner, George C. Bennet, ill at Hot Springs, Ark., with another for $10,000.

"There were other honoraria for Johnny Mayberry, Ham Keene and Jack the Ripper, who had a lot to do with bringing up Skillful to point in secret undercover. Nice job. But, as I say, the Climax.

"Two days later, down at Spa, little rosy cheeked Wonderly, fat and rich now as a lamprey, did not show up to ride a pretty undercover year-old-trick for Handsome Harry Robinson, owner of New Orleans' famous mudder, Death, a descendant of Leamington. The colt was scratched and another coup nipped in the bud."

(A lamprey, having once fastened on a succulent whitefish, must swell up as quickly as a jockey who breaks training. The fluid medium of inflation in the fish's case is blood, in the jockey's champagne. The brief introduction of the apparently extraneous Robinson story is for me a high point of narrative art. It marks the continuity of that world of intellectual combat from which the jockey has absented himself, like Achilles from the siege of Troy. Where, the reader asks himself, has Otto Wonderly gone?)

"Two other afternoons came and went with no Wonderly. He had eloped with petite, youngish and most personable Wendy Ellison. Month later, they were located at Amalfi, on the Italian Riviera. Hector Mackenzie, the Prince of Wine Agents, made the trip across the Atlantic carrying the Palms of Forgiveness but the rascals declined all overtures, and remained in Villa looking out upon the assuaging Monterey Blue of the Mediterranean for years."[2]

So much for the third element of a good news story. Now the Colonel darkens his canvas.

"They finally returned to America, but like all things mundane, the stalwarts, men and women, of a former day had passed from the scene and there had come the dolorous Ides of Charles Evans Hughes and the nullity in Racing—the charm had gone. Hildebrand, a great race rider, handled by Plunger Joe Yeager, succeeded Wonderly, who finally met his end in a shooting affray at Little Rock, Ark. It all happened in front of Chambers & Walker's palatial poolroom while the Don Juanish race rider stood talking to Dynamite Jack Thornby & Harry Brolaski. Long legged Red Booger strode up and Smith & Wessoned him to death with a soft nosed slug through the heart.[3] Dark visaged Dynamite, like his friend Bat Masterson, quick on the trig, wheeled and killed Mr. Booger. Next night the poolroom was dynamited as flat as Mattie Baldwin's proboscis.[4] McCarthy[5] Boy are you on the Listening Dept.? Yea Verily Verily."

That takes care of the blood.

---

[2] Not the Mediterranean Blue of Monterey, as Henry James might have expressed it. The Colonel is no servile deferent to extraterritorial scenery.
[3] Only the adjective Don Juanish applied to Wonderly hints at the cause of the tragedy.
[4] Nothing even hints at the cause of this. Who blew up the poolroom? Friends of Booger or friends of Wonderly? Or did the vigilantes simply blow it up as a menace to public health? In front of it was obviously a dangerous place to stand.
Matty Baldwin, as I have often heard, was a good Boston lightweight of the first

25 / A Little Journey to Pittsburgh Phil's

MY PREFERENCE for the Colonel's stories of his own life, or at least of the life in which he played a role, has frequently evoked the astonishment of my friend, who believes, like the authors of Greek tragedy, that only the lives of the illustrious are qualified to edify a large public.

To support his theory he cites the example of an old idol of his, Elbert Hubbard, known to Americans of the gas-log and hobble-skirt period as the Fra. Hubbard published an indeterminate number of volumes of Little Journeys to the Homes of Famous People, Good Men and Great, Famous Women (as distinguished from People), American Authors, American Statesmen, Eminent Painters, Great Musicians, and Great about everything else you can think of.

"He barely broke even on those," the Colonel says, "but he began to sandwich in Little Journeys to the Homes of Great Businessmen and Great Industries. For example he would write A Little Journey to the Home of the Hartford Lunch, or A Little Journey to Wanamaker's Department Store, or to Joseph Quincy Magruder, the shelled-pecan king. The Fra would publish the Little Journey in one of his magazines, the *Philistine* or the *Roycrofter*. The *Philistine* bore the whimsic device, 'Published Every Once In A While.' It was the equivalent of the marine expression, 'As cargo offers.'

"He would suggest that the businessman on behalf of his company purchase a hundred thousand reprints at ten cents, to distribute as the most flattering format of publicity. Soon a spirit of rivalry and emulation began. Unless you had been visited by the Fra you had little stature in the industrial world. The deals were arranged in advance; the boob signed up for so many thousand reprints before the Fra deigned to visit him.

"I served as a herald and intermediary, posing as one who knew the Fra intimately and thought I could arrange to get the boob visited if he consented to Mr. Hubbard's usual terms. It was all legal, nobody got hurt, and it was wonderful. I think you have the makings of another Elbert Hubbard, but you are in need of promotion. There is a millionaire I know

---

decade of the century, and his pictures show the exactitude of the Colonel's simile. The obscurity of the reference I hold as no subtraction from the pleasure of reading Stingo. The allusions in Milton and Spenser were similarly opaque to the uninitiate.
[5] Clem McCarthy, the radio announcer of turf events, an old friend of the Colonel's. They met in Seattle in about 1909, when the Colonel was conducting a medium of personal articulation known as the Seattle *Daily Sporting Times*. There was a boom in Seattle then, and a race track just outside of town.

of who manufactures poultry-laying feed down in Pennsylvania and feels he is a fitting subject for a biography in a national magazine. We could take him like the Dalton gang took Coffeyville, Kansas."

The Colonel is always trying to make something of me, but I let him down.

"I don't think I have the qualifications to be a Fra," I told him once when he was particularly urgent.

"You have, Joe," he said generously. "All you lack is self-confidence and a good advance man. Of course he had an advantage in appearance. He had hair that came down over his shoulders, and he wore a hat like Walt Whitman, with a Prince Albert coat and long-legged burnished boots.

"I remember the first time I met him out in San Francisco. He was on a lecture tour and I had been engaged to do some advance promotion. I had a committee of representative citizens and a brass band out to meet him at the Oakland Ferry. The crowd coming off the ferry cheered thinking it was Buffalo Bill, and as we drove off through the huzzaring plebes, the Fra put his hand on my knee and said, 'Little Mac, I've got them.' His creed was Sunshine, Fresh Air, Friendship, Calm Sleep, and Beautiful Thoughts,—the Sea, the Sun, the Smile, America, and the Love of the Farm. He was the sweetest, dearest human being that ever lived, and you would have loved him."

Colonel Stingo and I were in Joe Braun's Palace Bar and Grill on the evening of this particular discussion. It is a place which always disposes the Colonel to sentimentality. "There have been three Palace bars in my life," he says, "the grandiose dispensatorium dominated by the Pied Piper in San Francisco, the Palace Bar on the Bund in Shanghai, where I was entertained by Dr. Sun Yat-sen, who was then incubating the revolution, and this present Palace on Forty-fifth Street. It lacks the pretension of the first two, but it is more appropriate to my present portfolio of securities.

"This dear old Fra," he said, "perpetrated a tour de force called the *Message to Garcia*, which sold a couple of million copies. The fellow he said carried the message didn't even find the right Garcia. Cuba is full of Garcias. 'How the fellow by the name of Rowan took the letter, sealed it up in an oilskin pouch, strapped it over his heart, in four days landed by night off the coast of Cuba from an open boat, disappeared into the jungle, and in three weeks came out on the other side of the island, having traversed a hostile country on foot and delivered the message to Garcia,' the old Fra wrote, 'are things I have no special desire now to tell in detail.' That is just as well, because it didn't happen.

"The old Fra, though, used the suppositious exploit as an illustration of the kind of service employers didn't get in return for the wages they paid, in those days frequently aggregating a dollar and a half a day. He adjured the toiling masses to spit on their hands and prove themselves worthy of their bosses' benevolence.

"Sales were light among the objects of his exhortation, but this did not disappoint his anticipations. 'Slipshod assistance, foolish inattention, dowdy indifference and half-hearted work seem the rule," he fulminated, and the Pennsylvania Railroad bought the first million copies for distribution to passengers and employes.

" 'No man who has endeavored to carry out an enterprise where many hands were needed but has been well-nigh appalled by the imbecility of the average man,' that dear old humanitarian indited. 'A first mate with knotted club seems necessary; and the dread of getting the bounce Saturday night holds many a worker to his place.' But he was not incapable of sympathy.

" 'Nothing is said,' he suggested considerately, 'about the employer who grows old before his time in a vain attempt to get frowsy ne'er-do-wells to do intelligent work; and his long, patient striving with help that does nothing but loaf when his back is turned.'

"Dear old Fra," the Colonel said, swelling the tide of his Gambrinian with a tear. "He was the people's friend."

"He seems to have been a precursor of Westbrook Pegler," I said.

"He was more on the order of Al Jennings, the train robber," the Colonel said, "only he didn't need an equalizer."

Seeing him in a mood so softly reminiscent, I thought it might be a good time to bring up again the subject of his own career in conventional journalism after his discharge from the *Evening Sun* for scoring a sensational scoop.

"Did you achieve any scoops of note after your translation to the *Evening Journal*, Colonel?" I asked him.

"*Any* scoops?" the Colonel repeated ironically. "It was my function to provide at least four exclusive first-page stories a week while the horses were running at metropolitan tracks, and I may say I succeeded. Shortly after my advent to the Halls Hearstian, a Mr. Foster Coates was made managing editor of the *Evening Journal*, always under the superior aegis of that old fraud Brisbane, who retained guidance remote. Mr. Coates was said to be capable of swearing for half an hour without repeating himself. He was of a type prefiguring the hard-boiled city editor of *The Front Page* and many moving pictures.

"This Mr. Coates infected Brisbane and through him Mr. Hearst with the idea of a late edition of the *Evening Journal*, to be known as the Peach. It went to press at the unprecedentedly late hour of 7 P.M. By tacit agreement theretofore all New York evenings had put their finals to bed at five-forty. The Peach had a pink front page.

"In order to sell an otherwise redundant paper at an hour when the workaday crowds had already homeward wended, it was essential to have some startling daily item of headline import. It would in most cases concern sports, since it was difficult to assure a supply of murders or stickups between five-forty and seven. The race track would seem to be the most dependable source, since, as Mr. Coates observed, baseball did not interest women. He envisaged the Tenderloin and Broadway as the mart for the Peach, and a woman objects to the purchase of a newspaper by her escort unless she wants to read it too."

The Colonel reiterated his Gambrinian intake, and said: "The two fields that newspapers cover most inadequately are, indubitably, Wall Street and the race track. The reason is the same in both cases, hypocrisy. The motivation of both institutions is frankly acquisitive. There is however in Wall Street a sanctimonious fiction that the market exists as a medium of liquidating old ladies' estates. It is parallel to the Tartuffian claim that the pari-mutuels run to improve the breed of horses descended from the Darley Arabian.

"The professional journalists covering these beats have a jargon of veneerment which bedims rather than accentuates.

"MARKET WAVERS, for example, has not the same interest as $500,000,000 LOST. You look at Wall Street headlines and the only thing they seldom mention is money.

"Readers are not interested in trends, so denominated, but in tales of quick enrichment or spectacular impoverization—the saga of that vast gist of gelt.

"For racing news the same thing is true. People go out there to bet, and the betting is what they want to read about. The plungers of halcyon were not secretive. The income tax, with its incentive to discretion, had not yet been constitutionalized. So Pittsburgh Phil, Bet-a-Million Gates, and their ilk were public figures, outranking in interest the Russo-Japanese War and like contemporary events. By concentrating upon the ebb and flow of the oceanic tide of Tease, I was able to provide a bumper crop of headlines.

"Each day at five forty-five, when the other papers were away, I would send my Peach story from the track. Western Union facilities at the race track were limited, and, by agreement among the newspapers, no one message filed could run more than fifty-five words. There was therefore scant opportunity for fine shading and qualification. The copyreaders and make-up men, impatient to be off to their respective chatelaines, were indisposed to lavish time in the pursuit of the exact equivalent of my thought, in Gallicism, *le mot au jus*. The resulting headlines were in one or two cases the cause of embarrassment. But I survived."

The Colonel paused to help a fellow devotee of Gambrinus over a rough spot in a Sunday *Times* crossword puzzle. The puzzler, a graying fellow, had come to our table and asked: "What is an opera by Wagner in six letters, beginning with R and ending with *i*?"

"*Rienzi*," the Colonel said without hesitation. "It has an overture."

After the grateful puzzler had withdrawn, the Colonel said, "A pitiful case. He spent nine months in the Death House at Sing Sing, a victim of mistaken identity. There he became addicted to crossword puzzles. Now he wanders disconsolate, in search of a saloon without a juke box or television so he can concentrate. He misses the amenities of prison life.

"One morning at Brighton," he said, reverting to the good Edwardian time, "I was standing over near the racing secretary's office when I saw George Smith, known on the turf as Pittsburgh Phil, with his trainer ascend the steps to the pagoda, or stewards' stand. I used to get out to the course early in those days, since the time for digging was before or after the races. During their running my usual news sources were too engrossed to talk.

"I was therefore the only turf writer present. Mr. Smith's presence at the track at that hour was more unusual than mine. I sensed that something must be up, though when he descended from the stand his imperturbable countenance reflected no disgruntlement. He was a man of inconspicuous demeanor, like one of those fellows who sit at their desks in the front offices of banks, waiting for their prey.

"I therefore waylaid Mr. Harry Knapp, one of the Jockey Club stewards, a dear old fellow, when he in turn descended from the pagoda, and asked him what was up.

" 'We have refused the entries of Mr. Smith's horses until the miserable showing of one he ran yesterday is explained,' he said. 'There's an investigation in progress.'

"I naturally kept my information to myself throughout the afternoon. I knew Pittsburgh Phil would tell no one, and I was sure the Jockey Club would make no announcement until the result of the investigation was determined.

"After my colleagues had gone home, I sent my Peach story: 'Entries of horses owned by George A. Smith, better known as Pittsburgh Phil, were refused today pending result of investigation of Grand Opera's showing in the fifth race yesterday on which it is known western gamblers took the books for a cool quarter million. Such investigations have often led to stables' being barred from the turf.' It was all I could do in fifty-five words.

"I started for my office well pleased, traveling by electric train to the Sands Street station in Brooklyn, where I had to transfer to a streetcar for the trip across the bridge. At Sands Street, which I reached at seven-thirty, the Peach was already on sale, but with a headline which indicated I was in Blackstonian jeopardy: PITTSBURGH PHIL RULED OFF. The copyreader, anticipating the decision of the Jockey Club, had strained the legal limits of my innuendo.

"The next day's papers announced that the stewards had cleared Mr. Smith of complicity in the capricious conduct of his three-year-old Grand Opera, and that Pittsburgh Phil was now suing the *Evening Journal*, Mr. Hearst, and J.S.A. Macdonald, the *Journal* racing expert, for a hundred thousand dollars apiece, in my case, sheer flattery. Luckily the *Journal* had published the text of my despatch in full, so I was in the clear with my superiors, but it was the occasion of much mental anguish.

"I was interviewed by a junior member of the paper's firm of libel lawyers, a neophyte trusting only to written rote. He asked me what time I had seen Mr. Smith go up into the stand? I said eleven o'clock. He said, 'How do you know?' I said, 'Because I was just outside the racing secretary's office and all the hustlers and the touts and trainers were standing around waiting to see the entries for the next day's races.' He was unacquainted with the world outside Harvard Square. However, Mr. Smith was reported implacable. The paper was clearly at fault, even if I wasn't. I squared that one myself. I waited upon him in his suite at the Hotel Imperial, Broadway and Thirty-second Street, and explained that the fellow who wrote the headline was a Sunday-school superintendent and a force in the Anti-Saloon League and was, besides, the sole support of his mother, wife, and eleven children.

"The man was in real life established in sin with a member of the Ladies' Orchestra of the Atlantic Gardens *bierstube*, and his sole support for every day of the week except payday was the magnificent free-lunch counter at Furthmann's Saloon under the El on Park Row.

"Because of the paragon's blameless past, I told Pittsburgh Phil, he was unacquainted with the terminology of the turf, a country boy who thought a poolroom was a synonym for a natatorium, and if he lost this job he would be blacklisted and the children would become public charges, while all the drunkards on Park Row would jeer at this black eye for clean living.

"Pittsburgh Phil was a man who would bet fifty thousand dollars on the turn of a card and never indicate by the slightest contraction of the facial muscles pleasure or displeasure at the outcome. But, Joe, I had him crying like a baby.

" 'Thank you for coming to see me, young man,' he said when I had finished. 'You have prevented me from committing a grave injustice. I will instruct my solicitors tomorrow to withdraw my suit. And here is five hundred for you,' he said, the dear old fellow. 'And the next time one of my horses is a stiff I will let you in on it.' "

26 / A Little Journey to Sysonby's

"THE HORSES, like the men, were of superior stature in those days," the Colonel said regretfully. "These are degenerate times, in which the race horse, sensing himself a mere instrument of greed, has lost all sense of *noblesse obligée*. A horse like the great Sysonby, by Imp. Melton, winner of the Epsom Derby, out of Optime, would never let you down. Imported *in utero*, but foaled in this country, as I recollect, this equine knight of the

Table Round lost but once as a two-year-old, and then to the great mare Artful in the Futurity. As a three-year-old he won all save for one dead heat with Race King. That made fourteen firsts in fifteen starts, and the American public waited, agape, for his *rentrée* as a four-year-old in the season of 1906. He was the predilectory possession of James R. Keene, a mighty old man of money, a czar of Wall Street and preeminent on the American turf, having survived William Collins Whitney, his chief competitor. Keene and Whitney were two of the most rivalous men that ever lived.

"Mr. Keene was by then a valetudinarian, swathed in thick-carpeted luxury and surfeited with attendance in the old Waldorf-Astoria, on the site of the present Empire State Building. The triumphs of his horses were to him the most potent of tonics, accountable, according to his physicians, for his continued survival. But the doctors adjured the members of his suite to cushion him against shock as much as possible.

"The seasonal debut of this Sysonby," the Colonel said, "was repeatedly postponed. Jim Rowe, his trainer, said he was doing well, but he was scratched in turn from the Metropolitan, Brooklyn, and Suburban Handicaps, the Wagnerian Ring Cycle for three-year-olds and up of that era, and it was bruited about in hushed whisper that he was suffering from a mysterious rash that the veterinarians could not diagnose. A minor ailment, the vets said, but he could not endure a saddle blanket on his back.

"I was standing down by the finish line at Sheepshead Bay after the last race one day in mid-June, trying to think of something to send that the boys could hang a headline on for the Peach, when Dynamite Jack Thornby breezed up to to me and said, 'Jim, you'd better get over to Jim Rowe's barn. Sysonby is in a lather and shaking like a leaf, and they're walking him in circles. He looks one to ten and out to die in an hour.'

"I ran right over there and the facts were as Dynamite Jack had reported. The track veterinary, whom I knew, said, 'He's a goner of a certainty,' and the horse's groom was crying. I hustled back to the telegraph operator, who waited for me every day before putting up his bug, and sent the *Evening Journal* all I knew: 'The great race horse Sysonby was fatally stricken by illness at Sheepshead Bay after the last race this evening.' It was a scoop. When I reached Sands Street I bought a *Journal* with the headline across the page: SYSONBY DEAD.

"The boys had pushed up the tempo on me again, but this time I thought it was safe enough. Sunday morning's papers, however, brought trepidation. The morning papers, taken aghast by my scoop, had tried to confirm it but had been unable to establish contact with trainer Rowe. They had then sent reporters to the Waldorf to check up with Mr. Keene, but had not been allowed to see the old hidalgo. Instead, a gentlemanly understrapper, a kind of social secretary, had come out from the sanctum and informed them that Mr. Keene could not be disturbed, but that they might rest assured there was nothing the matter with Sysonby. 'If the horse had died we would surely have been informed,' he said, and dismissed them.

"Every Sunday sports page carried a headline: SYSONBY LIVES—CANARD DENIED, or TURF SCOOP PROVES HOAX—SYSONBY HAS HORSE LAUGH. I had a gloomy morning. But the afternoon was even more lugubrious. I was captain of the *Evening Journal* team in the Newspaper Baseball League, which played its games on Sunday afternoons at old Washington Park, the home grounds of the Brooklyn Superbas. There was no Sunday professional baseball, and they let us use the park. I pitched," the Colonel said, and added, modestly, "I was of big-league calibre. On this particular Sunday we were playing the *Evening World*, a deadly rival.

"All the *World* boys took the opportunity of riding me. Their witticisms were uncouth but effective,—they would for instance whinny when I came to bat, and yell, 'Run it out, Sysonby,' when I hit a bounder. While I pitched, their coaches on the base lines would ask me where I expected to work after the iron ball hit, suggesting I might find employment with my old associate George Graham Rice, then promoting mining stock in Nevada. I was so preoccupied that I allowed three hits and had to drive in the winning run myself with a double in the ninth inning.

"I was by now a married man and father, and my thoughts were dark indeed as I turned in that night, after an evening of spurious good humor designed to conceal from my spouse the foreboding which was, under the circumstances, appropriate. Fortunately she was not a sports-page reader and did not know what I was thinking about. On the morrow I dragged myself to the office, then on William Street, figuring I might better go there and receive the fatal news than straight to the track and receive the blow by telegraph.

"On entering the city room at noon, I saw by my desk the ominous figure of Coates, the Peach's only begetter. I made my way bravely toward him, prepared to submit my justification but not sue for mercy. Suddenly, on perceiving me, Mr. Coates, a man of generous dimensions, rushed in my direction. I threw myself into a posture of defense, but his intentions proved amicable.

"'That was a clean beat, Jimmy,' he proclaimed, and waved in my direction a paper with headlines stating: SYSONBY DIED SATURDAY NIGHT, TRAINER ADMITS. It seems that the great son of Melton had expired a few hours after my view of him, but the trainer, fearing the effect of such dolorous news on the cardiac structure of the octogenarian millionaire, had not imparted the information until late the next day. The social secretary, in denying the receipt of the bad news, had been veracious, but the news desks, eager to throw down Peach's story, had not pushed their enquiries far enough.

"We crowed over our beat for a week. Mr. Coates expressed his pleasure, and an office boy delivered at my desk a note from Mr. Brisbane congratulating me on my performance and alleging that I would be rewarded with a five-dollar raise as soon as Mr. Hearst's finances permitted.

"In my memories of equine immortals, Sysonby holds a special place. I sometimes dream of him, a great bay horse, charging down upon me as I lie flat on my back on an unidentified racing strip. As he comes thundering down upon me I hear him singing: 'Alive, Alive-o,' to the tune of 'Cockles and Mussels,' an air I never hear in my waking moments without a shudder of grim association."

It was now my turn to surprise the Colonel. I ordered up another round of the amber, and when we had filled our glasses I said, "I challenge. I propose a Little Journey to the Home of Sysonby."

I must explain here that as a small boy resident on the West Side I had been a habitué of the American Museum of Natural History, earning a familiarity with every stuffed seal and dummy Eskimo in the joint. I had ranged from mammals to meteorites, hummingbirds to horses, and the name Sysonby struck a familiar note. Sysonby's skeleton, I remembered, had stood in the Museum, plainly labeled, and that omniretentive repository must still hold it fast.

The Colonel, for once, looked at me with astonishment, but when I recounted my recollection he readily acceded to my proposal.

"I never thought to look on Sysonby again," he said. "He was a hell of a horse."

We got a taxi and made our way to the Museum. It was still midafternoon. When we arrived we had to fight our way in through a vast circular agglutination of school children in the rotunda, forming a human aspic around a miniature whale *sous cloche*. This was labeled "Oscar, the Baby Whale," and a card under the glass explained that Oscar's mother when killed had been sixty-eight feet long and that Oscar, if he had survived the ordinary period of gestation, would have been born twenty feet overall. Oscar and the children packed the rotunda. The Colonel made a way through the juvenile plankton, making effective though surreptitious use of his pointy shoes, for a few small shrieks of pain mingled with the gabble in his wake. I fancied that, following him, I stepped on one or two small prostrate bodies. However, these may have been knocked down by their playmates and trampled to death hours before our arrival.

A girl at the information desk said that all the horse exhibits were grouped. By consulting a map she was able to inform us that they were on the fourth floor, and we extricated our legs and buttocks from the pediatric jelly mold and headed for the elevators, the Colonel hitting one little darling a pip of a backhander as we broke away.

We found Sysonby, a spirited *squelette*, in full stride in the midst of his Museum playmates: the Przewalsky horse; the wild ass, or Kiang; Grévy's zebra; and a draught horse pulling a heavy load, all skeletons grouped for ready comparison. Sysonby, the sign within his glass case indicated, is shown at the instant when the right forefoot has left the ground, and left hind foot, right hind foot and left forefoot are to follow in that order, carrying him forward one full stride of twenty-six feet. "He's hanging in the stretch," the Colonel said. "Can't seem to get anywhere. It isn't like him."

The delicacy of the horse's bone structure impressed him. "He looks so small when he is divested of his outward integument," he said. "I remember him as a big horse. It is easy to see why two-year-olds go so frequently askew," he added, regarding the complex lattice of the rib cage. "They are of surprisingly fragile construction." Another card within the case gave the date of Sysonby's demise—June 17, 1906—and noted that the skeleton had been mounted at the expense of James R. Keene and presented by him to the Museum. There was a photograph of the great son of Melton-Optime,—the Colonel's recollection of his breeding had been precise,—passing a winning post in full flesh, with jockey up and Keene's polka-dot silks flattened to the boy's small torso by the breeze.

"He was a hot tip the first time he ever came out," the Colonel said, "and I passed him up. He was three to five, and that turned out to be the best price ever laid against him."

We began the return journey to Joe Braun's. Our path led through the Hall of Mammoths, a larger and more impressive catacomb between Sysonby's glass loose box and the elevators. The Colonel, ever curious, paused before several of the reconstructed mammoths and mastodons, and was particularly attracted by a South Dakota entry called the Megabelodon, which stood about twenty-seven hands at the shoulder and was slightly longer than a crosstown bus. "If a puny creature like Sysonby could stride twenty-six feet," he said, "imagine what that thing could encompass with a bound." He stood, contemplative, before Megabelodon for a moment, and then continued on his way.

"If we could get Sysonby out of here, some night," I suggested playfully, after we had got into the elevator, "we could enter him in the last race at Belmont and he could probably still take that class of horses."

"Sysonby hell," my courtly old friend said unsentimentally. "Do you suppose I could get racing papers on a Megabelodon?"

It was shortly after our Little Journey to the Last Home of Sysonby that I suggested a Little Journey to the Home of the New York *Journal-American*, the Hearst newspaper that encompasses in its identity the old *Evening Journal*, on which the Colonel scored his scoops, along with the *Journal*, its senior, and the *American*, its junior.

The Colonel had learned from a newspaper paragraph that there was at least one man at the *Journal-American* who had been an office boy in the sports department in his day. The paragraph had recorded a testimonial dinner celebrating the man's fiftieth year of service, at which fellow employes had presented him with a watch. The Colonel had passed on the information without comment, but it was my idea to promote the reunion, in the belief that some further details of the Colonel's career in the days of halcyon might accrue. He telephoned to the man, whose name was

Harry, and the mutual recognition, to judge from the Colonel's end of the conversation, was immediate. Harry, after all these years, the Colonel informed me, was now sports make-up man, a job replete with responsibility and tension, for it means putting the several sports pages together for each of several editions, rearranging them each time to feature the latest news. Four in the afternoon, Harry said, was a good time to come and see him.

At luncheon on the day set for this Little Journey my old friend was, not unnaturally, in reminiscent mood.

"The Hearst empire of my day was, like that of the Byzantine emperors, labyrinthian," he said, "and not without occasional instances of corruption stemming from its uncontrollable ramification. Each of the Old Man's objetti d'art, it was rumored, had been paid for at least three times by officials of duplicative functions, two of the three prices being split between the art merchants and the disbursing officers. A similar tropical profusion reigned in all other departments where gelt was to be laid hands upon, and this sometimes redounded to the profit of even the reporter.

"I well remember one winter when I was covering racing at New Orleans I received, in place of my regular weekly money order for $125, including expenses, a whopping one for $750. I had sent for no extra Tease, but there it was, all properly made out to me. After a period of trepidation, waiting for the home office to announce discovery of its error, temptation prevailed and I spent the money. There followed a period of more intensive apprehension, but this in turn receded into the subconscious recesses of my mind, and I forgot all about it. Full fifteen years later, protected by the statute of limitations, I was standing in the Palace Hotel bar at San Francisco in full sartorial splendor. I was riding high on the Great American Hog. The Syndicate was proliferating profit as well as pork chops. Down the bar from me I noted a man who seemed familiar. He was a seedy character however, in so advanced a state of disintegration that I wondered he had the temerity to brave the flunkey at the door. Upon further inspection I was horrified to recognize a man with an Irish name I now forget, who had once been auditor of the *Journal*, but who had been caught siding with the losing party in some court intrigue for the Old Man's favor. So he had had to suffer legal penalty for the peccadilloes of which his persecutors were perhaps equally guilty. He had embezzled around eighty grand, the price of a bogus stained-glass window, and so he got five.

"Upon his emergence from the stocks, he had found no ready victim and had made his way west, arriving in the debilitated format which had excited my commiseration. Putting my arm around his shoulder, I said to him, 'Mr. O'Calagan'—or whatever the name was—'I am *so* glad to see you again, and by the way, here is a small sum I have owed you for years,' and I slipped him a sawbuck.

" 'It is damned little interest on that 750,' he said.

"I then realized," Colonel Stingo said, "that the man had embezzled to gratify all his tastes. One of them had been philanthropy. Heaven knows how many employes' lives he had brightened with his unexpected gratuities. He may have prevented suicides, facilitated marriages, made possible appendectomies. And the Old Man would have blown the Tease on a bogus tapestry if O'Calagan hadn't diverted it."

We rode the East Side subway down from Grand Central to Brooklyn Bridge. When we came up out of the hole we were just outside City Hall Park and diagonally across the street from the Pulitzer Building, that monument to a great publisher's posthumous defeat. The building stared down, unkempt as a deserted eagle's nest, and the Colonel looked distressed. He remembered the park as the centre of the newspaper world, with editorial offices elbow to elbow all along Park Row. Even I could remember when five daily papers of general circulation clustered around the square,—the *Sun* at the northwest corner, the *World* and *Evening World* in the Pulitzer Building, and the *Journal* and *American* in the old rookery on William Street. Now there were none.

"The deterioration is pronounced," the Colonel said. "It is even worse than Times Square."

We started to walk to the East River to find the *Journal-American*, which stands on a wind-swept barren north of the Fulton Fish Market, a site so inaccessible the company runs buses from the subway railhead to the bleak door.

As we threaded the labyrinthian East Side streets the Colonel grew progressively more depressed. "It is the road to Siberia," he said. "I haven't seen a good-looking saloon for three blocks." When we came in sight of the Hearst newspaper building at Catherine Slip and the river, he stopped and surveyed the bare, nondescript rectangle of whitewashed concrete. "It's like a factory," he said, and wriggled his shoulders as if to shake off a revulsion. But he gamely got under way again. We entered the portal, under the eye of a house cop, and went up to the sports department, which is spread out, together with the city side, on one vast loft floor, like a garment plant before the unions got strong. The fluorescent lights overhead cast a wan glow on the sweat-pearled forehead of a man on the city side whom I recognized as one of the *Journal-American's* experts on Communists. The chap, a long-legged snollygoster with a profile like Andy Gump, looked intently at the Colonel, as if preparing to identify him as leader of a cell at Tanforan race track in 1937. The Colonel was unconscious of his peril, but I was beginning to be uneasy by the time we found the old colleague, Harry.

Since Harry had been a copy boy when the Colonel was already an established racing expert, I took it that Harry was about ten years younger than the stylist of the New York *Enquirer*, but they looked to be much of an age. They began almost immediately to enumerate the men they had worked with who were dead, their words expressing regret and their voices a guilty pleasure in their survival. Harry remarked that the Colonel had put on weight. The Colonel said he wasn't pitching any more. The Colonel said Harry had lost weight. Harry said the doctor had made him cut down on his eating. He had a family and lived in some place like Jackson Heights or Gibson, Long Island, and he came to work five days a week at some atrocious morning hour like eight or nine or ten and spent his day under the fluorescents, wondering whether there would be enough championship golf scores in to put a head on for the four o'clock edition.

As they talked, Harry and the Colonel measured each other with an affectionately actuarial eye. They were glad to see each other, but it was evident that their paths had diverged since 1907, and they didn't seem to have anything more recent to talk about.

"I remember how we used to sit around waiting for your exclusive from the track: PITTSBURGH PHIL SENDS BOOKS TO COVER, or something like that," said Harry, and the Colonel smiled graciously. But he seemed uneasy, and to my surprise, did not make his visit a long one. When he started for the elevator he was walking faster than usual, and by the time we got down to the functionally bare lobby, he almost sprinted for the door. He reached the sidewalk like a booster pursued by a store detective, and tore on for a block in silence, until he spotted a saloon. It was of dismal aspect, but he headed in like a Central Park riding horse going back to a warm barn.

"I would suggest a double bonded bourbon, straight," he said to the grimy-handed bartender wearing a shirt unlaundered for a month. He was suspending the Rule of the Great Transition.

While the bartender was fumbling among the bottles to find one that did not contain neutral grain spirits, the Colonel said to me:

"Joe, it was just like a prison. Newspaper life nowadays must be like working in a factory."

He got his drink, and after he had knocked it back with one swift, untypical motion, he began to feel better. His mouth lost its unwonted tightness, and the corners turned up in his habitual happy smile.

"Joe," he said, "affluence has not crowned my endeavors—as yet. But all I need is one good gold mine west of the Missouri. And I've certainly done a lot better than Harry."

The Colonel clasped his shot glass as possessively as if it contained fifty years of episodia.